T0209099

30 Days to NLP

AN INTRODUCTION TO NEURO LINGUISTIC PROGRAMMING

LAURELI BLYTH &
DR. HEIDI HERON PSY.D.

BALBOA.
PRESS

A DIVISION OF HAY HOUSE

Copyright © 2016 Laureli Blyth & Dr. Heidi Heron Psy.D.

All rights reserved. No part of this book may be used or reproduced by
any means, graphic, electronic, or mechanical, including photocopying,
recording, taping or by any information storage retrieval system
without the written permission of the author except in the case
of brief quotations embodied in critical articles and reviews.

Balboa Press books may be ordered through booksellers or by contacting:

Balboa Press
A Division of Hay House
1663 Liberty Drive
Bloomington, IN 47403
www.balboapress.com.au
1 (877) 407-4847

Because of the dynamic nature of the Internet, any web addresses or
links contained in this book may have changed since publication and
may no longer be valid. The views expressed in this work are solely those
of the author and do not necessarily reflect the views of the publisher,
and the publisher hereby disclaims any responsibility for them.

The author of this book does not dispense medical advice or prescribe
the use of any technique as a form of treatment for physical, emotional,
or medical problems without the advice of a physician, either directly
or indirectly. The intent of the author is only to offer information
of a general nature to help you in your quest for emotional and
spiritual well-being. In the event you use any of the information in
this book for yourself, which is your constitutional right, the author
and the publisher assume no responsibility for your actions.

Any people depicted in stock imagery provided by Thinkstock are
models, and such images are being used for illustrative purposes only.
Certain stock imagery © Thinkstock.

Print information available on the last page.

ISBN: 978-1-5043-0269-2 (sc)
ISBN: 978-1-5043-0282-1 (e)

Balboa Press rev. date: 07/14/2016

From both Laureli and Heidi, we wish to thank our trainers, colleagues, clients and most importantly our students for teaching us so much about NLP. Without all of you, our efforts within this field would be naught.

Laureli would like to dedicate this book:

To my grandparents who gave me love,
and encouragement to find my own path.

Heidi would like to dedicate this book:

To the one person, who without her none
of this would be possible. My mother.
Thank you for your encouragement and love.

What other are saying about
30 Days to NLP

Thirty Days to NLP is a clear, engaging, well-written overview of NLP. If you do the exercises, you will get the results you want. If you ever wanted to know what NLP is all about, this book is a great way to find out.

- Shelle Rose Charvet
Author of Words That Change Minds &
The Customer is Bothering Me

I like Thirty Days to NLP – its conversational style, logical building up of basic ideas and practical exercises make it a pleasure to read. Laureli and Heidi have congruently blended their values, beliefs and approach to training based on many years of experience in the field. If you are new to NLP this valuable resource will help guide you on your path of development.

- Penny Tompkins
Co-author of Metaphors in Mind:
Transformation through Symbolic Modeling

Laureli Blyth and Heidi Heron have written a great introduction to NLP. Their knowledge of the subject is impressive, and they share it in a clear, practical, and integrated fashion. I highly recommend it!

- Stephen Gilligan, Ph.D.
Psychologist and Author of The Hero's Journey &
The Courage to Love

I really found this book extremely interesting and very useful and informative in an organized way. Just what I have been looking for, as I have read quite a number of different books on NLP.

– Else Strom, Singapore

Reading this book was such a great way to introduce myself to NLP. It's like sitting down to a wonderful three course meal the book is the entree the gets you excited about the main course and dessert. Once you've read this book you'll be curious about more and wanting to learn more. Investing in this book and NLP was a decision i am so excited to have made.

- Jason Bourne, Australia

Overall an extremely useful book that can assist anyone in their NLP journey, whether you're new to NLP, or already have a level of skill and just need a refresher and to refine your skills, then this book lays it out for you. Overall, an excellent introduction to NLP, well done!

- Scott James, Australia

As you read this book, you understand yourselves first, then how you can deal with others in a manner that benefits both. It is simple, readable and easy to understand. This can be a reference book, kept and carried along with you anywhere.

- Haja Maideen, Singapore

This book gives a real and simple insight into that which NLP has to offer. It doesn't pretend to have everything NLP has to offer, but anyone new to NLP would certainly get a solid foundation from this book, and even more advanced NLP'ers will get plenty of benefit from reading it.

- Des Lowe, Australia

This book does a wonderful job of taking NLP and making it understandable for the average person. I have read several books on NLP but found none that explained the real benefits of NLP. 30 Days to NLP is written by professionals who have a deep understanding of this subject, decades of experience and who have the best intention for it's readers.

- David Benmayor, Australia

I love the chatty style of this book and the humour and warmth that shines through. It makes it so easy to read instead of slogging through like some other books on similar topics. The practical examples are welcome as you can appreciate how to apply it to your life.

- Natasha Crestani, Phillip Island, Australia

30 Days to NLP is just that - 30 days of to the point learning without any waffle. Really practical book for a Practitioner or Non-Practitioner. Highly recommended for anyone who wants to achieve more from life.

- Pauline Wright, United Kingdom

30 days to NLP is an excellent resource for NLP'ers and those who'd like to be. Heidi and Laureli have a writing style that is fun, practical and very easy to comprehend. Each day you get to discover more about yourself and what makes you tick in delicious bite size chapters. This is a book I refer to again and again.

- Joan Bell, Australia

The 30 Day to NLP book has been my go-to resource, practically my companion from the first time I got it. I've gotten so much use out of this book that I have a hardcopy at home, a PDF at work and a Kindle version to take with me when I travel. I find it so useful that I also purchased a copy for mother-in-law who has also taken on NLP into her life after hearing me rave about how it has transformed mine. This book is magical; each time I open it, I find new information to use!

- Sabrina Samsudin, Malaysia

This book created the foundation for my NLP journey. It helped to explain what NLP is and how it can help in all aspects of your lives. Its clear explanations and easy to follow processes helped me digest the concepts and enable me to try it on myself right away. Half way through reading the book, it piqued my interest so much that I signed up for Practitioner class immediately!

-Serene Nah, Hong Kong

We value your input, questions and comments anytime. Please feel free to contact us:

The Worldwide Institutes of NLP
Level 9, 143 York Street
Sydney NSW 2000
Australia
Phone: +61 2 9264 4357
Website: www.nlpworldwide.com
Email: info@nlpworldwide.com

Laureli Blyth
laureli@nlpworldwide.com
www.laureliblyth.com

Dr. Heidi Heron, Psy.D.
heidi@nlpworldwide.com
www.heidiheron.com

Global training and workshops conducted and sponsored by the Worldwide Institutes of NLP:

Training with Laureli Blyth and Dr. Heidi Heron, Psy.D.
- NLP Practitioner Certification
- NLP Master Practitioner Certification
- NLP Trainer & Presentation Skills Certification

30 Days to NLP

Welcome to 30 Days to NLP. Over the course of the next thirty days you are going to be embarking upon a journey through many of the skills of NLP. We purposefully call it a journey, because NLP can be just that.

In fact, the story of how this book came to fruition is also a journey and a great testament to some of the tools of NLP. Combined, Laureli and Heidi currently have thirty-two years of experience in the field of NLP. We have been working together fulltime for the past decade and have had thoughts of a book for many of those years. Yet, in the back of our minds we never knew what would set this book apart from the many hundreds of other NLP books on the market. We would start and stop writing, never quite having the right feel for the finished product.

We knew we wanted to write an intro to NLP book to provide to our students as pre and post learning materials, and to be a resource for other people throughout the world, but still had no concept of what would differentiate our book. Then, in late September 2010 we had an idea; a book that can be read one chapter a day which is written in the generative and conversational style that we train in. Now, how to get motivated and get it done? Another idea; there are thirty days in November. We put a call out to our students and colleagues and asked them to subscribe to the writing of our book. Starting 1 November 2010, 108 people began to receive via email one chapter each day of our book titled **30 Days to NLP.**

This book is based upon our successful and powerful NLP Practitioner Training programs that we have been conducting at our learning organization, the Worldwide Institutes of NLP, since 1994. We use generative learning and NLP techniques, which encourage learning by doing, openness, and systemic thinking. Many successful individuals and organizations effectively use this style of learning to transform themselves in the face of technological, social, and market change. This type of program enables you to learn as you apply and experience what you learned in a manner that will stay with you.

Being International NLP Trainers with private practices, we have seen thousands of people around the world make amazing transformational changes with NLP. We know and understand NLP from a practical application in business, life and coaching; not just a theoretical point of view. In our opinion, some of the benefits of learning and using NLP include the ability to:

- Clarify your goals, resolve conflicts and create a workable path to your outcomes
- Have resources available when and where you need them
- Clear unresolved negative emotions that hold you back
- Uncover and transform beliefs that limit or hold you back
- Create enhanced self-confidence and increased ability to clearly and specifically communicate

This 30-day program will provide you a complete NLP training. Each day you will be introduced to a different topic with explanations, examples, and some exercises. It is assumed that the reader has either little to no prior knowledge of NLP, yet if you do have prior knowledge you will find this book refreshing and a great resource for continued learning. The syllabus is set in the style of integrated and generative learning. Therefore, each day you learn something that can be carried forward to the next day and integrated. It is therefore recommended that you read this book sequentially; in the order it is presented.

The best way to learn NLP is in a classroom with supervised time to practice with other people and a trainer with ample experience to share the skills in a comprehensive manner; we offer such courses all through the world. If you decide to get your formal certification, you can use this book as a reference and pre-training manual, and of course as a post-training refresher.

In our trainings we purposefully keep the class number small; usually less than twenty students. We do this for the intention of ensuring we get personal contact and are able to build a relationship with every single student we train. We value the one-on-one rapport and connection with our students. As such, we want to build that same kind of bond here, in this book over the next month. To do that, let us properly introduce ourselves.

We are Laureli Blyth and Heidi Heron; founders, directors and principal trainers with the Worldwide Institutes of NLP. Laureli started the Australasian Institute of NLP in Sydney, Australia in 1994 and Heidi joined in 2000. With our commencement in the mid nineties our NLP training institute is one of the oldest in Australia. In 2002 we created the Worldwide Institutes of NLP which is comprised of the Australasian, American and European Institutes of NLP. We have the pleasure of traveling the world and sharing the skills and understanding of NLP with thousands of individuals. Both of us have a passion for knowledge and learning and a strong value for passing this information on to others to help people to live the best lives they can.

The NLP Institutes have taken our trainings globally with our courses taking place in Australia, New Zealand, the United States, Singapore, Malaysia, Poland, Scotland, England and Brazil. In 2009 we were privileged enough to train on a cruise ship that traveled from Sydney to Honolulu over seventeen nights! If anything, we are both proud and humbled by our accomplishments and lives around the world we are privileged to touch.

Very often we receive comments about our conversational style, expertise, integrity, vibrant presence and knowledge about human development. To be involved in a field that is still quite young and growing offers us both the opportunity to grow our skills and help contribute to the growth of this field. In the world of NLP trainers, we are highly visible and well regarded amongst our peers and colleagues. We are also a duo with more connections than just NLP. We are a dynamic training team connected by blood, Laureli is Heidi's mother; and while it seems they were destined to work together, this mother-daughter team never consciously planned it that way.

Originally from Colorado in the United States, Laureli worked for United Airlines and was introduced to NLP in the early 1980's by a work colleague. She began her NLP training with NLP Comprehensive in 1983 and used her skills for communication, leadership, family and business. She attributes her NLP skills to being selected to travel to the Asia Pacific region when United acquired Pan Am airlines in the mid eighties. In 1986 Laureli relocated and immigrated to Sydney Australia where she still resides.

Her love for NLP and its life changing tools spurred her on to learn more and more. She participated in several workshops and certified trainings and has completed a degree in Hypnotherapy. In 1994 Laureli decided to make NLP her full-time occupation and founded the Institutes and The Blyth Centre, her private therapy and coaching practice. She has an interest and love of people, the mind and human nature. With a great curiosity in holistic and spiritual aspects of life, she incorporates the whole person body, mind and spirit into her work. Laureli is the author five books including: Neuro Intelligence, Brain Power, Dream Power and Numerology of Names.

A sought after speaker, Laureli regularly speaks at NLP Conferences throughout the world, including the Institute for the Advanced Studies of Health (IASH) in the United States, the Australian Board of NLP Conference and the NLP Conference in London. Within our organization Laureli holds the official title of Director of Training and Research; she is continually improving our current training programs and seeking information for new courses and ways to share NLP with the world.

Laureli is the mother of two grown children and five grandchildren. She lives an hour north of Sydney in a fascinating pole home on the side of a rock hill surrounded by eucalyptus and the home of many wallabies. In her words "I look forward to my continued journey that has enriched my life all because I followed my calling and heart and took up NLP."

As we mentioned, it was never planned for Heidi to join her mother in the NLP business. Although Heidi was just child when Laureli began her studies in NLP, it wasn't until 1997 that Heidi picked up her first NLP book and learned more about this mesmerizing field. For her whole life, Heidi knew she was going to be a teacher. In 1986 she and her older brother joined their mother in Australia, immigrating to a new country. After completing high school in Sydney, Heidi returned to the United States to pursue her university education and become a teacher. Little did she know that she would become a teacher, just not of the small children that were in her mind. While at University, Heidi completed degrees in Psychology and Communication. Upon completion, instead of entering a classroom she entered in to a profession in Corporate Human Resources.

When returning to Australia in 1997 Heidi read her first NLP book with fascination and desire for more. While still working in Human Resources and Operations Management Heidi began her NLP studies and completed the NLP Certification courses and used her skills in her business and personal lives. In 2000, Heidi decided to follow her dreams and join Laureli as a trainer and start her own coaching and therapy practice, People Point. Since then she completed her Masters degree in Adult Education and has also completed her Doctorate in Psychology; making Heidi one of most highly educated NLP professionals in the world.

The structure and common sense of NLP appeals to Heidi and her training style. While she has a comprehensive and impressive educational background, it is her craving for integrity and knowledge and passion for people that makes her excel at what she does. Within our organization, Heidi holds the official title of Director of Operations; which allows Heidi to use her organizational and strategic skills.

Heidi continues to reside in Sydney and has been involved as a Board Member and most recently Chairperson of the Australian Board of NLP since 2006. She has been a guest trainer with NLP Comprehensive and has been a keynote speaker at the New Zealand NLP Association conference. As a leader in the field of NLP she is privileged to share her knowledge with others and inspire them to live an authentic life. You can follow her blog at www.heidiheron.com if you wish.

There you have it. Two self-motivated women who follow their hearts and dreams have created a purposeful, well established and highly respected NLP training institute.

We are honored to share the next month with you and our sought after delivery of NLP knowledge. If you would like to hear our voices so they can accompany you through this book, you can find a variety of videos on our website www.nlpworldwide.com. Above and beyond what we choose for our professions, we are real people with real lives. While you are traveling through your NLP journey with us over the next thirty days, if you have any questions or comments at all, please feel free to contact us at anytime! We are always more than happy to help.

It is our hope that you will find this NLP book refreshing, informative and inspirational. Unlike many other NLP books which are written like a text book, this book is written in the same conversational prose we use when training. It is a culmination of our experience, knowledge and years of practical application of NLP in the training room and in our private practices.

It is our pleasure to share our world of NLP with yours.

Contents

Day 1 – Introducing NLP 1

Day 2 – The Three Minds..11

Day 3 – Unconscious Mind Prime Directives............................20

Day 4 – NLP Presuppositions...26

Day 5 – Sensory Acuity & Calibration 34

Day 6 – Communication with NLP 43

Day 7 – Language..58

Day 8 – Meta Programs 72

Day 9 – Values...85

Day 10 – Meta Model 93

Day 11 – States and State Management..................................105

Day 12 – Reframing...116

Day 13 – Ericksonian Hypnosis...124

Day 14 – Using Hypnotic Suggestions..................................137

Day 15 – Eye Accessing Cues 147

Day 16 – Perceptual Positions 155

Day 17 – Rapport 165

Day 18 – Understanding Submodalities..................................172

Day 19 – Using Submodalities 183

Day 20 – Anchors 191

Day 21 – Using Anchors 201

Day 22 – Congruence and Parts 212

Day 23 – Parts Processes 218

Day 24 – Beliefs..233

Day 25 – Understanding Timeline 245

Day 26 – Timeline Processes 255

Day 27 – Strategies 267

Day 28 – Neurological Levels 277

Day 29 – Outcomes and Goals...286

Day 30 – Putting It All Together...297

Where to From Here 315

References..319

Day 1 –
Introducing NLP

Can you imagine a set of tools that will allow you to use your mind with optimum power to take control of your life? Neuro Linguistic Programming is such with the added benefits that have an ongoing personal development effect.

NLP is learning how your mind works and how to navigate and change it productively to make the improvements you want in your life. The added bonus is that you can also use the techniques to help others change their thoughts and behaviors too.

NLP has been described as the latest cutting-edge technology with a laser precision influence. These techniques, tools, and understandings can be utilized in business, education, sales, management, therapy, parenting, relationships, training, and more. In fact, NLP contains valuable skills which can be transferred to any area of life. Many call it the art and science of personal excellence. Over the years, millions of people from all corners of the world and all walks of life have benefited from NLP.

Nelson Mandela so eloquently stated, "Taking charge of our lives puts us in power of our actions, our light – our life."

Understanding NLP
When we teach an NLP Practitioner certification, we ask our students to tell us what they think NLP is. We share with you some of the most common definitions:
- The manual to run the mind, brain, and body
- A systemic approach to understanding human effectiveness

- Skills and techniques to have a successful and happy life
- Software for the brain
- Communication and modeling tools to achieve excellence at whatever you choose

In general, most definitions center around personal development. NLP can provide useful ways of improving performance and being even more competent and in control of thoughts, emotions, and behaviors.

Richard Bandler, one of the co-founders of NLP, has been quoted as saying that "NLP is an attitude, and a curiosity that leaves behind a trail of techniques."

It is also defined as a system of organizing human behavior into its smallest component parts, on both verbal and nonverbal levels.

We are fortunate to live in an age of science and technology as it helps us immensely to understand NLP. Much like a computer has programs, we too have programs – programs for learning, for selling, for parenting, managing, loving, speaking, playing, teaching; in fact, we have a program for everything we do.

These programs are created from our life experiences and are influenced by the language we speak to others and to ourselves, and through our non-verbal language patterns.

Utilizing the unconscious mind, where we store and operate these programs from, we can clear old, ineffective programs and behaviors as well as create new, beneficial and lasting programs that allow us to be on a direct path toward our goals and outcomes.

Although the name **Neuro Linguistic Programming** could imply almost anything, it actually encompasses the three most powerful instruments involved in the human experience, which are neurology, language, and mental programming.

The **Neuro**logical system is responsible for how we process information and regulate our bodies. The brain is the center of this magnetic field. It is controlled by the three minds and through thought impulses. Emotions trigger the chemicals that activate the nervous system and keep it regulated. All thoughts are the electricity of the system, and emotions are the magnetism of the system. The chemicals that are necessary for the nervous system come from the physiology of the body. All three are necessary for the brain, mind and body connection to operate.

Put simply, our neurology or nervous system processes our experiences via our five senses: what we see, hear, feel, taste, touch, and smell. We learned about this in primary school. We see, we hear, and we feel our external world, and in a nanosecond we internalize it.

Language or **linguistics** determines how we interface and communicate with ourselves and others. Interestingly, it is directly connected to our verbal and nonverbal language which describes our lives and experiences. Then we speak in terms of how we experience things.

Programming determines the kinds of models we create and act from. This in turn produces a physiology or body posture with muscle tensions and weight distributions. We organize our experiences in our programs, which are held in the unconscious mind which is holographic, therefore not only in the mind but also in our bodies.

All three work together simultaneously, continuously and in dovetail manner. One influences and affects the others all the time. When we change our internal image and language, then we change our physiology – your psychology is your biology.

Changing your language changes your neurology and your physiology.

Neuro	Linguistic	Programming
The neurology of your brain-body including neurons, chemicals, bioelectrical currents, and neural networks of connectivity.	Verbal and nonverbal communication based on your five senses and how you make sense of the world around you.	How your mind organizes into patterns, your beliefs, behaviors, emotions, and thoughts.

What Can You Do with NLP?

NLP teaches you to habitually take a systematic approach to life. To understand the different fundamentals that are part of the system and how they function. The system consists of events, thoughts, feelings, actions, and interactions with people and situations. Once you understand how the system is working, you have a means of navigating and operating it consciously, then unconsciously. In simple terms, NLP is like an electrician unraveling the wiring and bringing it up to code based upon the type of system it is supporting.

NLP is widely understood and used today in all areas of business, education, family, health, finance, and personal development.

NLP is a study of excellence; it is the latest technique of mind maintenance that comes from a person's desire to get more out of their life than what they have settled for and are usually achieving. As a thought system it gives you choices. What makes NLP so effective is its ability to break down functions into very small chunks or pieces and to find the internal processes that operate, such as thoughts and feelings, and at the same time determine the external behaviors or what the person is doing.

NLP is a very powerful body of knowledge, techniques, and processes. Hypnosis is interwoven throughout the fibers of most practices. Most of our programs are automatic or habitual. To be able to access your unconscious mind and clear and change your old, unwanted behaviors and limiting thoughts and beliefs seems magical. NLP offers you a way to deliberately use your brain and to have the life you want.

A Brief History of NLP

Historically, Neuro Linguistics comes from a long history of processes, techniques, and beliefs of the physical influences on the mind, using language dating back to as early as 1861 from the work of Dr. Paul Broca (1824-1880) and later studied by Alfred Korzybski, a general semanticist (1879-1950). Korzybski coined the term Neuro Linguistic in his book Science and Sanity, written in 1933. He also had a training called Neuro-Linguistic Training, in 1941. He saw it was a key element in developing a better understanding of the role and limitations of language and how we build our maps of the world. Much is attributed to Korzybski in NLP. As we now know, the world was not fully equipped to understand and utilize these concepts that became tools. As the computer age was born, the timing became ripe for NLP.

The basis of NLP we know today was originated in California in the early 1970s, primarily by John Grinder and Richard Bandler. Grinder was a Professor of Linguistics at the University of California, Santa Cruz, and Bandler was a student of Gestalt Therapy. As mentioned before, most of NLP was based on methods and understandings that were developed much earlier by countless doctors, researchers, educators, and philosophers. What these two men did was to:

- Replicate excellence with modeling techniques
- Systemize and make practical the tools for communication
- Unify these methods for success

By exploring how people excelled in their profession, they found patterns of behavior, thinking, and specific unified models to copy. They found that if other people could do something successful and excel, it could be replicated.

While Bandler and Grinder developed many of the early models and techniques, they were assisted by a committed core group of colleagues and students, including Leslie Cameron-Bandler, Judith Delozier, Robert Dilts, David Gordon, Frank Pucelik, Byron Lewis, Jim Eicher, Mary Beth Myers-Anderson and Stephen Gilligan, and many others.

What we do know is that the original foundations of NLP were modeled on the excellence of three professionals in the psychotherapy field.

 The first was **Fritz Perls** (1893-1970). A psychotherapist and one of the founders of Gestalt therapy, "Fritz" Frederick was born in 1893 in Germany. He earned his M.D. degree in 1926, and then worked at the Institute for Brain Damaged Soldiers in Frankfurt. Here he was influenced by Gestalt psychologists, and existential philosophers. Perls and his wife, Laura Posner Perls, founded Gestalt Therapy. They were not satisfied with psychoanalysis and wanted something different to help patients. Gestalt psychology, with its emphasis on the whole person, was a useful principle for the development of this new type of therapy. His work noted that many people split off from their experiences that are uncomfortable. One of his goals with his work was to move people into owning their experiences and developing into a healthy whole or gestalt. He moved to South Africa in the early 1940s and in the 1950s moved to New York City, where he and

his wife organized the New York Institute of Gestalt Therapy. In the 1960s, they moved to California where he continued to do Gestalt therapy workshops until his death in 1970. One of his most important publications was Gestalt Therapy Verbatim (1969) which describes his gestalt therapy work.

 **Virginia Satir** (1916 – 1988), a family therapist, is referred to as "The Mother of Family System Therapy." Born in Wisconsin on June 26,1916, her career spanned over 45 years. Rather than placing her focus on illness, Satir's style came to be based on personal growth. She was concerned with the health and healing of each individual human spirit by connecting with a universal life force.

As early as age five, she recalled that she knew what she wanted to do when she would grow up. She said, "I'd be a children's detective on parents." She was educated at the University of Chicago and received her master's degree from their School of Social Service Administration. She worked at the Dallas Child Guidance Center and at the Illinois State Psychiatric Institute. Later she helped start the Mental Research Institute in Palo Alto, California. She was instrumental in forming this country's first formal program in Family Therapy.

Satir has written or co-written twelve books. Her first book was published in 1964 and was called Conjoint Family Therapy. Peoplemaking was published in 1972. Another popular book, done in 1988, is The New Peoplemaking. She died in that same year, on September 10, in San Mateo, California.

According to author Steven Andreas, Satir helped people to reshape their way of problem solving into more positive ways. He quotes her as saying, "Problems are not the problem; coping is the problem. Coping is the outcome of self-worth, rules of the family systems, and links to the outside world." She recommends that a person pursue their dreams instead of trying to determine whether the dreams can be realized or not.

 **Dr. Milton H. Erickson M.D.** (1901-1980) was both a psychiatrist and a medical doctor, having received his medical degree and his master's degree in psychology simultaneously. He was the founding president of the American Society for Clinical Hypnosis, as well as the founder and editor of that society's professional journal. His professional life since 1950 has included both a busy private practice in Phoenix, Arizona, and constant traveling to offer seminars in hypnosis and lectures both in the United States and many foreign countries. What is less well known is the fact that Dr. Erickson has a unique approach to psychotherapy which represents a major innovation in therapeutic technique. For many years he had been developing effective and practical methods of treatment, which may or may not have involved the formal induction of trance.

Grinder and Bandler and their team studied the patterns of these therapists and refined them into models for effective communication, personal change, accelerated learning, and greater enjoyment of life.

The basis of their research and modeling was that people have three elements that make up how a person functions.
1. **How people THINK**
2. **How people FEEL**
3. **What people DO**

Everyone has ways of thinking, feeling and behaving that are individual and makes them either effective or ineffective in whatever they are involved in. Most people are completely unaware of these basic elements as they are automatic or unconscious patterns.

How Can I Use NLP?

There is a New Guinea proverb that says, Knowledge is only a rumor until it is in the muscle. This is true for almost everything that you want to learn in life, and NLP is no exception.

Often people come to the Institute with basic knowledge of NLP from books they have read or workshops they have attended, and they want to know more. They found that the missing ingredient was the actual trying out of the techniques. It would be like learning tai chi or yoga from a book without doing the poses. It's not impossible, but it's faster and more powerful when you have a coach or facilitator assisting your movements and learning.

First and foremost, we'd say that NLP should be used with yourself first. There are plenty of tools and techniques that will give you skills to maintain yourself in body, mind, and spirit. We have found that when people learn to do this, they then transmit an unsaid energy about themselves that translates certainty to others about who they are. Often, people will come up and say, "I've noticed how calm and at peace you are and I'm wondering how you achieved it." This is a general but common statement that can invoke a person to share with others some of the simple techniques for change.

With the millions of people who have learned NLP, there are unlimited possible uses and applications.

You can use NLP in business to promote top-notch sales and customer service results. It is also an effective way to implement and change organizational procedures and structures.

In schools, NLP can assist teachers with the teaching and learning styles of both verbal and nonverbal language of every child. It can identify how each one learns best.

Therapists, coaches, and counselors have more efficient tools to help people in a shorter time frame.

Medical professionals can use language and simple techniques to alleviate anxieties and fears, as well as assist people to heal with faster procedures.

When you learn NLP and use it in your life, you will enjoy far greater control and freedom over your own state of mind, responses, and interactions with others. You will find a greater degree of rapport and communication with others, recognize how others are using language to influence you and change unwanted habits and behaviors that hold you back. You will find it much easier to clarify your dreams for the future and identify barriers that may be keeping you stuck while changing the unwanted habits and behaviors that are standing in your way. You will understand your partner's and children's needs and communication styles more fully and you will find it easier to achieve your personal and professional goals, because you will gain greater access to your internal toolbox and resources.

Day 2 –
The Three Minds

In NLP we recognize and work with the three minds: our Conscious, Unconscious and Higher Conscious Mind. These minds operate simultaneously; in fact, one does not work without the other. Our understanding of the mind can influence how we run our lives and use our brains. In fact, how a person uses their mind with well formed communication makes the difference in how things are thought and acted upon and ultimately how a life is lived.

When we understand the mind, we can harness its power and expand our awareness. This is a part of developing the mind and taking responsibility for what is in it. Mastering the mind and your states of awareness is easy once you know how it works. Everything we are begins in the mind. This is where your programs are filed, chronologically and categorically and individually. It all starts with a thought.

Johnjoe McFadden, Professor of Molecular Genetics at the University of Surrey in the UK, believes our conscious mind could be an electromagnetic field. "The theory solves many previously intractable problems of consciousness and could have profound implications for our concepts of mind, free will, spirituality, the design of artificial intelligence, and even life and death." This may account for the "Law of Attraction," that happens when we have thoughts.

Most people consider "mind" to be all the conscious things that we are aware of. However, most mental activity goes on without conscious awareness. Actions such as walking, opening a door, or eating an ice cream can become as automatic as breathing. Let's look at the three minds in more depth.

Conscious or Thinking Mind

The conscious mind is the state you inhabit during waking awareness. It is your present time experience of environmental and internal sensations, feelings, thoughts, attitudes, and awareness of impressions entering your mind. This is where we think, perceive, judge, analyze, do and choose. Its thinking capability is limited to whatever it is focusing on at any moment as it is always anticipating what is going to happen next. It gathers information from the external world via the five senses. It then stores this information in the unconscious mind, otherwise you would have to continuously learn everything over and over again.

The conscious mind represents 10% of the mind, yet it "thinks" it runs everything. It is only as good as what is being received and filtered in from the external world and what has been stored in the unconscious mind. Being the awake mind, it is limited in how much it can be aware of at any one moment in time. The magic formula 7 ± 2 chunks of information is what George Miller claims an average human can hold in working memory. The conscious mind is responsible for logic and reasoning. When you think about taking any voluntary action such as crossing the street or calling a friend, it is activated by your conscious mind. When you are aware of the things that you are either doing or want to do, it is your conscious mind at work. Whenever there is logic or reasoning, you are using your conscious mind.

Unconscious Mind

The unconscious mind has more influence and power than the conscious mind. It represents 90% of the mind. It is the storehouse for memories, emotions, habits, values, beliefs, and behaviors. In fact, everything you ever saw, heard, felt, tasted, smelt, said to yourself, or experienced is stored here. It has an unlimited capacity for storage. It controls the autonomic nervous system, which acts as a control system that affects heart rate, digestion, respiration rate, salivation, perspiration, diameter of the pupils, urination, and sexual arousal. It is the part of your mind responsible for all your involuntary actions such as emotions and breathing.

It is important to note that it has no decision making facilities, therefore it does not know right from wrong, good from bad, it just accepts what is presented. It is said that the unconscious mind works through the Law of Attraction. It is a servant to follow your orders. It is constantly eavesdropping on whatever you say, do and think, and this becomes your reality; whether you mean it or not, it makes it true.

From birth to about age 7, a child is unconsciously gathering like a sponge whatever is around him and how it relates to him. This is a critical time when beliefs, values, habits, and behaviors are formed. The unconscious mind can be trained and reprogrammed. Using NLP we can identify unwanted and limiting patterns and unresolved negative emotions, in order to clear and replace them with solutions and desired states.

Albert Einstein, Milton Erickson, Sigmund Freud, and Carl Jung paved the way for us toward understanding the minds. They knew something that few realized at the time – most of what happens in our life is driven by our unconscious mind. More than 95% of the neural activity in your brain is unconscious. You don't have to think about breathing, blinking, digesting your food, balancing, hearing, and don't forget to breathe, swallow; it's endless. You don't have to think how you will walk across the floor or how you brush your teeth or dodge another pedestrian. You just do it. You don't have to think about much at all. In fact, when we do think during routine activities, we often interrupt the pattern.

For instance, can you remember the last time you tripped going up some stairs? It's because you thought about going up the stairs. You see, when the unconscious mind is doing its job the conscious mind is left to focus on whatever is happening, such as typing, talking on the phone, texting, or making a plan.

The Higher Conscious Mind

The higher conscious mind is part of the unconscious mind. It is knowingness, intuition, and information that come from the higher self and the collective consciousness. This is the part of the mind that knows your purpose in life, it is not judgmental or critical. It is there to guide you and assist you. Sigmund Freud calls it the Superego, Carl Jung the Spiritual part of the mind.

The unconscious mind is pivotal in its actions. It takes information from your higher conscious mind as intuition or knowingness and passes it on to the conscious mind. We communicate with this part of our mind when we relax and go within and let go. Mediation, trances, and light sleep or naps evoke this mind. The ah-ha or eureka moments spring from here.

Having a good communication with this part of the unconscious mind can be established through knowing how it sounds or feels and how it presents information to you. Keeping the unconscious mind free of limiting patterns and negative feedback loops allows the stream of data to come through with ease. And the more you develop the connection, the stronger the communication becomes.

Differences between the Conscious and Unconscious Mind

Conscious Mind...
- is only aware of 7 + or – bits of information at a time.
- is sequential. It likes logical order.
- is logical. It likes things to make sense – have a reason.
- is linear thinking. It thinks in terms of cause-effect.
- seeks answers to "why"?
- does your intellectual thinking. Is responsible for your self-talk.
- is associated with the waking, thinking state.
- can voluntarily move parts of your body.
- is only aware of the now.
- seeks understanding of problems and reasons that if it understands them, it can make them go away.
- is deliberate.
- is verbal (including self-talk).
- is analytical.
- is the place of cognitive learning and understanding.
- uses the intellect to come up with logical solutions for problems.
- will tell you when you're right because the facts line up.
- has limited focus.

Unconscious Mind...
- is aware of everything else.
- processes simultaneously. It multitasks.
- is intuitive and can make associations of information easily.
- makes associations and connections between many thoughts, ideas, and feelings.
- knows why.
- does your perceiving and feeling.
- is associated with the dreaming (including day dreaming), reflecting, meditating, and sleeping state.
- can involuntarily move parts of your body.

- is unlimited in time and space. It holds all your memories and future constructs.
- decides what it will do about it. It can forget (amnesia), distort (make false associations) or break connections (get over it).
- is automatic.
- is nonverbal (feeling).
- is literal.
- is the place of experiential learning.
- can access internal resources from memories of experiences, linking them all together – creating a resourceful state.
- will tell you when you are right because it will feel right.
- has unlimited focus.

Have you ever wondered?
- How do I know something is right or wrong, good or bad?
- How did I learn how to walk, eat, drive, and brush my teeth?
- Why do I love certain foods or dislike others?
- Why do I like some people automatically and with others it takes time?

All the answers to these questions are deep within your unconscious mind. And *everything that you say, do and think* comes from those programs that get built from infancy to now. You are a work in progress. Everything you are or think you are comes from how you learned how to be.

I (Laureli) was amazed when I had my children to realize they had to be taught how to eat and how to get them to sleep in a normal pattern. Now I know they primarily were responding with autonomic mind functionality. Most newborn functions are involuntary and work in tandem with the conscious mind. I honestly was bewildered that although a baby has an instinct to suckle and wants to feed, it has to learn how. Everything we know how to do we learned how to do it.

So what is learning? It is defined as acquiring new knowledge, behaviors, skills, values, or preferences. It may involve processing different types of information.

Things and activities that are learnt may thereafter be performed unconsciously. As children, we learn by observing and mimicking others. We do so by repetition and replication; with hardly a thought as to why or what the ramifications may be. Some learning is automatic and some can take time. Research tells us it takes anywhere from 3 to 13 times before something is learned or automatic. People naturally have a hunger for learning. It is one of the most natural things to do. So how do we learn?

Levels of Learning

The Four Stages of Learning come from the competence theory of Abraham Maslow. It shows how a person learns and progresses from unknowing to complete skillful knowingness. Knowing and understanding the process your mind goes through to learn a task no matter how big or small, we can learn anything we desire.

The Four Levels of Learning are as follows:
- **Unconsciously Unskilled** - You don't know that you don't know.
- **Consciously Unskilled** - You are aware that you don't know.
- **Consciously Skilled** - You know how but have to think about it.
- **Unconsciously Skilled** - You just do it without thinking.

Driving a car is an example of unconscious competence:

1. There was a time when the driver didn't even think about or know he didn't know how to drive.
2. The driver now practices and realizes he is unskilled. This is where the learner can learn fast and has the greatest room for results.
3. There is skill, however it is still with conscious thought, there is a need to concentrate.
4. The driver now can drive without much thought. Of course if something untoward happens, they become more conscious, but in general they just drive.

You don't have to think about walking, or eating, or reading; in fact, everything that you do without thinking has become automatic or unconsciously skilled.

Remember, it requires consciously doing a task first to become unconsciously skilled. Repetition makes it become automatic and a pattern. Once a task is automatic (unconsciously skilled), it frees up your mind to think new things and learn other skills and tasks. Practice and modeling are ways to accelerate learning.

Unconsciously – Consciously – Skilled
There is a fifth level of learning where a person automatically responds or does something, but has a reasonable thinking process available to know they know what they are doing. This is where mastery takes place. Teachers should be unconsciously consciously skilled. When you watch someone who is unconsciously – consciously – skilled, you can see how easy they make it look.

How to Unlearn
The same principle applies if you wish to unlearn something. You would start from unconsciously skilled back to unconsciously unskilled. Let's take smoking. This is a learned practice. To unlearn it:

1. Unconsciously skilled - A person smokes with little to no awareness they have lit up.
2. Consciously skilled – They start to take notice when, why, and how they smoke.
3. Consciously Unskilled – They begin to think about doing other things instead.
4. Unconsciously Unskilled – They don't even think about smoking.

Using NLP we make the unconscious conscious. In other words, when people are more aware of what they say, do and behave, they have the influence and power to manage what is in their minds; in other words, they have choice.

NLP is the practice of discovering and revealing new ways of thinking and behaving. It is a way of continuously learning and growing and is a key factor toward personal development. When you use NLP and understand how to manage your minds, you give yourself more conscious choice over what you do and how you behave. Instead of blaming others, environment or factors, you can make inner thinking changes that will change how you experience life.

Day 3 –
Unconscious Mind Prime Directives

The key to NLP is having an understanding of how the unconscious mind works. The main roles or functions the unconscious is designed to provide are called the prime directives. One of the presuppositions we have in NLP is that when a person knows better they can do better. When we know our mind and have the ability to communicate between our conscious thinking mind and our unconscious, then we can direct and manage it. Having this understanding also helps to realize why people do what they do.

An analogy that I (Laureli) like, which describes what and how the unconscious mind operates, was written by Jonathan Haidt, a professor of psychology at the University of Virginia. He says:

> "The mind is divided in many ways, but the division that really matters is between conscious/reasoned processes and (unconscious) automatic/implicit processes. These two parts are like a rider on the back of an elephant. The rider's inability to control the elephant by force explains many puzzles about our mental life, particularly why we have such trouble with weakness of will. Learning how to train the elephant is the secret of self-improvement."

In other words, the rider is like the conscious mind, making judgments, planning, thinking, imagining with conscious (thinking) awareness. The elephant represents the thousands of automatic habits, beliefs, pathways, and behaviors that exist outside of the conscious awareness. Thus, the rider has little influence on the behavior of the elephant. He can be an adviser, but in thought only. The rider or conscious mind thinks it is in control of the elephant or unconscious mind. Although he can foresee and imagine, he cannot order nor force the elephant to do anything. In most cases, the rider doesn't even realize there is an elephant and is baffled or upset with itself because it doesn't do what it thinks it should be doing. When there is conflict between the rider (conscious mind) and the elephant (unconscious mind), the elephant will always win. This is because it is programmed to do what it does without thought. However, it is possible for the rider to train the elephant and this is where NLP comes in.

As Stephen Gilligan says, "The unconscious mind is a wonderful servant but a terrible master." Knowing how to manage your mind and master your emotions is a very powerful skill.

The unconscious mind runs without your conscious thinking mind being aware of it. It is a magnificent organized structure that surpasses any imaginable sophisticated computer in the universe. This means it is unconscious (automatic) and is unlimited in its applications.

Here are several prime directives to help you understand more about how your mind works.

Prime Directives of the Unconscious Mind

1. **Stores and organizes all of your memories**
    Everything is stored unconsciously in some sort of order. Otherwise we would not know the difference between today, tomorrow, and yesterday. The memories with the most influence have some sort of gestalt or emotive feeling in them. The more distant a memory, the less it usually affects you. In NLP we have techniques for clearing past unwanted emotions and memories and creating futures that draw us forward.

2. **The domain of the emotions**
   Your experience in life creates how you respond to what happens. Emotions are a natural occurrence. As Deepak Chopra says, we either have pleasure or pain. All types of emotions are present and when we know what is in our unconscious mind and have the ability to communicate, we can control and maintain our emotions.

3. **Represses memories with unresolved negative emotion**
   The unconscious mind will do all possible to protect a mind that does not have the ability to deal with negative emotions. People will try not to think about these negative emotions. However, this will influence how they react towards things when these repressed emotions are triggered. Often the person doesn't know why they react because it's an unconscious response.

4. **Presents repressed memories for resolution**
   The uncovering of repressed memories often results in people having things they thought they had forgotten about or dealt with come to the surface. This happens when the unconscious mind is ready to deal with whatever has been repressed. It is always good news as the unconscious mind is resourceful in its own right and knows your mind better than you do.

5. **Runs the body and has a blueprint of the body now and the body perfect**
   The unconscious mind governs the body and the nervous system. It controls heart rate, breathing, digestion, temperature, blood pressure, waste removal, creates new cells and much, much more. Some of the other things it does for you without your conscious thought are:
   • The stomach lining is replaced every 5 days
   • New skin every 30 days
   • Liver every 6 weeks

- Entire skeletal every 3 months
- Every year 95% of the atoms are replaced
- Handles physical motion when walking, talking, standing, sitting

6. **A servant to follow orders**

   The unconscious mind is constantly eavesdropping and responding to what you think, say and do. It processes everything as true, real. It does not filter information for what is right or wrong, good or bad. It just accepts the information, feelings, and thoughts and does its best to follow orders. What suggestions are you giving yourself? In one day we think more than 60 thousand thoughts – and every thought is a suggestion to our unconscious mind.

7. **Controls and maintains all perceptions. Receives and transmits perceptions to the conscious mind**

   Generates a "Consciousness." It serves as a liaison for thoughts and intelligence to surface to a "now" awareness. It functions as a sorter, reasoning, intellectualizing component that forms our opinions from the data that is held in our existing programs or minds. The information comes in via the five physical senses, which are stimulated by the environment. It attracts and/or repels depending on what you are consciously thinking.

8. **Maintains instincts and generates habits**

   It surfaces back material to remember learned information when needed for "now" and interprets it in a meaningful way. Our instincts and habits then become automatic or unconscious responses. Knowing this helps us to realize that we can change our habits if they are not congruent or how we wish to behave and respond.

9. **Functions best as a whole integrated unit**
   Often people have multiple parts that can interfere or cause conflict. The mind works best when communicating the same message. If there are multiple commands or thoughts that are conflicting, it then becomes confused. Many people think they have a weak mind instead of realizing that their mind is doing exactly what it is being told to do. For instance, when there are conflicting thoughts or two different messages, instead of taking action it does nothing. We often jokingly refer to these as devil and angel thoughts. This is when the thinking mind talks to itself with words of encouragement on one hand and words of negativity on another. This confuses the unconscious mind into states of stuckness or no action. Generally, when two opposing thoughts come, the negative thought will prevail.

10. **Symbolic, uses and responds to symbols**
    It uses symbols, as it doesn't have conscious words to communicate to itself. It doesn't know the difference between fantasy and reality. It communicates with pictures and feelings. The doorway to the unconscious is through imagination. For instance, when you think of peace what do you notice? How about war? Whatever you imagine or feel is your symbol. In the dream world, the unconscious mind is controlling thoughts and perceptions. This is why dreams are so strange and iconic. When you begin to understand and know your symbols, they communicate information to you.

11. **Takes everything personally and literally. It is unable to judge**
    As it has no thinking or filtering capabilities, the unconscious mind accepts emotions, thoughts, and perceptions as true and literal. It is unable to make

judgments. Knowing this makes you more responsible for how and what you think and put into your mind.

12. **Is unable to process negatives (directly)**

This is possibly the most powerful prime directive to remember. Since the mind is literal, it does not have the capability of automatically deleting negatives. For instance, if I say, "Don't think of a cat" – you will notice that you have to think of a cat first in order to "not." This goes for how you speak to yourself as well as to others. Remember – always say it the way you want it! Avoid using "not," "don't," and similar words, because these simply don't deliver the results you want.

Day 4 –
NLP Presuppositions

The basic foundations and beliefs upon which NLP is understood and carried out are called Presuppositions. A Presupposition is simply an assumption. They are statements that are not necessarily true, however, they are useful as assumptions when modeling or working with ourselves and other people. NLP Presuppositions give a philosophical basis for understanding how people operate and offer an opportunity to better understand people. Through our own journeys in NLP, we have found over fifty different NLP Presuppositions via various websites and books. You may find many worded a bit differently from source to source, yet the ideas remain firm.

Today we will be sharing ten Presuppositions with you. We have chosen these Presuppositions because they can automatically act as filters, which help us to understand, respect and communicate more effectively. You don't necessarily have to believe or agree with these Presuppositions. Some will fit, some may not; they are just some of the guidelines and foundations that NLP is based on.

Presuppositions of NLP

1. **The meaning of communication is the response you get**. When you understand this presupposition it lets you know immediately if you are communicating or not. It also puts the responsibility of how you communicate back to you. Often we express ourselves with only a bit of information and expect the listener to understand or know what we mean.

For example: You tell a co-worker that the information they provided you was missing an essential piece of data. They respond with: "What do you mean you can't use the work I gave you." Now you never said that you couldn't use it, they made that deduction. However, what it does tell you is that perhaps they needed more specific instructions or detail from you. Therefore, this communication was not communicated effectively.

2. **The Map is not the territory.**

   This presupposition comes from the founder of General Semantics Alfred Korzybski. Simplified, this presupposition is saying that, as human beings, we cannot know reality, we can only know our perceptions of our reality; and it is generally not our reality that limits us, but rather our inner map of what we think is our reality.

   For example: a rainy day to a farmer may be exactly perfect, while that same rainy day to a courier could spell calamity – it is what is in our own beliefs that create our reality and our map of reality.

   "If there is any one secret of success, it lies in the ability to get the other person's point of view and see things from that person's angle as well as your own." Henry Ford

3. **Respect for other people's model of the world.**

   We each have a different map; this creates our model of the world made up of each person's unique personal history. When we are able to respect, yet not always understand, other people's models of their worlds, this allows us to create rapport on a deeper level and takes away the judgment component of the thinking process.

For example: Milton Erickson was a master at creating rapport and respecting other people's model of their world. When he worked in a psychiatric hospital, a patient who had been there for 9 years came to his attention. No one knew who he was, he did not communicate or have any conversations with anyone, and if someone would say "Good morning," he would reply in a word salad, "Not a good day, didn't go away, air in the wind," things like that… just irrelevant words all mixed up and made no sense at all. Milton was curious and got permission to work with him. He endeavored many times to communicate with the man, but only got word salad. So he sent his secretary to take down his word salad and transcribe it. Then he went through the word salad dictation and prepared a similar type of word salad. Then one morning he said "Good morning," and the man replied with a big word salad; Milton responded with his prepared word salad and it went on for a couple of hours. Finally, the man said, "Why don't you talk sense, Dr. Erickson?" Milton said, "I'd be glad to, what is your name?"; then was able to get the man's address, and then the man slipped back into word salad, so did Milton, however by the end of the day he had a complete history and rapport. Within a year, he was released from the hospital and had a job.

4. **People are doing the best they can with the resources they have available.**
   This presupposition takes away judgment allowing the ability to forgive and perhaps understand a person from a different perspective. We all have within us all the resources we need at each moment in our lives. We do the best we can dependent upon how we are programmed.

   For example: A young mother screams at her children and in effect they only respond to her when they hear that certain tone in her voice. She realizes that this is how she was disciplined (and not very effectively). She did not have a better resource available until she found a better one. Sometimes people never find a more effective resource. Moreover, we live in a day and age where people are changing and finding or recovering choice and therefore available resources. The basic assumption is that somewhere inside each person lies the resource to live a better life, and when we clear the limited beliefs and limiting language it frees us to accept these resources.

5. **There is no failure only feedback. As** Homer Simpson once said, "Trying is the first step towards failure." A successful person knows that failures are truly pathways to new opportunities and discoveries. Everything we have ever desired or thought of came from this principle. History provides us with numerous examples of the importance of adopting this NLP Presupposition. Without it, our lives are stagnant and offer little to no advancement. Modification and adjustments allow freedom to search, grow and have experiences along the way.

For example: Scientists use this strategy every time they invent or do research. They push and prod, because they know that whatever they are working on will only expose their strengths and weaknesses when pushed to the limit. Think about all the things you have done that you have accepted as feedback. Now ask yourself if you can allow yourself to know that in all things there is no failure, only feedback. How would that change your life?

"It is common sense to take a method and try it. If it fails, admit it frankly and try another. But above all, try something." Franklin D. Roosevelt

6. **A person is not their behavior.**
   Can you remember the last time you had a bad behavior? Now for what purpose did you have such behavior? Are you that behavior? Behaviors are what we do with our emotions. It is a normal human function. An event happens and ultimately it gives us a state or emotion. From our emotions, it goes through our body and we have an automatic physical reaction and our body posture mimics these emotions. This results in having behavior and it all happens within a nanosecond. When we realize people are not their behaviors, it gives us a bigger perspective from which to view others and ourselves.

   "Remember, happiness doesn't depend upon who you are or what you have; it depends solely upon what you think." Dale Carnegie

7. **When people know better they can do better.**
   As all NLP Presuppositions are subjective, this one assumes that as we learn we adjust our attitude and behaviors. There are times when we measure our success or failure by the fact we are not yet where we want to be. Considering our new behaviors and thoughts is growing and is a part of the journey of life. I would like to add one word to this presupposition, which is "they can do better." There is always choice.

8. **People have all the resources they need to succeed and achieve their desired results.**
   Without this assumption, it would be difficult to help yourself and others. Within each person is that inner flicker and flame of who they are at the wholeness of themselves. Perhaps it has been blocked or covered by negative experiences and limiting beliefs or unresourceful thoughts. A large part of NLP is based upon the recovery

of these resources that we can reveal and then make even better.

"Nurture your mind with great thoughts, for you will never go higher than you think." Benjamin Disraeli

9. **All procedures should increase wholeness and choice.** It is human nature to want to find solutions for issues and problems in life. It is important to remember that not everything is broken and that some things work well as they are. The adage If it's not broke, don't fix it is what this presupposition is all about. This allows for ecology to be taken into consideration as well. There should always be a moment of reflection before any technique or procedure is begun. A good way to do this is to ask, "Is this a solution for today that will cause a problem or consequence tomorrow?"

We once had a student ask us if it would be okay to clear a past memory that was happy or pleasant. The answer is "Does it increase wholeness and choice?" If not, then do not proceed.

10. **Resistance in communication is a sign of lack of rapport.** Too often, people blame someone else for "not being ready" or being stubborn when they communicate with them. If you have any resistance when you communicate from your point of view or from the other person's, it means that you have either not built rapport properly yet or you have lost it. As an effective communicator, when you have any resistance it is your responsibility to regain it. It only takes a few moments to get into rapport.

Interestingly, this Presupposition is often looked at only as rapport with other people. However, resistance with anything can be a sign of a lack of rapport with it. Think about it, have you ever had resistance with money? Or with time? If you have resistance with anyone or anything, it just might be that you do not have rapport. Therefore, you can then identify what is incongruent or missing and regain rapport with the person or with the thing or concept.

As we mentioned, we've seen over fifty different Presuppositions in various places. Each day we are using a variety of these Presuppositions in our own daily lives and we are discussing relevant ones with our clients. When we meet a challenging person, we are bringing to mind that people are doing the best with the resources they have available. When things in life are not going as we planned, we remember the law of requisite variety. When a project or idea doesn't work, we know that there is no failure, only feedback. Presuppositions can be everywhere they are useful.

Additional Presuppositions:
- Every behavior is useful in some context.
- Every behavior has a positive intention.
- You are in charge of your mind, therefore of your results.
- The most important information is about a person's behavior.
- The mind and body are connected and therefore affect each other.
- Everyone has the potential for genius.
- If what you are doing isn't working, do something different. Anything.
- Change makes change.
- You cannot not communicate.
- If it's possible for someone, it's possible for me.
- People work perfectly.
- Choice is better than no choice.
- Experience has a structure.
- Modeling success leads to success.

- If you want to understand, experience it.
- People respond to their experience, not to reality.
- Experience is not reality.
- Changing our experience of reality changes reality.
- Anything can be accomplished when the task is broken down into small enough chunks.
- The messenger never rests until the message is delivered.
- We learn something new every day. Most of it is unconscious.
- People constantly change.

Day 5 –
Sensory Acuity & Calibration

Have you ever been so involved in an activity that you have missed something else that was going on? Or maybe someone was even talking to you or saying your name and you didn't hear a word they said? How about this – have you ever watched someone playing a video game and that is all that exists in their world? Or someone so engrossed in a television program or book that they don't know you are even there?

We've all had this experience: someone is talking to you and it's time to go. You give them all of the polite signals like looking at your watch, taking small steps backward, shifting your posture, using closing statements like "ok then"

and "alright" – with that tonality you have which means to you "I'm done." Yet, no matter how subtle about going you are, or even how obtuse, the person talking to you doesn't get your message – and for the time being, you're stuck.

On the other hand, do you know people who are able to read others very well? They know when you mean no when you're saying yes. They know when you have a question before you even said you did. They know exactly the right tone of voice or volume or words to say based on a facial expression. They know when to leave you alone, encourage you to talk or invite you out simply on what they notice.

These people seem to have an innate ability to know what you are thinking or feeling without words being exchanged. They are great communicators, phenomenal negotiators, successful sales people, exemplary parents and wonderful role-models. Is there a 'trick' to what they are doing?

All of these examples have something in common – **sensory acuity**, and in the first examples, a lack of sensory acuity.

Sensory acuity refers to the ability to notice and be sensitive to what you see, hear and feel from other people. People who are skilled at sensory acuity notice when someone wants to wrap up a conversation, they notice when a person's mood may have changed based on a facial expression, breathing pattern, muscle tension, or shift in posture. People who are skilled at sensory acuity are able to know when someone has a question, is uncomfortable, is confused, is ready to move on – all from observation.

The person who doesn't notice the signals that you are ready for a conversation to end or doesn't notice the "don't talk to me" vibe that you are giving has poor sensory acuity skills. This person is so wrapped up in their own model of the world that a flying pig could float by and they wouldn't notice. Building your skills of sensory acuity will help you to notice not only obvious things like a flying pig, but also the more subtle messages and non-verbal communication aspects that a person is saying, without saying anything through words. This is one skill, which when you master will put you head and shoulders above your peers and colleagues in being seen as an exceptional communicator.

Sensory acuity is a skill you can build by being more aware and open to much more than just the words that a person is saying. When being sensory acute, the aim is simply to notice changes, not to make meaning of the changes you notice. We don't want to mind read, make a judgment or make an assumption, just notice. When you notice a change, you can then ask a question, calibrate for meaning or simply make note of the change for future reference.

A tip when using sensory acuity: a soft visual gaze or **peripheral vision** will assist you in noticing more of what you see, hear and feel.

When you are focused on something – with your eyes or ears, listening to or watching only the content being delivered, this is known as **foveal vision** or hearing. Foveal vision acts like blinders on a horse – so the horse can only see what is in front of him and nothing to his sides. When a person is using foveal vision when communicating, he is seeing only what is in front of him and nothing to the sides. This also means that in foveal vision a person is much more unaware of subtle changes to a person's facial expression, breathing rate, skin tone, body posture, and many other aspects which you can more easily see when using peripheral vision. Most of what a person is communicating is not in the foreground of awareness.

Peripheral vision, although aimed at the eyes and how a person sees, actually opens up the possible awareness of information in the background. By moving your eyes to peripheral vision, you will be able to see more, hear more and feel more. Therefore, having more information to filter communication and make better meanings from what you can see, hear and feel.

When using sensory acuity, the following are some of the traits you can be open to noticing:
- **Breathing rate and** location – you can notice if a person has started to breathe more deeply (from their stomach), if they are holding their breath or if their breath has become shallow (from their upper chest).
- **Blinking rate** – has the person started to blink more rapidly or has their gaze become locked on something.
- **Skin color** – watch for blushing or redness of the neck, cheeks, and nose, or be aware of when a person loses color and goes pale.

- **Muscle tension** – notice if someone's muscles become loose or tighten in their jaw, neck, shoulders, arms, hands, and legs.
- **Body posture** – has the person's shoulders just slumped, did they just sit up right, is their head leaning forward or tilted to one side, did they just cross or uncross their legs, are they still or fidgety?
- **Physiology** – in addition to posture, has their physiology moved? Did their leg twitch, eye twitch, did they smile, frown (with their mouth or eyebrows), did their facial expression change, did they cross or uncross their arms?
- **Voice tone** – you can hear if a person's tonality has changed – from neutral to angry, angry to calm, calm to frustrated, or many other changes and combinations.
- **Voice volume** – you can notice if a person's volume gets louder or softer.
- **Voice pitch** – listen to the pitch of a person's voice, notice if it got deeper or higher.
- **Eye contact** – has someone stopped making eye contact, are they now making sporadic eye contact, are they staring at you.
- **Head nod or shake** – is the person saying yes or no with their head movement.
- **Words** – when listening, you can notice if a person's words have changed, or if they have moved from first person (me, my, I) to second person (you, they, one).
- **Somatic syntax** – somatic syntax refers to how we represent the words we use with our body. You can watch how someone describes what they are saying through their hand gestures, body movements, and actions while talking. They may be using hand motions to refer to their future or past, a weight, temperature, location of a feeling, denseness/density or lightness of something.

As you get more skilled at sensory acuity, you can start to notice even the more subtle changes of a person. Dr. Milton Erickson was said to be a master at sensory acuity – he could apparently see the heart rate of his clients by watching their ankle; not by watching for it, but by being observant to it.

As we mentioned earlier – when you notice a change through sensory acuity, this gives you an insight into the person's unconscious model of the world. After noticing something, you can then: ask a question, calibrate for meaning or simply make note of the change for future reference. What we want to avoid when being sensory acute is mind reading. When we mind read, we are in effect making a judgment about what we have noticed from another person based on our own model of the world.

Has something like this ever happened to you: you are deep in thought about something and someone walks into the room and looks at you. They walk over to you and say, "You look really angry, what's wrong?" This then gets you thinking (and possibly angry), "am I angry?", "do I look angry when I'm thinking?" What has just happened? Someone saw you, used sensory acuity, stepped momentarily into your facial expression and made an incorrect assumption based on their model of the world. Unfortunately, this happens all the time.

Remember, the best option when you notice something is to ask a question, calibrate for meaning or make note of the change for future reference.

Not long ago, I (Heidi) was assisting one of my clients with some relationship difficulties she was having. When we talked about her partner, I noticed that her jaw tightened, her cheeks went red, and her eyes got narrow. I asked her about what I noticed: "Sue, when you started to talk about your partner, I noticed your jaw get tight, your cheeks went red, and you squinted your eyes – I'm curious, what was going on inside of you?" Her answer will tell me about her thoughts, emotions, memories, or whatever else she may have been aware of. Now that I have asked, I have more specific information based on her model of the world. I can, with fair accuracy, calibrate (make meaning) of these visual cues in the future. The next time Sue tightens her jaw, gets red cheeks and squints her eyes, there is a good chance that she is having the same internal reaction as this time. When you are able to make meaning of what you notice this is known as **calibration**. Your calibration will be more useful when you use clean calibration; that is, you ask or verify meaning of what you have noticed versus mind reading or making an assumption based on your model of the world.

As trainers we are very sensory acute to our students. In the first few hours of meeting a new group, we are noticing and calibrating for facial expressions, tonality changes, body changes, and anything else that will tell us that people are in a state of comprehension, understanding, eagerness to learn, and willingness to learn. We are noticing head nods, when people write notes, eyes registering understanding, eye movements to a space of visual remembered or visual construct, physical movement to the edge of one's seat, and any other external signs that someone is involved in their learning. When a person has a question, we notice their facial expression, what they do with their hands, their breathing rate, how they hold their eyebrows or lips. Then, the next time we are sensory acute and notice those same changes, we can presuppose that this person again has a question. This is how we often ask our student, "What question do you have?" before they tell us they have a question.

Not only are we calibrating for questions and for understanding, we want also to calibrate for clarity, tiredness (time for a state change or break), confusion, when someone has just had an epiphany, when we have just touched a nerve, or when someone is very excited about something. We can use all of this information to train better, communicate more effectively, and more importantly, to understand and respect our students' models of the world.

When communicating with everyone – no matter if it is your family, friends, colleagues, clients, or peers, sensory acuity and calibration skills will help you to be a better communicator.

You will be able to calibrate if someone is being truthful or if they are lying; there is not one recipe for this – you will need to use sensory acuity and then make meaning of what you notice by asking questions or calibrate for meaning. Sometimes simply asking a question will bring out the truth, because people are not used to others paying so much attention to how their body says something. A friend and I were talking about a new coffee shop the other day, I was asking if he had tried it and he said yes and he didn't like it. However, while he was saying this he took a deep breath and his chin went slightly backward and his eyes moved up and to my left (visual construct, we'll look in depth at eye patterns in a few days). This was different than what I had noticed in the past when asking him questions, so I asked him about it – "I noticed that when you said you didn't like their coffee you took a deep breath and your head moved back – what were you experiencing as you told me about this?" He sighed, shook his head and said, "I actually haven't been there, but I don't think I'd like it." I now know how to calibrate this friend for not telling the whole truth. This is a great example of why you shouldn't lie to an experienced NLPer!

In business, it is useful to be able to calibrate for understanding – without the ability to be sensory acute and calibrate there are two common issues. First, some people are prone to talking incessantly and giving too much information to make sure the person they are talking to understands what they are saying. Instead, this person could calibrate for understanding and actually save time, words, and energy by only talking until they calibrate "I get it." The second common issue is when people don't say enough and don't calibrate for understanding. They may say something which makes complete sense to them, like "Can you make a table of that information?" and just figure the person who now has that task understands what they want. When you are able to calibrate for understanding, you are at the same time calibrating for confusion, need for clarity and questions. After all, anything other than the person's signals of understanding may be a lack of understanding.

As a parent or friend, you can calibrate for when a person needs to talk about something or when they need to be left alone. We often hear news stories about people committing suicide and no one knew the person was in pain. However, there were most likely signs that something wasn't going right for that person. These signs may not have been blatant or obvious, but rather subtle and understated. However, by using sensory acuity, we have the opportunity to notice more and ask questions. On a not-so-serious note, we can usually calibrate for a sense of unhappiness, dis-ease, uncomfortableness, and unresourcefulness. When we can calibrate these states, we can potentially help people to move to a better and more resourceful state.

Business leaders, sales people, and great negotiators know how to calibrate for a 'yes' state. When talking to many sales professionals, there is nothing worse than 'over selling' a client. Over selling is when a person continues to persuade, sell or talk someone into something well after they have made their mind up to say yes. When this happens, the most common outcome is for the person to change their mind. People have a tendency to not like being sold to – when you can calibrate for a yes, you actually set the scene to have a better opportunity to sell conversationally without pressure or construed sales tactics.

While the days of this book progress, we invite you to develop skills of sensory acuity. Start to listen with more than just your ears. What do you see? What do you hear beyond the words a person says? Can you ask questions for more clarity or can you just make note of what you notice and calibrate for meaning based on a future event.

Throughout the next many days, and as you further develop your NLP skills, sensory acuity and calibration will become a key skill. If you are using an NLP technique to change a belief for example, calibration skills will be useful to know when and if a change has occurred, or if you need to continue to work on changing that belief or pattern or possibly work on another pattern.

One of the NLP Presuppositions we looked at earlier fits very succinctly into this topic of sensory acuity and calibration: *the more you know, the better you can do.*

Day 6 –
Communication with NLP

It has been said that you cannot not communicate. Is this true? We believe it is. Even if you are not communicating via words, there are other elements to communication including non-verbal cues, eye patterns, and physiology that continues to communicate long after words have stopped. Sometimes the entire message someone is trying to convey is not in their words at all, but in the tone of their voice, or how they are holding their body. In fact, a study was conducted by Ray Birdwhilstle at the University of Pennsylvania to determine how humans communicate. At the end of his study, he concluded that only 7% of communication between people has to do with the actual content of the words being said. The remaining 93% of our communication comes from *how* we say what we say, meaning the volume, pitch, tone, timber, and quality of our voice (38%); in addition, we communicate with our body and physiology (55%).

Over the next few days, we will be closely examining many of the NLP components that make up Communication. Not only will the next few days allow you to understand yourself better, therefore allow you to communicate at a higher level; but you will also better understand others. By understanding other people better, we are able to *respect their model of the world.*

Each of us has a different model of the world. This is how we view our lives, our surroundings, and ourselves. Our own viewpoint is likely to be different from someone else's. By respecting someone's model of the world, we are able to remove judgment and show an element of flexibility to both understand and be understood. We will be looking at language patterns, communication styles, questioning methods, modes of operating, and eye patterns in order to increase your effectiveness as a communicator, with yourself and with others.

Let's first look at how we communicate and then we'll begin to investigate some of the **filters** we use which create our model of the world.

Communication Model

As we have discussed, we all operate from a different model of the world. This model is the basis upon which we communicate and it is made up of our individualized filters comprising our primary representational system, memories, values, beliefs, and meta programs (programs beyond our normal conscious awareness).

The **communication model** within NLP is a systematic process that occurs continually within our lives, and specifically looks at how our own mind-body connection communicates with itself to create the outcomes in life. This model also illustrates how the output of an event can indeed be different for each and every one of us, and the end result of an event (our behavior) can be changed by changing aspects of the communication model at any step along the way. For example, if I am having a procrastinating moment, if I change or alter any facets of the communication model, I can alter my procrastinating behavior.

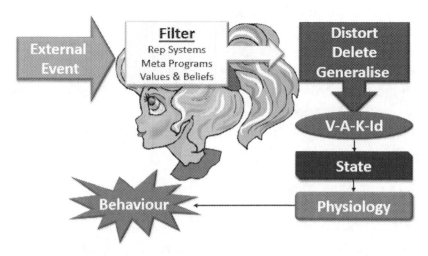

At any moment in time, there are approximately 2,000,000 bits of information being sent to us. This is compromised of everything you may see, hear, feel, touch, smell, taste, and think consciously and unconsciously. Out of those 2,000,000 bits, the human mind is only able to accept 134. Our unconscious mind chooses those 134 bits based on our own individual filters. Our filters including the elements of our life like our beliefs, memories, life experiences, representational systems, meta programs, and values (we will be looking at each of these filters individually). Instantaneously, our unconscious mind then makes the information fit for us personally by naturally distorting, generalizing and deleting details, allowing us to then chunk this information into 7 +/- 2 chunks of information (Miller, 1956).

These 7 +/- 2 chunks of information are then internalized, giving us an internal feeling, sound, or picture which creates a state (a mood or emotion), which gives us a certain physiology (how we hold our body), and ends in us having a specific behavior. This is a continual process that occurs every moment of every day.

Because this same process happens to everyone, and because each of our filters is different – each of us will have different internal representations of the same event leading to a different state, physiology, and finally, behavior. This explains why you and another person can have a completely different interpretation of the same thing. It doesn't at all mean that one person is wrong, it simply means that we notice different things, filter differently based on our own personal representational system, beliefs, values, programs, and memories. By understanding the communication model, this should assist us in respecting another person's model of the world.

Let's put some content around this model as an illustration: a single fifty-year-old man with no children walks into the birthday party of a two-year-old child with sixteen children aged two and three-years old. In an instant, he will filter this situation based on his history, beliefs, habits, meta programs, values, memories, and representational systems. This information is then quickly distorted, deleted and generalized in order to capture the 134 bits of information that will fit into his model of the world. Instantly he creates internal images, feelings, thoughts and/or sounds, which in turn gives him a particular emotion, mood, or state – which we can notice by immediate changes to his physiology and leads directly to his behavior. This behavior might be overt (for example, a wide-eyed man says, "Wow! This is a lot of kids"), or more subtle (he may just take in a deep breath) – what we may notice depends largely on our sensory acuity skills.

Even as you read this, as soon as you read the words "the birthday party of a two-year-old child with sixteen, two and three-year olds present" – your own mind filtered this information and took you through the entire communication model to a behavior. Every single moment, your mind and body is communicating with itself based on the stimulus outside of ourselves. Again, we cannot not communicate.

Today, we will start to look at the Communication Model in depth by investigating one of the elements of our filtering system, Representational Systems.

Representational Systems

Have you ever been in a situation where you have just said something that is as clear as day to you, but the person you were talking to didn't understand a word you said? Or perhaps you have been in a social situation and after words were discussing the event with someone else that was also there – and their description isn't even close to the party you were at? Or maybe in a business meeting you have gone round after round of meetings not being heard only to find out that everyone has actually been saying the same thing! What happens??

We already know that people communicate in different ways than each other. This we have known since birth. What some of us may not know is how to understand each other's communication styles in order to communicate at a higher level, and to be better understood.

Our **Primary Representational System**, which is sometimes referred to as our Communication or Learning style is how we represent ourselves to the world through the language we use and our physiology (how we hold our body). As a child we learned about our 5 senses – sight, sound, touch, smell, and taste. Our main communication style is also derived from theses senses – mainly sight, sound, and touch. The touch we refer to in NLP takes into account external as well as internal feelings. An example of an internal feeling is an emotion or mood – love, generosity, frustration, clarity. In addition to these three senses, we also include a 4th element – Internal Dialogue (Id) in NLP.

The four representational systems:
- Visual (sight)
- Auditory (sound)
- Kinesthetic (touch)
- Internal Dialogue

act as filters to what is going on around us. While each of us does see, hear, feel and talk to ourselves – there is one that you do more often. In fact, you will normally filter first through this system – this is known as your **Primary** representational system. The order of the other three creates your **4-tupple**, or systematic order of your representational systems.

As you begin to learn more about representational systems, you will be able to notice what someone's primary representational system is fairly quickly. Believe it or not, they will use a lot of words and phrases that will show or tell you what representational system they operate from the most. There are also physical signs you can look for. Once you are aware of what representational system someone is, you can mirror their language and physiology and begin to build rapport by respecting their model of the world.

Visual:

To spot if someone's primary representational system is Visual, there are a number of signs to look for. First you can notice the external clues. A primarily visual person may be fairly well presented, looking nice, having finely pressed attire on and be well groomed. They may stand or sit straight and tall, and they will breathe mainly from their upper chest. When a visual person speaks, the tempo of their words may be quite quick paced and contain a lot of visual words such as:

See, sight, look, view, picture, imagine…

Visual people will filter information first by what can be seen. They may make judgments about people and things by first appearances. Primarily visual people make up approximately 40% of the population.

"I see what you mean. I've looked over the reports and from my viewpoint, everything seems to be in line."

As a learner, a visual person will want to see something happening, see how something works or see information written down about what they are learning. If they do not get the opportunity to watch or view as they are learning, they may become easily confused. The best way to teach a visual person is to let them see something.

Tips when communicating with Visual people:
- Increase the speed of your speech to match that of the Visual person.
- Use Visual words along with your own as descriptors; show them what you mean.
- Use diagrams, mind maps, pictures, or charts to better explain something.
- Don't just tell a Visual person something – write it down!!!
- Look at the visual person while you are speaking to them.

Auditory:
Individuals with Auditory as their primary representational system make up only approximately 20% of the population combined with Internal Dialogue. These people will filter information based first upon what they hear. External clues include a sing-song almost melodic tonality, an unconscious need to shift their head or body near to someone who is speaking and they will also breathe from the middle of their chest. They may talk to themselves out loud and move their lips when they read. They may use Onomatopoeia when talking – this is using sounds as words (screech, boom, pow, zip, click, etc.). When speaking, primarily auditory people will use a lot of sound based words such as:

Hear, listen, quite, resonates, speak, talk, sounds...

"Listen, I've read this report and it speaks volumes about the progress we are making. Sounds to me like we are right on track."

As a learner, Auditory people want to hear about something. They may want some details or facts about what they are learning.

Often if you tell them something, they understand it. If you were to only show them something without explanation, they may not fully comprehend the information.

Tips when communicating with Auditory people:
- Add vocal variety to your tonality.
- Use auditory words along with your own; make sure they hear what you are saying.
- Don't expect the auditory person to look at you, they don't need to see you to hear you.
- Add verbal summary indicators when speaking to an Auditory person (yeah, uh hu, oh, etc.).
- Usually there is no need to repeat yourself to an Auditory person, they heard and will remember something from the first time you tell them.
- Have a conversation with them so they can hear you and you can hear them

Kinesthetic:
The primarily kinesthetic person is quite easy to pick out in a crowd and they make up approximately 40% of the population. This is the person that is comfortably dressed, possibly slouching slightly (or a lot), and is slightly slower in his or her speech patterns. This slowness is simply because the Kinesthetic person must make a connection of information before getting a sense of how to respond next. This often drives Visual people crazy! It's often that kinesthetic kids are labeled or mislabeled as ADD or ADHD because they are often fidgeting, moving around and not paying attention. Most likely, however, they are not being taught in a way that engages their senses and they are bored or not intrigued. When speaking, a kinesthetic person may use sensory based words such as:

Feel, touch, grasp, point, run, sense....

"I ran through this report and I get the feeling that we are really going to grasp this opportunity!"

As a learner, the kinesthetic person will learn best by doing something. They like a hands-on approach to learning and often feel out of place in a classroom based upon visual learning techniques. I often suggest to teachers and parents of kinesthetic kids to allow them to play with stress balls or "koosh" balls in the classroom (as long as they are not interrupting the class), in order to engage at least some part of their need for 'doing' while in a classroom environment. The kinesthetic person may not have many questions about what they are learning until they have had time to digest the material and know if it fits with them or not.

Tips when communicating with Kinesthetic people:
- Slightly reduce the speed of your words.
- Use kinesthetic words as well as your own to give them a good sense of what you are saying.
- If appropriate, touch the person on the hand or shoulder.
- Give the kinesthetic person plenty of time, don't rush them – they must feel comfortable about what you are communicating to them.

Internal Dialogue:
This person is sometimes most difficult to pick out of a group of people, until they speak. Combined with the Auditory person, primary Internal Dialogue people make up approximately 20% of the population. In our opinion, the need and desire to filter first through internal dialogue is a learned behavior. The other representational systems seem to be somewhat hardwired at birth. This person will filter based on information and will seek a lot of it. The basis of this person is to filter through a question of "Why." The Id person will want to know facts and figures, directions, and will normally share their model of the world in a fairly precise way. Id people will use words such as:

Generally, compute, understand, information, think, 1st, 2nd, 3rd...

"If I understand this report completely, I think we must first take a stand on this information and next we must follow

through. **Generally, it all computes and I believe we are standing on solid ground."**

Tips when communicating with Internal Dialogue people:
- Know what you are talking about so you can provide details to the listener, or be confident enough to say "I don't know."
- Use Internal Dialogue words that convey meaning and structure.
- Take a moment to think before responding to an Id person.
- Be as specific as possible in answering their 'why' questions.

Using representational systems

Once you are able to watch and listen to a person and ascertain what their primary representational system is, you can then use that information to understand them better, and to be better understood. Mismatching representational systems is the main reason for communication differences in relationships, careers, and families.

Example: A few years ago, a couple came to us for coaching. They had been together for a number of years, but Carol was feeling like Robert no longer cared about her or their relationship. After talking to them for a while, it became apparent that they were not respecting each other's models of the world. In fact, they were oblivious that it was okay to have a difference. Carol is a very visual person, and she made special effort to keep their house in perfect order. It always looked wonderfully manicured, organized and well kept. One way she showed her love for Robert was to make sure the house always looked great. However, upon arriving home each night, Robert would kick his shoes off, take his tie off – leaving it on the bench, put his feet up on the coffee table and watch television. He never commented on how good the house looked, never made comment on her new clothes or hair style – "he only ever looks after his needs," Carol told us. In fact, he came home and made a mess! Which to Carol was an insult. But you see, Robert is not a visual person, he is Kinesthetic. He wants to come home and feel good. He wants to take his shoes off, take his tie off and make himself at home. He didn't even notice how the house looked, or how Carol looked because he wasn't looking, he was getting comfortable.

Once they were able to recognize how the other viewed their own model of the world, it was then easy to respect the other's model of the world. Robert started to make a bigger effort to notice things around the house, including Carol more – and to put his shoes and tie away in the bedroom instead of wherever they landed. And Carol realized that she no longer cleaned the house for Robert, but for herself – it made her feel good. They were also able to define new ways of showing their love and appreciation for one another that fit into their respective models of the world.

Understanding the 4-Tuple

Because each person has elements of all four representational systems, Visual, Auditory, Kinesthetic, and Internal Dialogue – we each process this information in a different way. When you are able to not only ascertain someone's **Primary Representational System** but also the order of all four representational systems, you will then be even better equipped. A mistake many people make is to disregard a person's other representational systems.

A method used to note the structure of any particular experience is called a 4-tuple – or a 4-way sensory based description of cognitive processing. This is where all four representational systems are generated at any given moment. It is how the human mind processes information through the senses and makes sense of their world.

Any experience must be composed of some combination of the four primary representational systems:

V –Visual, A = Auditory, K = Kinesthetic, and Id = Internal Dialogue.

A human being processes information using all the senses all of the time, from a hierarchy of needed or preferred system to least preferred or needed system. For instance, someone may be talking to themselves (Id) and at the same time making pictures in their own mind (V) while considering how they feel (K) about it as they listen to someone else give their opinion (A). This is done in an unconscious way and is subjective in nature and influenced by what is happening. It forms our responses, memories, and behaviors. Not necessarily right nor wrong they are influenced by how our minds are wired.

Predicates & Predicate Phrases

Within the confines of NLP, predicates are process words (like verbs, adverbs, and adjectives), that a person selects to describe a subject. Predicates are used in NLP to identify which representational system a person is using.

Once you have ascertained what a person's primary representational system is, feed a few of the following words into your language. You will be amazed at what happens when you respect someone's model of the world! Do remember to be yourself and use your own words – just be flexible and use theirs too!

Visual Predicates:

Admire	Expose	Imagine	Sparkle
Appear	Eyed	Look	Spy
Attractive	Faced	Perspective	Vanish
Blurred	Flash	Picture	View
Clear	Focus	Preview	Visualize
Cloudy	Foresee	See	Vivid
Colorful	Glance	Show	Watch
Dark	Illuminate	Sight	

Visual Predicate Phrases:

An eyeful	Get a	Mental	Short sighted
Appears	perspective	picture	Sight for sore
to me	Get a scope	Mind's eye	eyes
Beyond a	Hazy idea	Naked eye	Staring off in
shadow of a	In light of	Paint a	space
doubt	In person	picture	Take a peak
Bird's eye	In view of	Plainly seen	Tunnel vision
view	Make a scene	Pretty as a	Under your
Clear cut		picture	nose
Eye to eye		See to it	

Auditory Predicates:

Announce	Discuss	Noisy	Talk
Answer	Explain	Outspoken	Tell
Argue	Harmonize	Question	Vocal
Asked	Harsh	Quiet	Yell
Call	Hear	Request	
Cheer	Inquire	Sang	
Complain	Listen	Shout	
Cry	Loud	Sighs	
Deaf	Mention	Sound(s)	

Auditory Predicate Phrases:

All ears	Hold your tongue	To tell the truth
Be heard	Inquire into	Tongue tied
Blabber mouth	Loud and clear	Tune in
Clear as a bell	Manner of	Tune out
Call on	speaking	Utterly
Describe in detail	Outspoken	Unheard of
An earful	Pay attention to	Voice and opinion
Give me your ear	Purrs like a kitten	Well formed
Heard voices	Rings a bell	Word for word
Hidden message	State your purpose	
	Sounds like	

Kinesthetic Predicates:

Angle	Firm	Irritate	Tremble
Beat	Fits	Pressure	Twist
Bounce	Force	Run	Unfeeling
Brush	Grab	Scrape	Warm
Comfortable	Grasp	Smooth	Wash
Concrete	Hard	Soft	Weigh
Exciting	Hold	Stuffed	Work
Feel	Hurt	Sweep	

Kinesthetic Predicate Phrases:

All washed up	Get a hold of	I'm touched
Be felt	Get a handle of	Keep your shirt on
Boils down to	Get in touch with	Lay the cards on
Catch on	Get the drift	the table
Chip off the old	Go with the flow	Light headed
block	Hand in hand	Pain in the neck
Come to grips with	Hands on	Run with it
Connect with	Hang in there	Sharp as a tack
Control yourself	Heated argument	Slipped through
Cool/calm/collected	Hold it, hold on	Stiff upper lip
Floating on thin air		

Internal Dialogue:

Categorize	Distinct	Motivate	Sum it up
Change	Frankly	Perceive	Think
Conceive	Generally	Process	Understand
Consider	Know	Sense	1st 2nd 3rd
Decide	Learn	Specifically	A – B – C

Day 7 –
Language

Everything that is happening around us – what we see, hear, think, feel, taste, touch and smell creates a chemical reaction. Similarly, the words we hear or think create this same type of reaction. Today, we are looking at language as a filter within the Communication Model.

Words have power. No matter where you are or who you are – when you hear a word that you know the meaning of, you have a reaction. When you hear (or read) the word calm and you filter that word and its meanings to you, your body reacts. Even if you think the word anger, you filter that word and its meanings and your body reacts. Your body will react based on your model of the world – your history, memories (conscious and unconscious), beliefs, values, representational systems, meta program, and other filters. An important note to make is that everyone will react in their own way – not right or wrong, just their own way; this again illustrates the importance of respecting other people's model of the world.

By understanding how the mind processes language, creates emotional responses and develops meaning of the words we use, hear and think, we can utilize words and the language of the mind more effectively and resourcefully with ourselves and others.

Within today's lesson, we will be exploring aspects of language including: presuppositions of language, limiting language, and modal operators.

Presuppositions of Language

If you recall the information we discussed previously about the unconscious mind, you will remember that the unconscious mind follows orders and constantly eavesdrops on what you say and do as triggers of where to go next. Language plays a large part in how we communicate directly to our unconscious mind. By listening to how someone says something, you can get a glimpse of his or her model of the world, and even into your own.

Because we have distorted, deleted and generalized aspects of the world around us to fit into our model of the world, our internal and external language is normally full of assumptions or presuppositions that are real to us. If we didn't do this, we would have to say too many words to express a simple thought.

The answer of "I'm good thanks," as a response to the question "How are you?", would have to be something like: "Subjectively compared to myself, I am better than average. Compared with yesterday when I was feeling slightly tired and achy in my neck – a few days ago, however, I was more productive, energetic and…" – you get the idea.

It has been said that we can easily compare communication with an iceberg. Only about 10% of an iceberg appears above the surface of the water. This means a whole lot of ice below the surface which we can't see. If we think about communication in that same way, we communicate at the **surface structure** – communicating through words, physiology, and tonality only about 10% of what our actual message is. The rest of what we are not saying or what we are implying is at the **deeper structure**.

When we are speaking to others, it is a natural tendency to presuppose that the other person knows what we are talking about, yet the reality of communication tells us that when we say a statement based on our model of the world, the person we are talking to creates their own meaning about that statement based on their model of the world. If you are talking to two people at the same time, that is three different meanings being made, if you are communicating with a group of people, that is even more meanings.

Let's take a look at some of the things you might presuppose based on the following statement:

> **I should exercise more.**
> What might you presuppose here? Maybe that I don't exercise at all. Perhaps you could presuppose that I have a desire to exercise. Or, maybe that I don't like to exercise. It could be presupposed that I know how to exercise, have a place to exercise, find importance or value in exercise. Maybe a thought could come to mind that I already do exercise, but not enough. And so many other presuppositions based on this one statement.

This is a good example of how after our mind filters an event (in this case a statement) we create an internal representation – we see, hear or feel something due to that event. This internal representation is based on our own personal model of the world. It is because of the missing information from the deeper structure that we as humans want to fill in the blank with what is in our mind based on our own world. In essence, we are mind reading, completing someone else's thoughts, and sometimes we are right, and often we can be wrong.

With the following statements – think of or list your initial reactions and then many of the different things you could presuppose:
1. My husband would die if he knew how much this cost.
2. I love a day at the spa.

The main intention of discussing linguistic presuppositions is so that you can be more aware of the assumptions you make when listening to others and to be aware when others may be presupposing something about what you are saying. When you are able to be more aware, this can offer you more choices. Choice to ask a question, to offer clarification and even to give more information if needed.

Just as the saying "don't judge a book by its cover," we can learn through understanding about linguistic presuppositions: don't judge a statement by its words. There is usually more information we can find out about someone else's model of the world, therefore, communicating more effectively.

What can you presuppose from the following statement?

> *Children of today have no manners. It seems there isn't any discipline in schools or at home anymore. I can't imagine how bad this generation's children will be! How are they going to learn??*

- Compared to past generations, this person thinks children do not have manners.
- There is no discipline in schools.
- Parents are not disciplining their children.
- Children go to school.
- Children should get disciplined at school.
- This generation of children will have children one day.
- There is something to learn about manners and discipline.

We are always doing it. We are making meaning, mind reading, presupposing and somewhat imposing our model of the world onto someone else's. When we know more, this allows us to do better.

Sales and marketing use a lot of presuppositions. Next time you watch commercials on television think about what the commercial is getting you to presuppose. Maybe it's that if you buy that car, you will have a more exciting life; if you eat a certain brand of yoghurt, you will gain more health; or perhaps it is if you use a certain bank, you will earn more interest than any other bank. Linguistic presuppositions are everywhere!

In a few days, you will be learning about a questioning technique which will help you to presuppose less and find out more.

Limiting Language

"The most important things you will ever hear is what you say to yourself when you are by yourself, about yourself " – Al Walker

Language is possibly one of the most influencing important factors of our life. As we mentioned before, you cannot not communicate. However, we do have a choice in how we communicate via language. To ourselves and to others, our language patterns can either help to excel us, or greatly hinder us in progression and momentum toward our goals. In fact, our language can simply keep us stuck when it limits us.

In respect to language, remember these prime directives of the unconscious mind:

- **The unconscious mind is a servant to follow orders.**
  Imagine your own little version of "Mini-Me" or little butler inside of you. Maybe there is just one or perhaps there are hundreds of Mini-Me, all waiting for an instruction. This is like your unconscious mind. It is a servant that waits for instructions and then follows those instructions – often perfectly. This can be very empowering because it gives you the opportunity to give yourself the instructions that you want. However, what often happens is that we are giving ourselves inept, incorrect or unuseful instructions.

  Have you ever heard someone say something like, "I always forget things." This person's Mini-Me is waiting, on alert for this instruction and low and behold, Mini-Me hides things from the person by deleting them from their awareness. This creates a self-fulfilling prophecy of losing things and makes the Mini-Me feel great because he/she has fulfilled an order.

Think about some of the commands you give yourself. Here are a few that we hear regularly from clients:
- I'm just stupid
- I'm a slow learner
- I'm not good at relationships
- No matter what I do, I never have enough money
- No one would want to be in a relationship with me
- I can't control my children

We can guess that whatever these statements are, the person who said them has evidence of the statement in their life.

Because the unconscious mind functions in this way, we actually gravitate in the direction of our dominant thoughts, and our lives will reflect a self-fulfilling prophecy – we see the proof of out thoughts. We can see daily evidence that we get what we think about most of the time.

In our NLP practice, we listen to language patterns a lot – we hear people telling us all the time through their language where their issues and problems stem from. When working with a young woman suffering from Anxiety and Panic attacks, she was explaining her work situation. In her company there were a few people that she had personality clashes with – she kept saying the words "he just makes me sick." Remember, the unconscious mind is constantly eavesdropping on what we say and it follows those orders. It doesn't know when you are being serious or joking. Nor does our unconscious mind understand sarcasm. Her language, to herself (internally through her thoughts) and externally to others, tells her what to do – get sick. It is then up to her unconscious mind to do that. It is almost as if there is a butler in your mind that has the job of just doing things for you – anything that you constantly tell it – and it has so many ways of doing that.

- **The unconscious mind takes everything personally**
Another function your version of Mini-Me has is it takes everything you hear, say, think or feel personally. It is unable to differentiate a thought for you and someone else. Your unconscious mind can't tell the difference between a conversation that you overhear and one that you belong in – and it will provide an internal representation (you will see, hear or feel something) based on your model of the world.

If you overhear someone saying they are tired, your mind will let you try on being tired for a moment, and there is a chance that you too will become tired. If someone asks you if you are nervous, your body will respond with nerves so you can make a comparison to answer the question. If someone tells you not to be a smart-aleck, your internal servant will demonstrate your wonderful smart-alecky behaviors. If you tell yourself that you are always late, you will always be late. If you tell yourself that you're bad at spelling – you'll prove yourself right every time. If a little girl overhears an adult talking about boys being better at science than girls, her unconscious mind will most likely store that as a truth.

The unconscious mind also doesn't understand humor, sarcasm, or irony. It has a simple function which it fulfills expertly. So how can you use this information? First – listen to what you are telling to yourself and others. Say it how you want it to be replicated in life. Second – if you become aware of something limiting that you have said, heard directly or over heard, be mindful to change what you have in your awareness. The last thing in your unconscious mind is the last thing your body will respond to. Therefore, if you overhear someone say, "you'll be sore after this massage," notice the message and think what you want instead – "I'll be nice and relaxed after this massage." A different message gives different chemicals which produces a different result. You are in charge of your mind and therefore your results.

- **The unconscious mind is not able to process negatives directly**
  The human mind is unable to not process something which it has been given. As you read this, don't think of your favorite desert.

Now, what did you not think about? Cake, cookies, fruit, pie, ice cream? Maybe you even thought of where you had this desert last – or what kind you had last night, or what kind of desert you would like to have right now.

Although the sentence said don't think of your favorite desert, you did. In fact, you had to. Remember from the communication model – your mind takes an event (even just the word desert is an event), and it filters it, deletes, distorts and generalizes the event and then creates an internal representation of it. It does this automatically. Ultimately, your unconscious mind negates the negative and hears think of your favorite desert. You cannot not create the internal representation. Let's try with a few other words.

Dog. Anger. Love. Zoo. Rain. Television. Ferrari.

With each of those words, your mind has to get an internal representation of it. Automatically. Some of those words are also infused with emotion – it's part of your filtering process.

Now, understanding that the unconscious mind is unable to process negatives, we can use this information usefully. It seems to be human nature to think about what we don't want. However, if we dwell upon what we don't want, guess what happens – we get it. We get what we think about most of the time. Therefore, because the unconscious mind is unable to process negatives and because it takes everything personally, often what we are telling ourselves and others that we don't want is exactly what is happening in our lives right now.

I might ask a client what they want and I hear from them, "I don't want to be lonely. I don't want to be negative. I don't want to be angry anymore." None of these statements actually tell me anything about what my client does want. In fact, I can presuppose that if a person tells me they don't want to be negative that they are a negative person. Their statement presupposes it.

In your own life, start listening and being aware of negating language you might use – don't and can't are two key words. Here are a few types of statements we hear people use and find quite interesting:
- I can't forget about the meeting I have in the morning.
- Don't forget to remember your homework.

When you notice yourself use don't or can't – start to change it. The best rule of thumb is to say it like you want it. Instead of "don't throw the ball inside," say "only use the ball outside," or "don't speak to me like that," say "use a nicer tone when you speak to me." The more direct you can make your statement about what you want – the fewer filters someone needs to use and the more efficient their mind will be in creating the internal representation you want.

When you notice someone else use negating words, ask them what they want instead. For example, if someone told me, "I don't want to be negative," I would ask them, "If you weren't negative, what would you be." This will give the person you are speaking to a direction of what they want, versus what they don't want.

Limiting language is always easier to hear from someone else than ourselves as we are used to it – it's part of us. However, if you find the patterns in your life that are holding you back, you are very likely to find limiting language.

The NLP Presupposition *communication is the response you get* not only relates to communication with the other, but to yourself as well. If the words you say to yourself are self defeating – telling yourself you can't do something, or don't deserve something, then that is what you will get.

It sounds simple, and it is. We are not going to tell you that if your language (internally and externally) is flowered with positive words then that is what you are going to get – because we know there is more to a good life than just words. For example, you need action behind those words. If our words were telling us one thing yet our behavior was doing the opposite, we would be incongruent and therefore not whole in ourselves. The two go hand in hand. Actually – language, behaviors, and feelings are all interconnected. What you say/think affects your behavior and how you feel; how you behave affects how you feel and what you say/think; and how you feel affects what you say/think and your behavior.

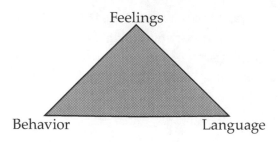

Modal Operators

A Modal Operator is another form of 'linguistic tip-off' that will clue a listener into the motivation behind an action, behavior or belief. From a linguistic standpoint, Steve Andreas (2001) described Modal Operators and how they work:

> "Since a verb always describes an activity or process, a Modal Operator is a verb that modifies 'how' an activity is done. A Modal Operator functions in the same way that an adverb does, and perhaps should be called an adverb. An adverb sometimes precedes the verb that is modified, and sometimes it follows it, while a Modal Operator always precedes it, and this is part of the power of a Modal Operator. A Modal Operator sets a general orientation or global direction 'before' we know what the activity is."

We will discuss two types of Modal Operators: **Modal Operators of Possibility** and **Modal Operators of Necessity**. Both utilize words as clues to motivation, potential stuckness, and beliefs. When we are able to recognize a Modal Operator, we can better understand someone's model of the world, and therefore communicate or assist in a more productive and beneficial manner. One of the presuppositions of NLP states *All NLP should increase choice and wholeness. When we can communicate more effectively, with others or with oursel*ves, we are automatically allowing ourselves more choices.

A **Modal Operator of Possibility** creates a belief or set of rules about what is possible or impossible. When a person is using more possible based words such as can, possible, could, might, able, desire, want, may, we know that their model of the world is giving them permission and movement toward their desires. "It is possible for me to be successful" is an example of a positive Modal operator of Possibility and most likely will not be challenged.

However, when someone uses words such as can't, don't, couldn't, and impossible, they are going away from their desires. If someone were to say, "I can't be successful," this illustrates a limiting belief or view that may keep him stuck or limited based on a set of rules. When we notice these limitations, we can challenge the Modal Operator by asking questions. The intention of the questions is to understand more about someone's model of the world and uncover choice. Some potential questions to ask include:

- *What would happen if you did?*
- *If you could, what would that be like?*
- *What prevents you from doing that?*

Each of these questions **reframe** the person you are communicating with, allowing not only you to understand them better, but also for them to understand themselves better as well.

A **Modal Operator of Necessity** is similar, but instead of telling us what is possible, these are words that tell us what is needed, necessary and appropriate about an action, behavior or belief. They are words such as have to, should, must, must not, ought, and need. Modal Operators of Necessity are limiting in that they take away an element of choice. "I have to stay late at work" tells us that there is no choice but to stay at work late. "I must eat all my vegetables" illustrates a lack of choice once again. Just as with Modal Operators of Possibility, you can ask questions which will allow someone to make a choice, and move from a Modal Operator of Necessity "I have to go to school" to a Modal Operator of Possibility "I choose to go to school." By allowing someone to see a choice, they can then regain their own responsibility and control. A few questions you could ask to challenge a Modal Operator of Necessity include:

- *What would happen if you did/didn't?*
- *According to whom?*

Example: When speaking with people, it is easy to tune your ear in for these key words. Heidi was working with an individual that had a desire to start her own business. A bit of their conversation went as follows:

Client: I really do want to start my own pet grooming business (Modal Operator of Possibility)

Heidi: That sounds great!

Client: Yeah, but I don't think I can do it. (MO of Possibility)

Heidi: What prevents you? (challenges the don't)

Client: I have a stable job. I should just keep that and be safe (MO of Necessity)

Heidi: What would happen if you didn't keep it and you started your business? (challenge 'should just keep it' and used as if frame)

Client: Well, that would be great! I know it would be successful! (MO of possibility) It would take a little time, that's all.

Heidi: So, what prevents you from starting it? (challenge previous don't)

Client: I guess I don't really know where to start. (MO of Possibility)

Heidi: And how could you find out where to start?

Client: I have a friend that started a business, I could ask him.

In this example, Heidi was able to ask beneficial questions that retrieved more information and was able to help her client uncover a choice, to ask her friend for assistance. Notice that Heidi only asked questions, she didn't offer advice or assistance.

By applying the NLP Presupposition *everyone has the resources available to achieve their desired results* tells us that sometimes people just need a small nudge in the right direction, but they don't need to be led in that direction.

When someone is stuck due to Modal Operators, sometimes the easiest thing to do is nothing. In the above example, the client was making excuses about needing stability in her job, when the real issue was not knowing how to start her new business. It is easy to delude ourselves and others with Modal Operators. However, once we start to purposefully challenge those Modal Operators, we then are living and choosing based on a Modal Operator of Possibility and Choice.

Being aware of the modal operators that people are using offers us the ability to ask better questions and find out more about a person's model of the world. In fact, looking at today's lesson in its entirety – the main focus has been about being aware that what you are seeing, hearing, saying or thinking is creating an internal and chemical response that you can be more mindful of and control in a beneficial way.

As you continue with your day, and as we continue with our daily lessons, we invite you to become more aware of what you say (externally and internally), and what others say. When appropriate, ask questions and above all, do your best to respect the model of the world of other people by not imposing your own presuppositions, beliefs, or mind reading on their world.

Day 8 –
Meta Programs

Today we are going to be looking at another filter of the unconscious mind – Meta Programs.

Many people who are interested in NLP are very curious about people and very curious specifically about why people think and behave in the way they do. **Meta Programs** help us to gain an insight into a person at a deeper unconscious level.

We've already discussed that we have programs for everything we do – a program for waking up in the morning, motivating ourselves and others, procrastinating, eating, exercising, moving, even brushing our teeth. The word **Meta** is a Greek word meaning beyond, above, about. So, when we are talking about Meta Programs, we are looking at our programs beyond our programs – above our conscious awareness. For the most part, Meta Programs are largely unconscious – programs of thought and behavior that are truly running on autopilot.

Meta Programs can help us to better understand why people think and behave in the way they do and therefore respect their model of the world. From there, you can communicate more effectively because you can then use a person's Meta Program when communicating. Finally, understanding your own Meta Programs will help you to respect your own model of the world and gain a better perspective on your own patterns.

In the world of NLP, there are many different Meta Programs. Dr. L. Michael Hall looks at 60 Meta Programs in the second edition of his book *Figuring Out People: Design Engineering with Meta-Programs*. In the NLP Worldwide Practitioner training course we look at eight, and in Master Practitioner we investigate a further dozen Meta Programs. Today, we will discuss eight different Meta Programs.

In addition to the NLP specific Meta Programs, there are also many forms of non-NLP based Meta Programs. Because a Meta Program gives us insight into what is beyond our conscious programs, there are many tools and ideas which could be loosely defined as Meta Programs. Ultimately, anything which helps to explain a person's model of the world can be classified as a Meta Program, including Astrology, Ennegrams, Myers-Briggs Type Indicator results, DiSC, Spiral Dynamics, and many more tools.

When talking about Meta Programs, it is sometimes important to remember the NLP Presupposition *when people know better, they do better.* This presupposition is important with Meta Programs, because as we probe into the Meta Programs of ourselves and others, we begin to know more; more about ourselves and why we do what we do, and more about how other people operate.

Meta Programs tell us information about a person, such as if they prefer working with plans or more spontaneously; if they are more in touch with their feelings or more dissociated with themselves; if they seek validation internally or externally; if they are prone to an all-or-nothing way of acting. With most things in life, balance is key; a balanced and healthy individual generally will not be at the extreme of any Meta Program spectrum but rather be somewhere within the spectrum.

The following is an example of a dichotomous (extreme) pattern of a specific Meta Program:

John is a self-proclaimed workout-aholic. He goes to the gym every day for a 60-90 workout. His thought is that if he doesn't go every day, he won't get the benefits of working out. If something stops him from going to the gym, he doesn't go at all that week – he'll start over the next Monday and go hard core each day. Unless something comes up.

We can map this Meta Program of **all or nothing** behavior on a scale:

All _X_____ Nothing
John's Meta Program about exercising
All _____X_ Nothing
John's Meta Program if he misses a day of exercise

As you will continue to understand, for something to be long lasting the Meta Program may be more useful further to the left or right of each extreme.

There are some Meta Programs which stay fairly constant in a person's life – for example, a person who tends to be more extroverted with their energy (that is, they desire to recharge their batteries with other people), will tend to always be this way. There are also are many Meta Programs which are context specific. For example, we will be looking at the Meta Program of being more prone to seeing the big picture or details. One person may be more detail oriented in a specific task at work, but at home they may prefer the big picture. The Meta Programs we will be learning are all in the category of context specific. Please keep in mind that Meta Programs are not personality traits, they are the answer to why you think and behave the way you do when a certain event is happening.

We can use the information we elicit from other people's Meta Programs to communicate more effectively with them. Using the above example of a person who is more detail oriented, when I know this preference I can communicate in a more detailed manner, working toward the big picture. Conversely, if I know someone is more oriented to the big picture, I can speak more in generalities and big chunks of information.

A dynamic tool that we use incorporates a conversational model of tailoring responses to an individuals Meta Programs is the *Language and Behavior (LAB) Profile* developed by Shelle Rose Chavet. As you continue to learn more you may wish to explore the LAB Profile to help develop just the right type of influencing language.

With the vast number of Meta Programs available to us, it is interesting to know that we can use Meta Programs not only to communicate better with others, but also as a way of modeling yourself. If you are able to do something well in one area of your life, you can elicit some of the Meta Programs that you use for that task and map them across to another task or area of your life. For example, if in your professional life, you find it easy to meet new people, yet in your personal life this is a challenge, you can find out some of the Meta Programs that you use in your professional life and start to use them in your personal life.

The Meta Programs we have chosen to look at today are some of the most versatile and useful Meta Programs that span across personal development, business, and coaching. As you are reading this information, we encourage you to be thinking of your own life and some of the people in your life. This way you will be better equipped to respect their model of the world and use some of their Meta Programs next time you are communicating.

Chunk Size – *Global/Specific, Big Picture/Detail*
This Meta Program refers to the size of the 'chunk' of information a person prefers to learn, communicate and think in. Generally, a person will start on one side of the spectrum and move toward the other. Some people start **globally** (big picture) and move toward more detail, while others will start with the **detail** (specifics) and move toward the global. One of the easiest ways to identify this Meta Program is to see if you need to ask any questions to obtain specific information about what the person is saying. If so, they are most likely speaking globally; if not, then they are most likely

speaking in detail. Communicate back in their preference to best be understood at an unconscious level.

> **Global:** My computer isn't working. I can't get the program to open.
>
> **Detail:** When I open a program in my computer, I normally click on the icon that appears on the lower left side of my screen. When I double click this icon, the program is supposed to open. It is not opening.

-- -- -- -- --

> **Global:** We had dessert earlier today.
>
> **Detail:** We had cookies, cakes, and pastries earlier today.

-- -- -- -- --

> **Global:** I was productive this afternoon. I did homework, shopped, did some laundry and worked outside.
>
> **Detail:** This afternoon I completed a paper, did the grocery shopping, did two loads of laundry and cleaned the car. I was productive.

Direction Sort – *Toward/Away From*

Direction Sort tells us what motivates someone. In any circumstance, someone will go either **Toward** what they want, or **Away From** what they do not want. Neither is good nor bad, and both can greatly help to facilitate motivation and drive in a person. The person who prefers the Toward direction sort may be viewed as more of a positive person, as compared to the Away From motivated person. Many times, the Toward motivation factor can be seen as "toward pleasure" versus "away from pain." When communicating to this Meta Program, think of pleasure and pain factors which suit the individual.

> **Toward:** I love how I feel when I exercise – fit and healthy.
>
> **Away From:** I exercise so I don't have to buy bigger clothes.

-- -- -- -- --

Toward: I get good grades when I study for tests.

Away From: I study for tests so I don't fail.

-- -- -- -- --

Toward: I enjoy having time on my own and recharging my batteries.

Away From: If I don't have time on my own, I get grouchy and grumpy.

Scenario Thinking Style – *Optimist/Pessimist*

This Meta Program looks at if a person assesses first for possibilities, opportunities, excitement, and the best case, or if they assess first for potential danger, threats, problems, or the worst case. Sorting for **best-case** scenarios provides the tendency for optimism, hope, and empowerment. Sorting for the **worst-case** scenario provides the tendency for pessimism, negativity, and problem focus. When communicating to this Meta Program, respect the other person's model of the world by expressing either their optimistic or pessimistic points.

Optimist: These shoes are on sale, what luck!

Pessimist: Even on sale these shoes are expensive.

-- -- -- -- --

Optimist: That person was very friendly and asked me some great questions.

Pessimist: That person asked too many questions, I think they are an employee from one of my competitors.

-- -- -- -- --

Optimist: The A380 airplane holds so many more people; that is so exciting.

Pessimist: With so many more people on an airplane surely that makes it more likely to crash.

Emotional State – *Thinking/Feeling*

The Emotional State Meta Program identifies how a person makes a decision most naturally. The **Thinking** style person will tend to rely on facts, information, data, and an objective and dissociated analysis to make a decision, while the **Feeling** person will make a decision based on their emotions, how the decision impacts others, and a more subjective and associated point of view. Thinkers tend to believe that conflict is a natural part of life, and Feelers will try to avoid conflict even if it creates discomfort for them. When communicating to these different styles, use more logic and dissociated words with Thinkers and more emotive and associated words with Feelers.

> **Thinker:** There are going to be changes in the company at all levels.
> **Feeler:** We are going to be making company changes and not everyone will be happy with it.
>
> -- -- -- -- --
>
> **Thinker:** I know I'll get a good grade if I study for five hours this week.
> **Feeler:** I want to do well on this test so I will put in the time to really get the information in my muscle.
>
> -- -- -- -- --
>
> **Thinker:** A few of us are going for a drink after work.
> **Feeler:** Joanne, Amber, and Rick are coming for a drink after work; you should come, it will be fun!

Philosophical Direction – *Why/How, Origin/Solution*
This Meta Program identifies how a person desires to solve a problem which is most natural to them; an emphasis on the past and understanding **why** something happened or emphasis on the future and understanding **how** to find a solution. The assumption that drives the Why mind is that if they can understand where something came from, they can gain mastery over it. When communicating using this Meta Program, emphasize either the problem and its origins or the solution.

> **Why:** Not enough paper was ordered in our last shipment, so we cannot print the letters today.

What: We need more paper than we have, so we've placed a new order so we can print the letters tomorrow.

-- -- -- -- --

Why: Because of three nights of rained out practice last week, we lost the game today.

What: Starting next week we will be having more practices and we'll create a contingency plan in case of bad weather.

-- -- -- -- --

Why: The economy has been heading south and our sales are down because of it.

What: Our entire team needs to brainstorm some ideas to bring our sales numbers back up.

People Convincer – *Trusting/Distrusting*

This Meta Program investigates how people relate to other people. By default, some people are more **trusting**, while others are more **distrusting**. People who are instinctively more trusting come across as more friendly and warm and will be quick to act trustingly, feel connected and open up. Conversely, people who are more distrusting may come across as jealous, guarded, and defensive. They will immediately wonder, question and explore a person's motives and intentions. When communicating using this Meta Program, use verbal and non-verbal language to convey a sense of trust or distrust to match their model of the world.

Trusting: Mark said that the movie Inception was good; we should go see it.

Distrusting: Mark recommended we see the movie Inception, but I don't know, he likes some strange films. What do you think?

-- -- -- -- --

Trusting: I'm happy to give you the information you need.

Distrusting: Before I give you the information you want, can you tell me what you'll be using it for?

-- -- -- -- --

Trusting: Ask me anything and I'll tell you what I know.

Distrusting: If you have any questions, let me know and I'll see how I can help you.

Relationship Sort – *Matching/Mismatching or Sameness/Difference*
This Meta Program looks at how we make sense of new information. Someone who sorts for **Sameness** (Matching) will identify how the new information or situation is similar to what they already know. A person who sorts for **Difference** (Mismatching) will notice how it is different. According to Michael Hall, this Meta Program plays a role in determining our world-view. People who sort for sameness tend to value security, do not like change and can be seen as conservative. Conversely, people who sort for difference will value change, variety, and newness. When overdone they will only notice differences, problems, and things that do not fit. When communicating this Meta Program, identify the sameness or differences that relate to the topic for this person.

Sameness: When you continue to learn your multiplication tables, you'll become very good at it.

Difference: Keep practicing a little bit of math each day, some multiplication, some division, some algebra; the more you know, the better you'll be at it.

-- -- -- -- --

Sameness: We have sold this new product to many companies in the Real Estate industry.

Difference: You want to set yourself apart in the Real Estate industry – this product will help you do just that.

-- -- -- -- --

Sameness: Last year we had a winning marketing campaign that brought in many new clients. Let's do it again this year!

Difference: Last year we had a great marketing campaign, what are we going to do this year to make it even better?

Frame of Reference – *Internal/External*

The Frame of Reference Meta Program identifies how a person evaluates a situation, idea, experience, or other person; internally or externally. That is, who (or what) do we use as a frame of reference. A person who references **internally** will evaluate things based on what they think is right and will often validate their own actions and results and be self-motivated. A person who refers **externally** will seek external validation from what others think and will often require the guidance of others and may feel lost without external feedback. Often, externally referenced people use the word "you" when they are talking about themselves, as compared with the use of "I" by internally referenced people. When using this Meta Program to communicate, elicit the internally referenced person's ideas and give the externally referenced people your views (without giving advice or telling them what to do).

Internal: You know how much you need to study in order to get a good grade and feel happy with your result.

External: Some people need to make a plan to study and create structure in order to get the grades they want.

-- -- -- -- --

Internal: She seems to me like a good candidate for this job, what do you think?

External: Have you checked her references to hear what others have to say about her past performance?

-- -- -- -- --

Internal: You know that you will look amazing in that dress, you really should buy it!

External: Look in the mirror, I think it's just an amazing dress on you! Your husband is going to love it, you should buy that dress.

This is just a brief overview of a few Meta Programs. Some additional Meta Programs include:

- **Stress Response Pattern** – Passive/Aggressive
- **Response Sort** – Active/Reflective/Inactive
- **Choice Sort** – Options/Procedure
- **Modal Operator Sort** – Possibility/Necessity
- **Preference Sort** – People/Activity/Places/Things
- **Energy Rejuvenation** – Introversion/Extroversion
- **Affiliation Sort** – Independent/Team/Management
- **Comparison Sort** – Quantitative/Qualitative
- **Closure Sort** – Closure/Non-Closure
- **Dominance Sort** – Power/Affiliation/Achievement
- **Instruction Sort** – Strong-willed/Compliant
- **Self Esteem Sort** – Conditional/Unconditional
- **Time** – Past/Present/Future
- **Ego Strength Sort** – Stable/Unstable
- **Temporal Operator** – Judger/Perceiver

With all Meta Programs, there is not good or bad. Some preferences may work better for some people than for others, but we do not judge them as good or bad. At an advanced level of NLP, we are able to change a person's preference using a variety of tools including belief changes, parts integration, submodalities, value changes, and more. From a level of learning and understanding NLP, the most important information to know about Meta Programs is that we can gain more understanding about how and why people do what they do and use this information to better understand, communicate and be understood.

Meta Program Elicitation Exercise

As an exercise today, elicit your Meta Programs about being motivated to complete a project or task:

Meta Program	Question to Elicit	Your Response
Chunk Size	When you were motivated, were you thinking mainly of the overall goal you were working toward or each step you needed to complete?	
Direction Sort	When you were completing this project, were you moving toward completing it or away from not doing it?	
Emotional Response	When you were doing this project, were you more associated to the feelings of being motivated or were you more just doing it without much feeling?	
Philosophical Direction Sort	When you were getting this project done, were you more interested in why you needed to do it and the problems you were solving or more interested in how to do it and finding a solution?	

Relationship Sort	When you were motivated, were you recalling how this project was similar to what you have done before or was it different and completely new?	

You may like to compare this with procrastination or something else which is similar yet has an opposite outcome. It is interesting that, often, our Meta Programs are in contrast between opposite types of events. This gives us an opportunity to model ourselves and provides a template for how something works well for us.

Day 9 –
Values

What is important to you about love? What is really important? Is respect important? Trust? Commitment? Honor? How about friendship, companionship, or personal growth?

In each area of our life, be it relationships with others or yourself, money, time, health, our career, and even common sense – those things which are important to us are referred to in NLP as our **Values**. When we ask the question, "What is important to you about a career," what we are really seeking is more understanding about a person's values. Each person has their own values which is one of the filters within the NLP Communication Model.

As NLPers, we find it very useful to find someone's Values. Values are motivational driving forces in one's life and form a major part of a person's identity. By understanding what is important to a person, we can identify why people do some of the things they do and we can use their values to motivate and inspire them more effectively.

If there is incongruence in a person's life or if something is *not quite right*, we can discover if some values are not being met or if the person has old or outdated values. As a manager, leader, or parent, I can learn what is important to someone and do my best to help get those values met. In a relationship, I can deeply honor and respect my partner's model of the world by respecting and meeting the values which I am directly related to. As an individual, I can identify what is important to me and this will help me recognize when my values are not being met, in order to restore fulfillment, happiness, and harmony in a specific area of life.

As an example, one of our recent coaching clients (Diane) wanted to change jobs because there was something "not right" in her current job, but she was unable to put her finger on the problem. One of the first NLP tools we used with her was Values Elicitation. We simply asked the question, "What is important to you about a job?" Values are greatly unconscious, that is, we don't often consciously think about our values. When eliciting values, we are listening for one to three-word phrases, phrases that are longer than this tend to be beliefs (we will discuss beliefs in the next coming weeks). This client told us the following things were important to her in a job:

- Use/Learn Skills
- Respect
- Independence
- Work/Life Balance
- Good Money

Once we elicit someone's values we ask if the values are being met. Here is what we found out from Diane:

Value	Is this value being met?
Use/Learn Skills	Yes
Respect	*No*
Independence	Yes
Work/Life Balance	*No*
Good Money	Yes

Two out of her five values are not being met. If even one value was not being met, there would be a sense of disharmony, incongruence, or a feeling that something isn't right. For Diane, she explained that her job was now taking a lot more of her time and interrupting the time she wants to spend with her family. With all of the extra time she has been working, she hasn't been thanked for her efforts and feels disrespected by her manager and teammates. Six months prior to our coaching session, Diane told us that she felt respected and that she did have work/life balance.

Values were something that Diane had not thought of before. She kneople who have a lack of money (yet desire to have more) to have few values for money. A fascinating aspect about money values as in this example is that normally the few Values a person does have for money are attached to many unresourceful patterns and beliefs. For instance, the following illustrates the possible Values and Beliefs of someone who is lacking money yet desires more:

Values for Money	Beliefs and Patterns
Freedom	- When I have money I'll be free.
	- Freedom only comes from being financially independent.
Help Others	- People who don't help others are greedy.
	- I have to help my family and friends when I can.
Recognition	- My family will be proud of my accomplishments.
	- I don't want to be taken advantage of.
	- People with money are recognized for their efforts.

As we can see from above, this example illustrates many beliefs that are in conflict with not only each other but with the overall desire to have more money. Remember, the unconscious mind is a servant to follow orders and the beliefs we have, that come from our values, are important beliefs. As we mentioned earlier, values form a basis of our identity. Let's do a little bit of mind reading about the above person to gain more understanding. Of course, we would normally verify or validate our presuppositions about someone by asking questions and not just making assumptions.

Based on the beliefs of the above person, we can presuppose that there is some sort of internal conflict happening. On one hand, they have a belief that says, "people with money will be recognized for their beliefs," and from this the unconscious mind has a rule that says, "when I have money I have to help my family and friends"; and on the other hand, there is a belief that says, "I don't want to be taken advantage of," further presupposing that if they have money they will be taken advantage of. This internal conflict can create incongruence and confusion for the unconscious mind. If you imagine your servant inside of you, it is getting many mixed messages. Having money is good. Having money is bad. The easiest thing for the unconscious mind to do is to get stuck in this pattern. One of Heidi's clients had very similar Values to these – he actually made very good money at his job, but never had any. He had a belief that any extra money he had at his disposal should go to help his family (parents, siblings, etc.). His own needs were put last – he had credit card debt, was in want for many things, but his family came first. We were able to identify where and when these beliefs were created and we made alterations to his set of Values and the beliefs that were supported by his values. The end result, he was able to become financially strong with no debt, he looked after his own needs and still helped his family when he could, but now because he wanted to instead of having to.

As you can already see, Values hold a lot of power into how and why we do some of the things we do. Today we will be investigating values – how to elicit them and how to use them with ourselves and with others. Let's first find out where values, which are mainly unconscious, come from.

Based on the work by sociologist Morris Massey, it is believed that by the age of thirteen the majority of our values and beliefs that we operate on as adults have been created. Massey has described three major periods in which values are developed.

Imprint Period – ages 0-7
From the time we are born until around the age of seven we are like sponges. None of our filters are yet in

place and we are taking in and accepting as truth most of what we see, hear, feel and think. This is especially true if we learn something (or overhear something) said by someone of importance to us like our parents, grandparents, teachers, doctors, clergy, and even our siblings. During this period, our mind does not process good and bad, right and wrong; this is something that we are developing and learning. It is during this period of Massey's Development Stages that we learn many values and generate beliefs from these values.

Modeling Period – ages 8-13

During this period, we are modeling and learning from the people around us. By the age of thirteen we have modeled and have learned to be almost everything we will ever need to be – a parent, a friend, a worker, a saver, a spender, a thinker, a feeler, a spouse, a teacher, a leader, etc. We learn these skills and traits from observing the people around us. During this time, more Values are being instilled in us as we try on different things.

Socialization Period – ages 14-21

Between the ages of fourteen and twenty-one we are strongly influenced by our peers. Peers can be found in our schools, religion, on television, in the media, and online. Values and beliefs about responsibility, work ethics, learning, sharing, independence, and socializing are created during the Socialization Period.

A value is what is important to us. It is what drives us forward or stops us in our tracks. We value different things in our lives at different times. For example, a young person may value energy in their health to ensure they are able to do what they want to do; while in older age, a person may value having mobility and independence.

Because values are what is important to us, when our values are not being met we are faced with challenges, incongruence, and we may feel unhappy or incomplete. As we saw with the above example about Diane's work values; now that Diane knows about her values, she can work to ensure they are being met. Additionally, Diane's manager also knows what is important to her and he can respect her values by ensuring she is learning and using her skills, she is being respected for her work, that she has autonomy, that she is being paid well and that she has work/life balance.

This is the case for every area of life. Once you know your own personal values, you can continue to do things, change what you are doing or start doing something new in order for your values to be met. When you know someone else's values, you can do your part to help those values to be met.

In a relationship, if it is important to my partner to be appreciated, I can do my part to ensure that I show my appreciation of him in small and big ways. If I don't know what my partner's values are, then I can't help to get those values met. And if I'm not showing him appreciation, his value may not be met and this may cause unhappiness in our relationship. While it is ultimately up to the person who holds the values to get them met for themselves, if I know more then I can do better for my partner.

In an effort to better know and understand yourself, sometime today elicit your values on three of the following areas of your life:

- Relationship with your partner
- Relationship with your parents
- Relationship with your siblings
- Parenting

- Health
- Family
- Problem Solving
- Teamwork
- Career
- Finance and money
- Education

- Time
- Religion
- Success
- Goal Setting
- Identifying Conflict

Once you have elicited your values, ask yourself if the value is being met. For those values which are not being met, the following questions will help you to find ways to get those values met:

1. What can you start in order to get those values met?
2. What can you change in order to get those values met?
3. What can you continue in order to get those values met?

You can also easily elicit the values of other people through general conversation. Simply ask the question, "What is important to you about X?" and listen for the key one to three-word phrases. Keep asking the question until you have elicited 3-6 values; a Values Worksheet can be found on the next page.

From a coaching perspective it is useful to know and understand the values of your clients so you can help them to ensure they are met. As a manager or leader, knowing the values of your team helps you to motivate, lead and manage your staff as individuals helping to get their values met. In your relationship, you can ensure a healthier and more vibrant relationship by knowing each other's values. As a parent, you can better motivate and teach your children with the use of their values. And as a friend, you can better connect and be an even better friend when you know the values of your companion.

Values Worksheet

Area Assessment _____

Values Elicitation: List 3-6 values, once they are elicited, tick the values that are being met. *Question: "What is important to you about _____?"*

Values	Values Prioritized	Being Met?

Based on the values not being met, answer the following questions:

What can you start in order to get those values met?

_____

_____

_____

What can you change in order to get those values met?

_____

_____

_____

What can you continue in order to get those values met?

_____

_____

_____

What are some of your beliefs or unresourceful patterns related to those values?

_____

_____

_____

Day 10 –
Meta Model

Every moment of every day we are unconsciously distorting, deleting and generalizing information. Recall from the Communication Model that of the two million bits of information coming into our awareness every moment, our mind is only able to take 134 of those bits. Imagine all of the details or feelings or awareness that you don't have because it was deleted, distorted and generalized.

As we discussed earlier, words make up only approximately 7% of communication. Those words, however, contain incongruence, limiting language, and clues to limiting beliefs, stuck states, and limitations. Recall from Day 7 we introduced the analogy of an iceberg. Most of what we speak is on the surface structure of meaning. When we say, "it is a nice day," we could possibly actually mean that the sun is shining, it is 80 degrees Fahrenheit, there isn't a cloud in the sky with a slight northerly breeze which is bringing a light aromatic smell of wild flowers into the room. However, to say all of this information is overwhelming for the conscious mind, remember we can hold only 7 +/- 2 chunks of information at one time in our conscious minds. Therefore, we distort, delete and generalize information based on our model of the world, our memories, perceptions, values, beliefs, and internal programs.

Before we go further, let's define what is meant by distortion, deletion, and generalization:

Distortion
Distortion is the process by which we shift perception of reality to fit into our model of the world. When we attend a fantasy or science fiction movie, we are able to distort time and reality to

believe what is happening. The same is true in day-to-day life. Examples of statements with distortions include:

- We don't communicate anymore.
- I know you'd like to eat Italian tonight.
- I can't go to school because I'm tired.
- Popcorn fills me up.

Deletion

Deletion is the process by which we exclude aspects of the world around us. For example, if you are talking with a friend in a noisy place, you are able to exclude the noise around you in order to hear your friend. Examples of statements with deletions include:

- He's a better person.
- Friends make me happy.
- Exercise is hard work.
- People don't understand me.

Generalization

Generalization is the process by which the mind categorizes information to represent one rule or universal truth. Examples of generalizing statements include:

- All women like to shop.
- Men are good problem solvers.
- Children have good imagination.
- When people get older their memory gets worse.
- Teachers are compassionate.
- I always get lost.

When you see this picture – what do you see?

Our mind automatically distorts, deletes and generalizes all information. So you will either see a young woman or an old woman in this picture. Most people are able to see both. Here's an interesting thing; once the information which you have distorted, deleted, or generalized has been uncovered, you cannot only see one woman anymore. This relates to the presupposition: *the more you know, the better you can do.*

Our mind is an amazing thing; it wants to help us, to do the best for us, to make sense out of the world. Take a look at this 3-D chalk drawing:

The artist of this sidewalk drawing is getting into his pool! It makes sense to the mind, because we want it to make sense.

This act of distorting, deleting and generalizing is happening all around us too; other people are distorting, deleting and generalizing what you say. This means that your full message is not getting through the filters of other people's minds. But what you say is important, isn't it? This means that people delete important things. So how do we retrieve this information which has somehow been lost in translation? Wouldn't it be great to have a simple tool that could help you to uncover what a person has distorted, deleted and generalized? When we can uncover this information, we are able to find a wealth of potentially hidden information – this allows us the opportunity to better understand someone's model of the world (or our own) and allow them access to more choices based on this new information.

This technique to uncover what has been deleted, distorted, and generalized is not new to any of us. In fact, we have been using this technique from the time we could talk. Today you are going to learn structure and intentionality to your already developed skill of asking questions.

The Meta Model is a questioning technique which allows us to go meta and find out what is beyond our model. We can use a variety of questions to purposefully uncover what a person has distorted, deleted and generalized, in order to understand and reveal more about a person's model of the world.

Because our mind automatically distorts, deletes and generalizes, it is important to be able to recover the information that has been lost in translation. Originally based on the work of Alfred Korzybski (Science and Sanity: An Introduction to Non-Aristotelian Systems and General Semantics, 1933), and also modeled on the linguistic patterns of Virginia Satir, the Meta Model is a set of twelve language patterns and questions that reconnect language with experience. Korzybski thought that we could understand each other better and behave better, if we were clear about who, what, when, and where.

This model was developed by John Grinder and Richard Bandler and can be used for gathering information, clarifying meaning, identifying limitations, and opening up choices. It is based on Transformational Grammar and identifies common distortions, deletions, and generalizations, which obscure the original or deeper meaning.

So often, we listen to what a person says and take their words at face value. At the same time, we automatically distort, delete and generalize what has been said and create meaning based on our own model of the world.

Imagine someone saying to you: *I need a new job.*

Based on your model of the world you make meaning of this statement and presuppose what is meant by saying this. You may also respond to this statement – again, based on your model of the world. You may be right; and there is also a great chance that you may be wrong.

By asking some simple, yet specific Meta Model questions, you can get to know much more about what this statement really means to the person who has said it:

Statement: I need a new job.

Meta Model Questions:
For what purpose do you need a new job?

What will happen if you get a new job?

What do you mean by a new job?

How do you know you need a new job?

What kind of a new job do you need?

As you can see, even without the answers to these questions, they have the ability to elicit a wealth of information just by asking them. Of course, you would most likely only ask one of the above questions and then possibly another question based on the answer you receive.

Meta Model Questions

While there are twelve Meta Model Patterns which we will discuss in detail, the most important information about the Meta

Model are the questions that uncover information and choices. Primarily, those questions are based upon the following:

- How do you know?
- According to whom?
- Who specifically?
- How specifically?
- What specifically?
- When specifically?
- For what purpose?
- What would happen if you didn't?
- What would happen if you did?

Always? Never? All? Everyone As you can see from these above questions, the Meta Model digs deeper to find more specific information. When used with purpose, these questions will not only help you understand another person or yourself better, but will also assist the person you are speaking with to see another point of view, recover choice and recognize a limit. In NLP, this is known as shaking up someone's model of the world.

The Meta Model Patterns

From a transformational grammar perspective, Bandler and Grinder defined twelve basic "syntactic" categories that represent patterns of distortion, deletion, and generalization. The following information is presented as a basis of understanding these categories. We have found that knowing these distinctions is much less important than knowing what question to ask in order to uncover what has been distorted, deleted and generalized.

Deletions

The Meta Model Questions asked for deletions should be aimed at uncovering what has been deleted in the statement.

Unspecified Referential Index - statements where the subject or noun is missing.

- She doesn't understand me
  - *Who is she?*
  - *What doesn't she understand about you?*

- Pets take too much time
  - *What kind of pets specifically?*
  - *What is too much time?*
- People should take care of the environment
  - *How specifically?*
  - *Which people should do this?*

Unspecified Verbs – statements where an action is not implied and fails to identify specifics of how something should be done.

- A family should love each other
  - *How specifically should they love each other?*
  - *How would you know if they love each other?*
- I want to have more responsibility
  - *What kind of responsibility do you want?*
  - *Where do you want to have more responsibility?*

Deletions – statements with information missing which could enrich or change the meaning of the statement.

- He is generous
  - *Generous at what?*
  - *Who is he?*
  - *Compared to whom is he generous?*
- Your education is better
  - *Better than what specifically?*
  - *How do you know my education is better?*
- I have a large house
  - *Large compared to what?*
  - *How large is it?*

Distortions

The Meta Model Questions asked for distortions should be aimed at uncovering what has been distorted in the statement.

Nominalization – statements where an activity or verb is represented as an object or noun.

- We stand for justice
  - *How specifically do we do that?*

- ○ *What kind of justice do we stand for?*
- You can take on more responsibility
  - ○ *How can I take on more responsibility?*
  - ○ *What kind of responsibility specifically?*
- I want to communicate better
  - ○ *What do you want to communicate better?*
  - ○ *How specifically do you want to do that?*
  - ○ *How will you know when you communicate better?*

Complex Equivalent – a statement where two experiences are tied together making them equivalent or equal to the speaker.
- The economy is bad so our sales will go down.
  - ○ *How do you know your sales will go down?*
  - ○ *Does a bad economy always mean sales will go down?*
- Bob and Anne divorced, they don't get along.
  - ○ *How do you know they don't get along?*
  - ○ *Do they not get along because they are divorced?*
- I can't learn a new language; it takes too much time.
  - ○ *How does taking a long time mean you can't learn a new language?*
  - ○ *Specifically, how much time does it take?*

Presuppositions – when an assumption must be made for the statement to be true.
- If my friends understood me, they wouldn't like me.
  - ○ *How do you know they wouldn't like you?*
  - ○ *What would they need to understand to come to that conclusion?*
- I'm not the type of person he would fall in love with.
  - ○ *How do you know what his type is?*
  - ○ *What type of person is that specifically?*
- They'll never hire me without a degree.
  - ○ *How do you know that?*
  - ○ *What makes a degree so important for this job?*

Cause and Effect - statements where a cause-and-effect relationship is either implicitly or explicitly implied between two experiences.

- Having a degree will help me get a better job.
    - *How do you know that?*
    - *Do you know people with good jobs and no degree?*
- If I don't do this project perfect, my boss will think I'm incompetent.
    - *How do you know that your boss will think you're incompetent?*
    - *How does an imperfect project make you incompetent?*
- I'll never find a wife because I don't have enough money.
    - *How does having money mean you'll find a wife?*
    - *Are all people who don't have enough money single?*

Mind Reading – statements in which the speaker claims to know what the other person or group feels, thinks or means.

- My sister hates going to work.
    - *How do you know that?*
    - *I know you are interested in learning more about language.*
- How do you know what I'm interested in?
    - *You're going to laugh when I tell you this.*
    - *How do you know?*

Generalizations

The Meta Model Questions asked for distortions should be aimed at uncovering what has been generalized in the statement.

Lost Performative – statements where an unmeasured evaluation is made with words such as: good, bad, right, wrong, just, etc.

- It's a bad thing to not eat all the food on your plate.
    - *Bad compared to what?*
    - *According to whom?*
- You're just waiting to be swept off your feet.
    - *How do you know that?*
    - *Is that all I'm doing?*

- Waking up early is a good habit to have.
  - *According to whom?*
  - *A good habit compared to what?*

Universal Qualifier – statements which create gross generalizations and create 'universal' truths from using words such as: all, every, never, always, only, everyone, no one, everything, etc.

- All Christians are God fearing.
  - *All Christians?*
  - *How do you know?*
- Men always want to find solutions to problems.
  - *Always?*
  - *Are there some men who can just listen?*
- You never give me the respect that I deserve.
  - *Never?*
  - *How do you know that I don't?*

Modal Operators – statements that include words such as: should, can't, must, have to, necessity, impossible, etc., which create a limiting situation by asserting a claim about what is possible, not possible, necessary, or not necessary.

- I can't speak to my father about this topic.
  - *What would happen if you could?*
  - *What prevents you from speaking to him about it?*
- You have to work hard it you want a promotion.
  - *What would happen if you don't work hard?*
  - *Is there another way to get a promotion?*
- It's not possible to be successful at work and be a devoted father.
  - *What would you need in order for this to be possible?*
  - *How do you know this is not possible?*

Meta Questions

In addition to basic Meta Model Questions, we would like to introduce you to Meta Questions. Meta Questions were defined by Dr. L. Michael Hall as a technique to uncover even more of the deeper structure within communication. Simply stated, Meta Questions are questions about questions.

Meta Questions are useful to find more information specifically about a certain theme. We will be looking at six different Meta Question themes.

Meaning/Significance – questions that uncover what a word or concept means to someone.
- What does this mean to you?
- What significance does this hold for you?

Permission – questions that identify ideas about permission versus prohibitions and taboos.
- Do you have permission to experience this?
- Can you allow yourself to do (have, be, feel, etc.) this?

Prohibition/Taboo – questions that identify ideas about what we do not allow but rather prohibit or taboo.
- Would it enhance your experience to taboo this?
- Who has prohibited this for you?
- Is this idea prohibited to you?

Beliefs - questions which identify what beliefs are held about certain ideas, words, emotions, or behaviors.
- What do you believe about this?
- What do you believe about this belief?

Value/Importance – questions about what we value, find important and treat as important or significant.
- What do you value about this?
- What is important to you about this?
- What is important that you can count on?

Intention/Desire – questions which identify motives, intentions, desires and wants.

- What is your highest intention about this?
- What intention is driving your response?
- What do you really want and desire about this?

No matter what questions we are using, the overall intention of asking the questions is to gain more information about a person's model of the world. When you are able to understand a person's model of the world, you have a better opportunity for improved communication, negotiation, and ultimately you can better respect that person's model of the world.

Day 11 –
States and State Management

We are fortunate to get to know people from many continents and countries as we teach NLP. These people have a variety of backgrounds and experiences; however, they seem to have the same basic wants, needs, and desires. When we ask people what they want, the most common response is "to have a good life." This makes me wonder, are they getting that good life? In NLP we know the key to how you live your life, make decisions, and feel about yourself comes from your state of mind. I (Laureli) remember when I was first learning NLP and the trainers kept saying, "The key to NLP is all about state." I soon found that this was a valid comment.

For instance, have you ever gotten off to a bad start or let external events determine how you feel or woken up on the wrong side of the bed? Sometimes we just feel bad and don't know why, no reason or rationale behind it. These states or moods are often habitual or automatic, and when you don't pay attention and intervene they can overtake you and affect your thinking capabilities and drain your physical energy levels. In fact, your physiology has a large part to play in the way you feel. It's not only our thoughts that control what we feel, it's also the condition of our bodies. Think back to a time when you had the flu or were not feeling well physically. What was your decision making facility like? How did you feel about life then?

An NLP presupposition says, *You are in charge of your mind therefore your results.* Therefore, we can intervene at any time and change how and what we think and how we hold our bodies. When we do, it will alter our state and mood.

Imagine attending a conference and you walk into a room full of people you either don't know or barely know. What emotions do you notice? How does it affect your body? How do you hold yourself? What do you say to yourself?

Let's look at someone with anxiety who allows their state to control them:

They feel self-conscious and uncomfortable with tension in their shoulders and a knot in their stomach. They have sweaty palms and a dry mouth. They are saying to themselves, "No one will find me interesting; I look silly; someone may notice me sweating." They are struggling to think of anything to say and either stumble over words or blurt things out really fast.

This example is only one of many possibilities, as each person has their own experience. However, has this state allowed them to be the true person they could be at that moment? Probably not. When people pay attention to the unresourceful effects of their state, it only replicates and influences the behavior of what they are focusing on.

What is a State?

A **State** is an emotional condition or mood a person has at any given moment in time. This means that when you have a thought, it gives you an emotional response and neurologically something happens inside of you. This state causes your body to react in a corresponding body movement and/or posture (physiology).

Deepak Chopra stated that "For every thought there is a corresponding chemical dripped into the blood stream." This is something that happens without our conscious awareness, and it affects how we feel and most generally how we react. States become habitual and automatic responses that are programmed from early childhood and can change from moment to moment.

It can be empowering to understand how to be in charge and master your own states.

We have both resourceful and unresourceful states. There are two main components to a state:

1. Your internal state or how you see, hear, feel, and what you say to yourself
2. Your physical state or how you hold and move your body externally

In day six, we discussed the communication model. It showed how a person gets into a state. To recap: Any given moment in time we are surrounded by external activities and situations, and from moment to moment we take these events and automatically run them through our internal filters.

*   First, the event goes through the five senses.
*   Then other filters such as values, beliefs, and meta programs, etc.
*   Some of the information is generalized, distorted and deleted.
*   From here we internalize it as it becomes coded as a picture, sound, or a feeling.
*   This in turn causes the brain to make corresponding chemicals which creates a mood or state.
*   The body responds by matching the mood with how it holds itself in muscle tone and stature.
*   This results in a behavior that can become a pattern.

All of this happens outside our conscious awareness. Keep in mind all this happens in a nanosecond and it can change just as quickly.

We often tolerate our undesired states or avoid situations that trigger them. Some people do not realize or believe they can change their states and how they feel. They hide behind their emotions as an excuse for behaving badly. They say things like: "You know how I am, so don't make me angry." Or, "I'm just an emotional person." It is not enough to wish you did not respond or behave a certain way. By determining how we behave, it is easier and more effective to change our behavior. A large part of NLP teaches how to manage and maintain your state. This results in people having more flexibility and control in their lives.

Have you ever had an incident where something happens and you wondered "why did I respond like that?" Did it make you think "where did that emotion come from?" Emotions are naturally occurring phenomena and are necessary for communicating; having control over our emotions is an essential characteristic which sets humans apart from other mammals. Emotions cannot be seen or touched; they are felt in a powerful form both physically and mentally. Emotions are an indicator of how we are experiencing each moment in life. When encountering beliefs and behaviors, we find they are wrapped and sometimes saturated with emotions. Some are good and some are not so good. It is a fundamental manifestation of the life force.

Emotions, when experienced, become a state of mind and body. We often refer to what a state we or other people are in; for instance, take a moment to think of something that concerns you. Now, notice how it makes you feel; and how you hold your body; where your eyes are looking; and what you are thinking or saying to yourself.

For most people, when they do this they will be looking down either to the right or left, and they usually feel something somewhere in their body. There is no right or wrong, however the body will react and be in some sort of state when engaged in any thought that has emotion in it.

Once you have noticed how you reacted, then think the same thought, but this time sit up straight and tall and have your eyes look up. When you do this what happens to the thought? And the emotions you notice? For most people the thought is still there, but it is often less intense and sometimes less important and sometimes it even disappears.

Now, try to feel annoyed as you smile. Be happy as you look down and frown.

Most likely this is challenging or difficult to do. The reason for having you do these exercises is for you to experience how your thoughts, emotions, and body respond together. By just changing how you hold your body, it can and does affect your emotions. Of course, there is more to managing your emotions than just this. By understanding how states are formed and how they affect people, we can learn how to manage our own states. When we know more we can do more.

Meta-States - What Makes a State?

Have you ever given much thought to what states make up a state? Or how many states you have at one time? Dr. L. Michael Hall takes the concept of states one step further by looking at **Meta-States**, the states about states.

Let's think about love for a moment. The romantic kind of love. When a person feels this kind of love they are actually experiencing a wealth of states all at once, coalesced together. For example, this kind of love may be made up of passion, friendship, kindred spirit, compassion, understanding and sexual desire. These various states are the meta-states of romantic love. Meta States help us to distinguish not only the finer details of a state but it helps us to understand the difference between similar states. This kind of love wouldn't equate to the love of a pet, the love of ice cream or the love of a child. Each of those types of love would be made of their own meta-states. To elicit meta-states you can simply ask "what states are included in that state?"

We can also use meta-states to build or amplify a state. If someone wants to be confident when public speaking, for example. To make this a more robust kind of confidence you might be curious about what meta-states they want with confidence. Instead of just being confidence (Michael Hall would call this a Plain Vanilla State), you can texture states with richer and fuller states. Just plain confident becomes: engaging confidence, authentic confidence, playful confidence, courageous confidence, natural confidence, intelligent confidence. Which would you rather have?

State Management

If something is distressing or challenging, we are often more aware after the event of how we could have felt or reacted more resourcefully and differently. Knowing how to be in control of your state even under duress is a great skill. We call it state management.

State management or utilization means you have the power to alter and access your state when you want to. Your mind is full of many tools that you can use, and state management is one of the most powerful tools you can learn to use. State management is where you choose to control your state versus it controlling you. When this is done often enough, it becomes automatic. When your state is controlling you, it automatically reacts while you watch helplessly.

There are three essential components for state management.
- **Acceptance** of the state you have, taking responsibility for it.
- **Awareness** of a new state you would rather be having.
- Take **Action** and to do something to change your state rather than only think about it.

These three components enable you to change an unresourceful state by applying a resourceful state when you need it. Resourceful states are states which are positive and useful including: feeling good, powerful, happy, content, helpful, loved, and wise. These words are more than just descriptions; they have internal feelings that go with them. Remember, every word we hear creates a chemical reaction which our body responds to.

If you should enter a situation that triggers an undesirable emotional state, you can decide to go into a resourceful state by just recalling what resourceful state you want to be in and stepping into that state instead. This requires you to think about and let yourself experience that state. Often we anchor these states so you can get into them easily and quickly (we will discuss anchoring in a few days). When you learn to get into resourceful states, you will be more in sync with the moment and can better focus on what you want instead of coping with unpleasant, unwanted emotions. You are in charge of your mind and therefore your results.

Resourceful States Exercise
The following exercise will help you to practice getting into resourceful states. As you get into each state, allow your body to move naturally to demonstrate the emotion. When you are in each state, hold it for two or more minutes and notice what you feel internally and how you are holding your body externally.

State 1: Composed
- Close your eyes and take a deep breath, as you relax readjust your body posture.
- Remember a time when you were composed. Truly composed. Let your mind create an image and feelings that represent being composed. Remember what it's like.
- Step back in time for a moment and let yourself feel and see and hear what you heard when you were composed.
- Hold onto this state for two or more minutes.

State 2: Amused or Pleased

- Can you remember a time when you were amused or pleased? Amused so you wanted to laugh or smile? Pleased so that a grin has to happen?
- Remember what it's like to be amused. Let your body remember too.
- Step back to a time when you were amused and pleased and let your body remember too – see what you saw, hear what you heard, and really feel what it feels like to be amused. Let that smile come to your mouth. Notice what it is like.
- Hold onto this state for two or more minutes.

State 3: Curious

- Curiosity is interesting. Can you remember a time when you were curious? What was it about? If you can't remember a time you were curious, maybe wondering about it now can help you to become curious now.
- Let your body and mind become curious. Notice how your head shifts, your shoulders move, your breath changes as you become curious.
- Notice what you think, what you feel, what you see and what you hear. Notice how you hold your body, even your arms and hands.
- Hold onto this state for two or more minutes.

When you are able to get into these resourceful states by just thinking about them, you can tap into them easily and at any time you want. Practice this exercise as a way to get in touch with your emotions and to program yourself to easily change state.

Everyone has and needs emotions. Emotions are normal and important for our balance and harmony. It is when they are repressed and not dealt with, or kept deep inside, that they are dangerous to your well-being in body, mind, and spirit. Repressed and unresolved emotions may manifest themselves into harmful health aspects like weight gain (or loss), high blood pressure, high cholesterol, and even cancer and other diseases. When we have unresolved negative emotions, not only do we suffer mentally, emotionally and physically, others are affected as well. These negative emotions can become contagious. You can learn to use state management and manage your states instead of spreading negative ones.

State Management Exercise

1. Be aware that you are the one in charge and in control of your life and your thoughts. Take a few moments to quietly think about what state/s you want to take charge of. As you consciously change your mind and thoughts, you will notice how it will change your physical and emotional state.

2. Take action. Decide how you wish to be instead and begin. The key to state management is repetition, repetition, repetition. Practices being in the state you want to be in. Spend time in this new state as you sit, walk, talk, hold your body, facial features that mirror the state you want to be in. Do this often and perhaps at the same time everyday. This will give your mind and body the blueprint of how to be in the state. This is especially true when you are managing old unresourceful states which have become habitual over time. You need a new positive habit.

3. Be confident in yourself and calmly take deep breaths. Tell yourself you can do it.

4. If an unwanted thought comes in, say to it, "cancel, erase," and then replace it. Take some time to think about three things you would rather think instead as a replacement. For instance: I can do it, I am happy, I am working on it. Make these replacement statements before you start the exercise so you will be ready.

Remember: Your mind has the ability to self organize, self stabilize, self replicate, self reference, self mirror and self modify.

State Elicitation

There are many NLP techniques that use state elicitation as a step and also many which notes what state a person wants to enhance or change. This is because when we are helping to clear unresourceful behaviors, thoughts, or feelings, or when enhancing or creating a new resourceful state, we need to be able to know how it feels. We call this state elicitation. The body and mind always need to be involved with any change.

When we elicit a resourceful state, we know the most effective and powerful states are the pure or real emotions a person has experienced and felt before. However, let's say someone wants to have a state of contentment but they don't know what it feels like, because they have never had the experience of it before. We get them to imagine how it would feel. Ultimately, your mind doesn't know if something is real or imagined.

In addition to NLP techniques, it is often useful to be able to help other people elicit a state which might be more useful for them. For example, when assisting a child with their homework, a parent may find it helpful to elicit a learning and fun state from their child. To do this, the parent could use a simple state elicitation script:

1. Can you remember a time when you learned something new and it was fun to learn?
2. Go back and remember that now, step into that memory like it's happening now and let yourself see what you saw, hear what you heard and really feel what it feels like to have fun while you learn, and what it feels like to learn something new. Let your body feel it now.

Eliciting a state can be quite simple. Something to keep in mind is that to make it even easier to elicit a state from someone else, you should be in that state too. If you want to motivate someone, make sure your voice is upbeat and that your body displays a motivated state.

> *Remember a time when you were motivated. Really motivated. Go ahead and take yourself back there, and act as if it's happening now.*

States and state management puts you in charge and responsible of yourself. As people learn to be aware and make conscious changes, their lives change. Or, as someone once said, "We change our tools and our tools change us."

No matter where you are, what you are doing or who you are with, you have a state. You literally can't leave home without it. Every moment of every day you have a state. While you cannot be without a state, you can have more personal power about your states. If it is by acknowledging your state, using state management, eliciting states in others or understanding meta-states, you have an arsenal of tools to help you to continue to do even better when you choose to.

Day 12 –
Reframing

Sometimes looking at something from a different perspective helps us to find a solution or even find a better option. Yet, too often, people get stuck in their own model of the world; held tight by the map they have created for themselves. Yet, that map isn't real. Each and every one of us has a malleable map. It's changeable. And words have the power to change it.

Have you ever taken part in a conversation with someone who just lost their job or their relationship just ended? Normally that person is standing in front of a now closed door just looking at the closed door. A simple suggestion that this door closing means that other doors can now open has the power to change a person's map.

Have you ever planned something that didn't work out? How do you handle it? There are really only a few options: (1) you can let it go and just move on, (2) you can get upset, or (3) you can see it from a different perspective.

Last year, one of our clients got a new job in a different state. He resigned from his old job, found renters for his house, started relocating his family to the new state and was excited to start his new job. At the last minute, the new company made some major changes and were unable to hire him after all. They did pay his relocation expenses and paid compensation for undue stress, but this man was still in the process of relocating and had no job. He could have easily gotten angry – his wife did. In fact, his wife had also left her job and was in the process of transitioning her life to the new state too. She was arguing about the unfairness of it, the lack of consideration the company had in hiring him in the first place; arguments that she had every right to make. Her husband, however, had a different way of looking at it. He pointed out that this was a great opportunity to start all over for the family. Maybe they could move somewhere totally different, not even to the city they had planned. Perhaps they could take this time to learn more about their world, their life, and each other. In fact, after much deliberation, with all of their belongings packed, mortgage being paid and some savings in the bank, the family did just that. They spent two months traveling through Europe and learning about the world, their lives, and each other. They were able to take one situation in life and view it from a different perspective.

This simple art of changing our map of the world, of being able to look at something from a different perspective is known as **Reframing**. It is aptly named because we are changing the frame of reference we are using to view our world. Recall the NLP Presupposition, the map is not the territory. The landscape of our lives is not actually real. What is real is what is actually happening. And, what is actually happening is never two dimensional; there are always more options, choices, routes, and possibilities. Reframing helps us to see those.

Ultimately, anything that creates a new point of view can be termed reframing. A metaphor, a life example, an episode of Oprah. In NLP, we use words as statements or questions to ourselves or to another person to offer a chance to reframe a current view. Today we are going to talk about two different kinds of reframing: **content** and **context** reframing.

Content Reframing

The content of someone's story tells us about the actual *story*, the what happened in the story. If someone has a relationship that just ended, the break-up and relationship ending is the story. If a picnic is cancelled because of rain, the picnic and the rain are the content of the story. If someone misses a flight, missing the flight is the story.

We can use a content reframe to identify *what else the story could mean*. When we can identify even one new meaning for a person, this opens up possibilities and the person's map of the world starts to shift and change. This also presupposes that content reframing is used to shift someone from an unwanted to a desired state. There is little reason to shift an already desired or positive state.

There are two things that we keep in mind when using a content reframe. The first is the NLP Presupposition *every behavior has a positive intention*; this helps us to remember that no matter what the story, there is a positive intention somewhere. And second, we are constantly thinking what else could this mean? This second question is where the content reframe comes from. Automatically this question allows you to see different possibilities.

If a relationship has just ended, that could mean that a new person is waiting just around the corner. Or it may mean that someone even better is out there. Or it may mean that now you have the opportunity to grow in different ways. It may mean that you have permission to move on. It may mean the universe has something better planned for you. The possibilities are limitless. Even just one reframe helps to shift the model of the world.

Now it's your turn, create 3-4 content reframes for the following stories, remember the magic content reframe question: *what else could this mean?*

1. A family picnic has to be cancelled because of the rain.

    * _____
    * _____
    * _____
    * _____

2. You've just missed a flight and the next one is tomorrow.

- _____
- _____
- _____
- _____

When working with another person, you can either offer your listener a statement like you've created above, or you can just ask them the question what else could this mean? Either way provides a reframe, and reframes can be very powerful.

A few years ago, we had a female client who was having bad period pains and came to see us for NLP assistance. One of the things we often do with physical pain is to find the meaning of the pain, to reframe it from pain to positive; remembering that every behavior has a positive intention. So we asked her, "What does this pain mean?" After much contemplation she said, "It reminds me that I am a woman." We discussed this for a while and then again we asked, "What does it mean to be a woman?" She then told us about her mother who was very strong and a feminist and that women who are not strong are weak. She saw herself as weak. We then asked, "What does it mean to be weak?", and she described a very kind, caring and compassionate person, in fact the kind of person she was and that she wanted to be, but apparently had not given herself permission to be. We then worked on allowing herself the permission to be the kind of woman she wanted to be, and the next month she reported a very calm menstrual cycle.

The meanings we put on things have power. This is why content reframing can be so very useful, everything can ultimately have more than one meaning.

Context Reframing

The context of someone's story tells us the *setting or scene* of the story, the where the story happened. Using the example of the break-up, the context could be a break-up in a park, in a restaurant, on an anniversary, or simply at home. For the picnic that had to be cancelled because of rain, the setting could have been at a park, in the mountains, on a boat, or on the beach.

We can use a context reframe to identify *where else something could be useful*. One Presupposition of NLP states *every behavior is useful in some context*. Offering a context reframe shifts a person from the current setting of their present state to somewhere else. By shifting the setting, the mind is now engaged in a new topic and it is easier to continue from there.

For example, the rain which cancelled the picnic could be useful if we need rain, it's useful to water the garden and flowers, it's useful to top up dams. A conversation within context reframing might sound like this:

Sad picnicker: I really wanted to go on a picnic, but since it's raining we have to cancel it.

You: Well, at least you won't have to water your lawn and garden this week.

Now, this example doesn't move someone to their desired state specifically, but it does shift their frame to a new topic. With this same example you could use a context reframe on the picnic itself; after all, there are no rules about where a picnic should take place! This conversation might sound like:

Sad picnicker: I really wanted to go on a picnic, but since it's raining we have to cancel it.

You: Have you ever picnicked inside?

As you can see here, we offered a question instead of a statement to reframe this. Either will do. Sometimes a question is better with context reframing, so the person you are talking to can shift their own map and find their own answers. As NLPers we do not offer advice, so it may be more useful here to ask a question instead of tell the picnicker where to go and have the picnic.

In addition to reframing the stories in people's lives, context reframing is particularly useful in reframing emotions and behaviors; especially emotions and behaviors which are seemingly unresourceful. Remember again, every behavior is useful in some context. We have found that some people deny themselves permission to exhibit or feel certain emotions or display certain behaviors. We can use a content reframe to reframe the meaning, and we can use a context reframe to identify *when else might this be useful?*

Let's take anger for example. We meet a lot of parents who get upset at themselves for getting angry with their children. In fact, many of them would like the opportunity to take anger out of their biological register all together. Yet, would that be useful? Probably not long term. Anger is a useful emotion to have as it sets up and protects our boundaries and rules for ourselves. If someone tries to steal my bag, hurt me, hurt someone I care about, encroach upon my values, tries to take advantage of me or someone near me, or is in anyway being harmful to me or someone around me, anger is a great response. To deny one's self of this emotion is to just accept that our boundaries don't amount to much. When working with people who don't like the emotion of anger, we start to point out (either by statements or by asking them questions), where anger could be useful. This redirects the mind to think of anger in new terms and gives new direction to when anger is more permissible to display. In other words, we are reframing anger.

It's your turn. Provide a context reframe for the following statements, remember to ask yourself where else could this be useful?

1. A friend of yours feels guilty for calling in sick when she wasn't sick. (here you'll either reframe guilt or being dishonest, try both)

    - _____
    - _____
    - _____
    - _____

2. At a staff meeting you raised your voice and showed your frustration to your team.

    - _____
    - _____
    - _____
    - _____

At the end of the day, it doesn't really matter if consciously you know if you are offering a content or context reframe. What matters is that you are able to help a person see a different point of view and shift their frame of reference to move toward a more resourceful desired state. Reframing is a skill that you already have, and you use with yourself and others every day. Now, you have more conscious knowledge about reframing which will assist you in the future.

Reframing Examples

Initial Frame	Reframe
I am in a tunnel and I can't see a way out.	_Every tunnel has an entrance and exit._
I am _too_ anxious to study.	_Being anxious can help you to do better. It means you care enough to do your best._
I know I will never be confident.	_Having confidence starts with having insights about our own limits._

When she looks at me like that she hates me.	*Some people cover up their feelings by putting a scowl on their face.*
I yell at my kids too much, I'm a very bad parent!	*You want to keep them safe and teach them right. It takes a good parent to do that.*
He is out at night and that means that he does not love me any more.	*Absence does make the heart grow fonder. Your private time can help you to appreciate each other more.*
She is so boring, stays in all the time and does not have a mind of her own.	*Stoic people are often a great port in a storm, a great source of security.*
He doesn't want to work. He is no good and a layabout – a typical waster – a drain on us all.	*A lack of jobs sometimes forces good and honest people into unemployment. This sometimes takes away their hope and breaks their spirit and belief in work.*

Day 13 –
Ericksonian Hypnosis

Dr. Milton H. Erickson is considered the father of modern hypnotherapy and is attributed to bringing legitimacy into hypnosis. Ericksonian hypnosis is one of the fastest growing and influential branches of hypnotherapy today. His methods have inspired short-term strategic therapy and the rebirth of guided imagery.

In the early 1970's, anthropologist Gregory Bateson introduced Dr. Erickson to Richard Bandler and John Grinder. They were particularly interested in the patterns of language and behavior that effective psychotherapists used with their clients to effect change. They found Ericksonian hypnosis fascinating and a perfect fit to use with NLP.

Ericksonian hypnosis is very conversational and uses metaphors as it communicates with the deeper unconscious mind. Erickson believed that when subjects were in a relaxed state or trance, the unconscious dismissed confusing ideas and accepted the essential underlying truth. Perhaps the best way to gain insight into Ericksonian hypnosis is to follow Erickson's lead and use stories, starting with Erickson's own dramatic life story. A story of courage, determination, and one that confirms that there are no coincidences.

Milton Erickson was born in a pioneering and rural farming country in 1902. The schooling he and many of his brothers and sisters received was basic, thus it is not surprising that nobody noticed that young Milton was experiencing the world in a rather unique manner: he was color blind, tone deaf, and slightly dyslexic. These perceptual abnormalities may have led Erickson to a road less traveled, but it wasn't until his teenage years that his life would take a truly pivotal turn that would affect his destiny and the evolution of hypnotherapy, as we know it.

In the summer of 1919, at the age of seventeen, he was stricken with his first attack of Polio (his second would come at the age of fifty-one). It was an extremely severe infection and he was not expected to survive; his parents were told that he would be dead by the following morning. He lapsed into a coma and when he awoke three days later he found himself completely paralyzed, unable to move except for his eyes, and barely able to speak. Since there were no rehabilitation facilities in their community, there was no reason to expect that he would ever recover.

Milton kept his still active and keen mind occupied as he played mental games by himself. He learned to notice the difference between his family's verbal and nonverbal communications. He noticed that sometimes people would say "no" with their mouth, while their body was clearly saying "yes." His parents, who took care of him as best they could, fashioned a crude potty for him and left him strapped into his chair for hours. He was sitting somewhere in the middle of the room, looking longingly at the window, wishing he could be near it so that he could see what was happening outside. As he sat there, seemingly immobile, intensely wishing and imagining being outside playing, the chair began to rock slightly. This excited him greatly and he endeavored to make it happen again. He gave himself direct commands: "Move legs! Rock the chair!" Nothing happened. Finally, he gave up, sank back into his daydreams and once more imagined playing outside. Again, the chair began to rock! It was the indirect suggestion, that vivid imaging, which produced a response. Using this discovery, over the following two years, Milton taught himself to walk again (aided in the task by closely watching his baby sister who was only then learning to walk), and closely observed how human beings communicate and how the unconscious mind works. Thus, one of the hallmarks of hypnotherapy was born: *indirect suggestion.*

Erickson said, "Everyone is as individual as their own thumb print." In his practice, he tailored every induction to the client's individual needs and perceptual dispositions. He believed in the wisdom of the unconscious mind, and the theory that people have all the resources necessary to make changes inside themselves. He believed that the job of the therapist is to help the clients re-establish their connection with their inner resources and to develop a rapport between the conscious and the unconscious mind.

To Erickson the unconscious mind was not a repressed Freudian entity but part of everyday life that was always aware. The indirect and embedded suggestions of Ericksonian hypnosis would bypass the relaxed conscious mind and slip directly into the unconscious where, if phrased correctly, they would be accepted without resistance.

When we bring up the topic of hypnosis, many people automatically think about a group of people sitting on a stage with their heads down, shoulders collapsed and someone about to tell them they are chickens. This kind of hypnosis is known as direct or clinical hypnotherapy. It is used as a direct therapeutic approach and in stage shows, but is not the kind of hypnosis we use in NLP.

Instead, we use **Ericksonian Hypnosis** which was modeled on the work of Dr. Erickson. Also referred to as indirect or utilization hypnosis, Ericksonian hypnosis is a method of inducing and controlling trance states without any explicit authoritative commands. Instead, it relies on indirect suggestions and a high degree of rapport with the subject, compared with traditional Clinical Hypnotherapy which uses commanding and direct language. Indirect suggestions are harder to resist, because they are often not recognized as suggestions by the conscious mind. It is often referred to as "artfully vague" language that is ambiguous and abstract. This makes the listener begin to unknowingly (and unconsciously) associate their experience to what was being said, while at the same time accepting the directions or boundaries of the speaker.

What is hypnosis? Before we go much further, it might be a good idea to define what we are talking about and in a way normalize hypnosis. A general definition of hypnosis is the use of suggestion to change a person's sensations, perceptions, thoughts, or behavior. When a person is hypnotized they enter an altered state of consciousness to make this change possible.

If you have ever watched a television commercial for pizza and got hungry, or overheard a conversation about a person's vacation and wondered when you'll get away next, or watched a movie and cried, or got so engrossed in a book you missed your bus, or if you've ever changed your mind or behavior based on what someone said, you have been hypnotized. In the world we live in, we are being hypnotized all the time. Every day throughout the day. Hypnosis is a natural phenomenon that we can use with conscious purpose to help yourself or someone else reach a desired state.

When used appropriately and ecologically, the use of hypnosis can help you to be an even more influential communicator. As we have talked about before, you cannot make someone do something they don't want to do, especially if it is against their core values or beliefs. Used with integrity and positive intention however, you are able to communicate more directly with the unconscious mind in an indirect way.

One of the great things about Ericksonian Hypnosis specifically, is that it is very conversational and can be used in every situation in life, not just as a therapeutic approach.

There are three main components of Ericksonian Hypnosis; over the next couple of days we will be investigating each and how they operate:
- Metaphors or stories
- Indirect Suggestions
- Ericksonian Hypnotic Language

Metaphors

Erickson's sessions would often begin with an apparently simple chat or metaphor as the subject relaxed. Erickson would observe the subject's reactions and tailor the indirect and embedded suggestions specifically to the person. Very often they would find themselves deeply relaxed and in a suggestive state without even realizing that anything had happened. These metaphors were the core of the work Erickson did with his clients. He used metaphors to create positive internal representations and to help the client reframe whatever they were working on.

The mind is an amazing mechanism. Erickson knew how it worked and he utilized his client's natural tendencies to help them. When something is being listened to, the human mind automatically does what is called a Transderivational Search (TDS). This is a psychological term that means a search is being conducted in the unconscious mind to find a match or meaning that the listener can relate to or understand. It is a normal part of how people process information cognitively, which allows the brain and mind to automatically generalize information so it can be learned and model the outer world from what is in their internal world. It is an automatic and an unconscious state of internal focus that induces or deepens a trance state.

For instance, when people watch, listen to or read a story, their unconscious mind automatically does a TDS to search for similar meaning or experiences. When they do this, their conscious mind seems to stop listening to the story and the person goes into a "trance" where they are in a daze or daydream like state, thinking about their common story and experience that applies to their life. This explains why you think of examples of things when people are talking. We often have someone come up to us after a seminar and ask how we knew about their issue, as they believed we were talking directly to them.

Erickson delivered positive constructive messages to his clients called *embedded messages* that if heard consciously they might resist. He consistently used quotes, imagery, stories, and examples as part of his metaphor narratives.

Quotes

In most cases, if you attribute your statement to someone else, you can say anything you want without having to accept responsibility for it. In using quotes, you establish some distance between you and the statement or story you wish to convey to your listener. This allows their unconscious mind to displace the reference to them as they automatically go inside and do a TDS. Here are two examples:

- **I was talking to George in marketing the other day, and he told me that someone in your department said that you were really being a jerk about overtime...** In this example it is communicated as hearsay, however it still allows the listener to do a TDS and perhaps view the incident from another point of view versus head on.
- **One of my friends was a champion ballroom dancer. She was also a successful manager at a bank. One of her favorite sayings was that "Dancing and managing people were exactly the same. If you could keep in time with whatever is happening, you can overcome anything."** This example is allowing the listener to compare how they keep things in time or manage things.

Imagery

Erickson knew the power of the unconscious mind and the imagination. He used imagery to help people access states they desired and access resources they needed. He often used "imagine" or "what happens when" statements to work as indirect commands to the unconscious mind. For example, "imagine how easy it will be to relax," or "what would happen if you began to relax?" The unconscious mind is very receptive and will imagine through pictures and feelings whatever is being said.

Stories and Examples

Probably the best known tool of Erickson is the use of stories and examples (metaphors). We will be examining metaphors in depth in a moment. A story or example of people in situations that may or may not mirror the client's issue can be very useful. People don't like being told what to do, but like to know that something is possible. A metaphor displaces the reference to the client (it's not about them), so they can do a TDS and come up with a solution or needed resource. One of our clients wanted to stop worrying about everything and be calm and relaxed. We could use any story that would convey overcoming something and achieving a release of emotions. The story does not have to be about worry or being relaxed. We will discuss this further in how to construct a metaphor.

Recall the NLP Presupposition that states *when you know better you can do better.* Now that you know how powerful language is and the way people unconsciously do a TDS, you have a responsibility to make what you say as clean as possible.

Recall from day 7, we learned that everything we say has an influence in our state and behaviors; not just in a therapy, coaching or training sessions, but all the time. The unconscious mind is constantly eavesdropping on what you hear, see and say and providing a chemical reaction to absolutely everything. Has anyone ever come up to you and said something like, "Gee you look tired today." Maybe you didn't feel tired, but all of a sudden - pow – you feel tired. These comments seem to be nothing, but are loaded with suggestions. Now we can use language even more influentially to assist people to find resources, solutions, and more choice.

It has been said that metaphors are an NLPer's way to give advice. As we said earlier, people don't like to be told how to do something, but we do like to know that it is possible to do something. The use of metaphors is a great way to reframe a person's current way of thinking and provide them with a new perspective or way of looking at something.

Stories and metaphors are magic in a therapeutic way, as they influence a person's inner mind and world. As Freud said, "Words and magic were in the beginning one and the same thing." Throughout the ages, stories have been passed down from generation to generation. The best teachers and communicators in the world use metaphors: Jesus, Mohammed, Buddha, the Dalai Lama, Nelson Mandela, and Einstein, just to name a few.

Metaphors can be either **shallow**, like a short example or quote, or **deep** like a story with a beginning, middle, and end.

In a shallow metaphor, the story will be similar to the situation being discussed.

- **Last year, I had a student who thought that he could learn everything at the last minute...** Then proceed to tell the short story of how they solved their problem. *This shallow metaphor could be good for someone who had a tendency to procrastinate.*
- **Over the years, I have watched hundreds of nervous students give speeches, but none was as bad as a young woman named Jane...** Then proceed to tell the short story of how Jane solved her problem. *This shallow metaphor could be good for someone who suffers from anxiety about public speaking.*

Deep Metaphors can be taken from movies, television programs, fairy tales, books, or any story real or fiction. A metaphor allows the listener to go inside and do a TDS, to compare their experiences with whatever they may relate it to. Depending on each person's experience, they will have different meanings from each metaphor. Metaphors are powerful reframes and serve to shape perceptions and perhaps have a greater choice in how we act.

Creating Metaphors

When creating metaphors, remember the best ones are often the real stories people can relate to. You can find metaphors everywhere, from things you observe, read or hear about, they are little slices of life. Ultimately, a useful metaphor should be fairly short and succinct, lasting anywhere from 30 seconds to a few minutes. These short stories are more effective because people can relate to them quickly, and it is easier to hold a person's attention for a short amount of time. A story that takes too long to tell may be too involved and people are more apt to get lost in the content or drift off. You can collect metaphors, or just let your unconscious mind be creative and remember things that are relevant. Learning how to create metaphors is fun and very rewarding.

The best kind of metaphors are those that are told for a purpose. We all have a friend who is a great story teller, they have a story for everything; yet their stories don't always have a purpose. If we overuse metaphors, we become redundant with metaphors, meaning that although a metaphor may have meaning, people get used to our stories and may stop listening. The metaphors you use with purpose should be created based on the desired state of whoever you are telling it to and conclude with a resourceful outcome. "And then he died" usually isn't the best way to end a metaphor!

An effective Metaphor has the following characteristics:

1. It displaces the reference of the person you are telling the story to. This enables them to accept or reject the information. Erickson had many stories about his friend John.
2. It paces the listener's challenge with similar characters and experiences in the story. Their unconscious mind will go inside and do a TDS and find the similarity and resource.
3. It has a resourceful ending with a way for the person to see other points of view and achieve their desired outcome.

Constructing and making Metaphors work:

1. Determine their present state; this is what they are having issues with.
2. Determine their desired state or the flip side of their present state.
3. Displace referential indices; use reference to other people key character/s in the story.
4. Establish similarities of the characters in story; mirror but not usually the exact situation, otherwise it may seem like a lecture.
5. Establish new resources; be creative and use simple but positive steps or ways to reach the desired state.
6. Use direct quotes and be ambiguous; this helps the subject do their own TDS and try on the story.
7. Future pace the outcome; end the story with some triumph or victory.

Remember:

- Use stories of your own experiences, especially times of transformation.
- Use other people's stories.
- Read stories to get universal experiences.

- Use fairy tales, books, history, movies, television shows, news.
- Use your imagination to revamp stories to match the person.
- Anyone can be a good story teller; it takes practice, but it is very rewarding. Once you start to listen and collect stories and examples, it will become easier to remember them when you need them.

Here's a story that was constructed for a person who was having problems at work with her supervisor. She wanted to be assertive and calm when he spoke to her, instead of nervous and detached.

I had a friend Bob who was stationed in West Germany for a while. He loved the Bavarian Alps, the beer, and the rich history. Bob had housing off the base and dealt direct with his landlord who was loud, not friendly and at times even critical. He began to avoid him as much as possible. One day his landlord phoned him, accused him of all sorts of things, and demanded he bring the money over immediately. Not wanting confrontation, he devised several ways he could pay the rent without seeing the landlord. The next day he drove over very early in the morning to put an envelope with the rent money under the door. When he got there, he saw through the window the landlord carefully brushing his six-year-old daughter's hair. He looked so tender and loving, nothing like what Bob thought of him. It reminded Bob of his relationship with his kids who lived with their mother in the USA. He decided to ring the bell. The landlord came to the door, brush in hand; Bob asked him about his daughter and found out that he was a single parent bringing her up alone. It was as if without any words they formed a kinship. They had a coffee and realized that they had many things in common. From that day onwards they became good friends who went fishing together and to this day stay in touch.

A few years ago, when Heidi's nephew Tommy was staying at her place for a few days, she was having trouble getting him to stay seated at the table while he ate. Finally, Heidi decided to use a living metaphor with Tommy. She asked him, "Tommy, are you four or five?"

"I'm five," he replied.

"Really? Are you sure, that is surprising I really thought you were four. Normally when boys are five they can stay at the table while they are eating, it's usually little boys who are four and younger that get up and walk around all the time. Huh, maybe that will come when you're six."

That is all that was said. Yet, she did not have to comment or ask Tommy to sit down at the table at all for the remainder of his stay. His unconscious mind did its own TDS and he created a meaning and a new choice. This was a much more powerful way to create change – internally versus externally. That's what metaphors do, they provide a person with the ability to see possibilities and come up with their own solutions. The story teller doesn't have to tell the "moral" of the story, that will come from the listener; and there is a chance that everyone will create their own meaning.

Sometimes the change or choices derived from a metaphor will be immediate, sometimes it may take some time. As with all other NLP tools, you can't push someone toward a solution, they need to find it in their own time. Metaphors provide not only the opportunity to find a solution, but to want to make a change in the first place. A few years ago, we worked with a teenage boy who was spending more time on his computer playing games than on homework. He did not have a desired state to do otherwise until he heard a story about someone who had balance of work and play and became a successful gaming programmer. This provided him with the motivation to focus more on school and study than on games; we then could use many of the NLP techniques to help him get to his desired state. Interestingly, he has just completed his university course with a degree in business.

If a person has a secondary gain, needs more resources, is stuck, wants to change, has an unresourceful behavior, can't see a solution, then a metaphor could be useful. If you want a person to make a certain decision, change their behavior, access a certain state or change their current state, a metaphor will be useful to influence them to start the change process. We suggest you collect stories and start to think about how to formulate them. You can use them anytime, with anyone, anywhere. I wonder how many metaphors you have already been involved with today?

Day 14 –
Using Hypnotic Suggestions

The immortal words "you're a Wizard, Harry" sparked a possibility of greatness in an 11-year-old boy and opened the imagination of a world audience. These four little words were powerful and led him to discover and develop his innate talents as well as astonish millions of Harry Potter fans. Real or imagined, whether spoken or thought, words  can uncover potential and activate emotions. As you recall from yesterday, Sigmund Freud said, "Words and magic were in the beginning one and the same thing." In day 12, we looked at reframing and learned that the right words at the right time can change the course of a person's life for better or worse.

Today, we will be exploring Ericksonian language patterns and methods of communication that allow the mind to go beyond or to go **meta**.

Dr. Erickson used language in a systemic and often remarkable way. A specific set of phrases that Erickson commonly used was called **The Milton Model**. It was also referred to as the reverse of the Meta Model, which came from the work of Virginia Satir. The difference being, the Meta Model was used to gain more specifics, while the Milton Model uses words that require the listener to fill in what is left unsaid or ambiguous.

You can use the model in its entirety, or as we will see today, you can use parts of the model in conversation to create hypnotic suggestions. Similar to metaphors, this side of Ericksonian hypnosis can be used anywhere and at anytime. As usual, keep integrity and positive intention in mind. One more tip while learning and using hypnotic language – less is more. If you attempt to use hypnotic language in everything you say, your words will become less potent, similar to what we discussed yesterday about using too many metaphors.

Indirect Suggestions

Erickson utilized indirect suggestions, which are useful not only for trance but also in normal conversations. They assist in pacing a person's reality as a way to access unconscious resources while gathering information. These suggestions lead people to an altered state of trance by passing the conscious mind while the person does a TDS to make sense or compare what is being said. We will be begin with three that are called Indirect Elicitation Patterns, which are particularly useful in getting specific responses indirectly without overtly asking for them.

1. **Embedded Commands** are suggestions that you can embed directives within a larger sentence instead of giving instructions directly. By doing this, you communicate more effectively, as the listener will not consciously realize the command has been given.

   - *Can you feel the feelings of peace as you breathe more deeply?* This suggestion is sometimes more useful that saying "relax", as the person could easily say no. This embedded command simply asks "can you feel…"
   - *As you learn more you can enjoy the experience.* Instead of saying, "enjoy learning," this suggestion provides a textured state without contemplation.

2. **Embedded Questions** are commanding questions that are embed_ded within a larger sentence structure. Useful

statements to start are, "I'm curious," "I wonder," "I don't know," "I realize." They presuppose interest and the listener responds without realizing the question was not asked directly. It provides a gentle way to gather information.

- *I'm curious to know what you would like to gain from this project.* This question will elicit an internal or external response, but it will elicit a response. If you just ask "what do you want to gain from this project?", you will elicit a conscious response.
- *I wonder how soon you will notice the change you have made.*

3. **Negative Commands** work on the premise that the unconscious mind is unable to process negatives. When a command is given, the positive instruction is what is generally responded to. For example, if someone says, "Don't think of a purple cow," you have to think of a purple cow to understand the sentence. Negative commands can be used effectively by stating what you do want to occur and preceding this statement with the words don't, can't, or not.

- *I don't want you to feel too happy.*
- *Don't feel the need to tell us how you are enjoying this book.*
- *I'm not sure how excited you are to use hypnotic language!*

Ericksonian Hypnotic Language

The Milton Model has many patterns that induce trance and help you communicate more directly with the unconscious mind. They are not meant to make grammatical sense, but to deliver messages to people to facilitate inner change. The following are some examples of how to use language to help people make these changes and recover resources.

- **X and Y choices** are useful when you want to lead a person into a state, behavior, or an awareness. Examples would be: The more your eyelids blink, the easier it is to close them. The less you try, the easier it becomes.

- **Awareness Predicates**. These are words like: know, notice, realize, aware, find, understand. They bring the communication to where the person is aware of the point you are making.

The more you learn about NLP, the more you want to know. The less you try the easier it becomes.

- **Placing –er at the end of a word** implies continuity in the same way words such as more or less give a direction to change.

You can feel happier tomorrow. When you trust your unconscious mind you can have a deeper level of understanding.

- **The use of –ly words** presupposes even more of whatever the word means. For instance, deeply, easily, happily, curiously, fortunately, simply.

Learning NLP from this book happens easily. You can add the skills of NLP into your life simply.

- **Double Binds** offer a free choice of two or more possible comparable alternatives. The person has free will and voluntary choice between them. Words such as **or** and **because** link these alternatives.

I wonder what you'll use first today, a metaphor or an embedded command? This presupposes that both will be complete, but it gives choice of order.

- **Compound Suggestions.** A compound suggestion is made from two separate suggestions that join a grammatical conjunction such as and, but, or, until, since, because, though, if, so, as, after. Often delivering them with a slight pause between the two parts adds a slight emphasis. The first statement is generally true, something the person cannot deny.

  With every chapter of this book you read, it becomes clearer that since you are learning NLP… you will be using NLP each day to make your life better and better.

- **Overloading the unconscious.** This is sometimes called stacking, as you use words such as and, however, because, linking them together in a series of suggestions or tasks. They may be related or unrelated. It increases confusion and therefore overloads a person's conscious mind. This overload forces the information to be processed at the unconscious level. Therefore, you can consciously overload the person to make them more receptive.

  *While you are reading about hypnotic language **and** thinking about how to use it in your life **because** being a more influential communicator **and** using language in an indirect way is important to you **however** knowing that you can take the time to learn this and master this is something that you can allow yourself.*

- **Temporal language** phrases, tag questions, and lack of referential index are used to give more impact to whatever is being said. They distort how time is perceived with what is being said. Dr. Erickson used these liberally throughout his conversations and metaphors. Practice putting them into your metaphors, indirect suggestions, and trance inductions and notice the influence they have.

Here are three categories that can be used with amazing effect.

- **Unspecified Predicates are words that lack description.**
    - And you can...
    - And you do...
    - As you continue...
    - If you knew...

- **Tag Questions are added after a statement and displace any resistance.**
    - Can you not?
    - Haven't you?
    - Didn't you?
    - Hasn't it?
    - Isn't it?
    - Doesn't it?
    - Aren't you?
    - Don't you now?

- **Lack of Referential Index is a phrase that deletes whomever is doing the action.**
    - One can you know...
    - You can you know...
    - You know the feeling...
    - You have, and you know it...
    - That's right.

That's Right is a phrase that Erickson used to mean anything. Generally thought to let a person's conscious and unconscious mind know that whatever they are doing at that moment was right. It puts their conscious mind to rest. That's right.

Here is an example of how to use all of the Ericksonian language we discussed.

As you sit there listening to me you are learning many things. I wonder how often you will use these skills... that's right. You can let yourself remember easily as you let yourself be calmer now. Can you not? Since you started reading this book, you may be aware of how much you already know... haven't you? That's right. I don't know if you will start to incorporate these things now or next week... however, when the time is right, that's right... and you will know it, because something will happen and your mind will say, this is the moment.

You may wish to take sometime to look through this hypnotic trance, and when you do you will notice that each hypnotic language phrase was used.

Posthypnotic Suggestions

Posthypnotic suggestions enhance and solidify a person's outcome while simultaneously reorganizing their experience. These suggestions often stay with the person for a period of time. A few examples of posthypnotic suggestions are:

- *After you finish this book you will find how easy it is to continue to use your new NLP skills.*
- *Whenever you feel a breeze, you can realize how wonderful it is to have a fresh new day.*

Hypnotic Language Techniques

The "art" of delivering a hypnotic message utilizes some simple techniques that go beyond building rapport. Taking time to use these tips will enhance your technique and help you go beyond mediocre and well on your way to being a wizard now, aren't you? That's right.

- **Voice tonality tempo.** Match your voice, tone, and tempo with whatever state you want to induce. During a trance induction, it is common to have a variety of voice variations.
- **Use pauses** to punctuate meanings or to let the other person have time to do a TDS. These pauses are powerful.
- Use the other person's positive key words or phrases. This makes the trance personalized and more meaningful.
- **Pay attention to the other person.** As you use your sensory acuity watch for relaxation cues, for responses,

abreactions, or anything that assists you. Follow along not just lead.

- **Use powerful words** that have positive meaning such as dreams, hopes, talents, resources, thoughts, trust, unconscious, love, etc.

- **Avoid double meaning words.** These words keep the unconscious mind from following and can create a negative response. If you have sensory acuity, you will notice if your subject pops out of trance or has an abreaction. For instance, if you are working with someone who wants to lose weight, if you are using a deepening exercise, you may want to say, "As you relax you are feeling lighter and lighter..." instead of "heavier and heavier." Or if someone has lost something, you may choose words other than lost or lose.

- **Handling Abreaction** can happen when a person has an emotional or significant physiological reaction to a past memory. It is important to assist them in releasing the abreaction, otherwise you could leave them with a distorted perception of real events, which can cause emotional problems and disturbances now. When they can release their own emotions, this can create more empowerment in "real life." This is a great time to employ your skills in state elicitation to help get the person to a more resourceful state. If you don't have the permission or time right there and then to create full resolution, at least create partial resolution and an agreement to resolve the memory or emotion at a later appropriate time and place if there are interferences to completing the session. I (Laureli) worked with a man who had an aversion to speaking in front of more than two people. He resisted any timeline type of release and just would not let himself release the negative feelings no matter what or how it was framed. Since he was very visual, I had him observe as the older, wiser man he is now the much younger self when the problem first began. He was able to dissociate and go back to when he was a small boy in school and his teacher made fun of him when was unable to recite something from his homework. He was able to edit and make the changes that allowed him to have a different viewpoint and state of mind. Realizing there are more ways to approach and help people is always an option.

Utilization

Erickson was a wonderful model of Utilization; that is, using what is in the surrounds to add to hypnosis. For Erickson and his clients, this might mean utilizing the nearest peak called Squaw Peak for people to walk up while contemplating an idea, or utilizing something in a person's sight, feeling, or hearing range.

A few years ago, I worked with a client who was seeking motivation and a spark in her life. She felt she was in a rut and had nothing to give and at times just felt like running away. We used a few NLP techniques and made some adjustments and then decided to complete the session with a little trance work. We were progressing quite well, and I was noticing how she seemed to be following along, when all of a sudden a trumpeter started playing directly under my window of my office the theme from the movie Rocky. My first reaction was sheer horror, I was tempted to throw open the window and shout at the person. Then my unconscious mind reminded me to utilize the situation. So I started to make my voice a little stronger and used words such as "you can do it, you are the champion, you have the power." Then as quickly as it started, it ended and I decided to complete the trance and bring her back to now.

When she opened her eyes, she said "Wow! That was so powerful, how did you know that was my theme song?" And she proceeded to turn on her cell phone and show me her ring tone was the Rocky theme song.

As you have seen over the past two days, the use of Ericksonian Hypnosis is vast and useful in so many situations. If words have power to alter a state, engage an emotion, change a behavior and influence people, then it is fair to say that everything is hypnotic. And we wouldn't be too far from the truth. With the new skills you have, we encourage you to find your own congruence with these types of language patterns. Having a positive intention and using these tools with ecology is a must in our minds. Remember, you can't get someone to do something they don't want to do or something that is directly outside of a person's values. A good way to think about the hypnotic tools that are taught in all NLP trainings is that hypnosis is useful to help facilitate a change not create the change.

We wonder how much hypnosis you will notice around you in your day-to-day life, and even how you will be using your skills now. One can you know, make an impact and be even more influential just by choosing their words with purpose. You have, haven't you, already decided which of these tools fit best. Now or later, you can choose to begin to develop your skills even more as you enjoy adding more intentional hypnotic language into your life. That's right.

Day 15 –
Eye Accessing Cues

When I (Laureli) attended my very first NLP seminar, I was struck by how watching people's eye patterns meant something. I was astounded to think that people's eye movements had relevance versus randomness. I could not wait to learn more about how it all worked.

Everyone has their own model of their world. For instance, something can happen to two people at the same time, and their memory of that event can be very different depending upon how they filtered the experience. The memories of these events are stored as an internal representation; that is, the event is stored as a picture, sound, feeling, or thought. In fact, each of our memories is stored as a specific set of images, sounds, feelings, smells, and tastes (VAKOG). This is how we distinguish one set of memories from another. We mentally recreate and recall our experiences (memories) with these stored pictures, words, sounds, and physical feelings as we think.

In 1890, Williams James, American psychologist, in his book Principles of Psychology, wrote, "In attending to either an idea or a sensation belonging to a particular sense-sphere, the movement is the adjustment of the sense organ (eye), felt as it occurs. I cannot think in visual terms, for example, without feeling a fluctuating play of pressures, convergences, divergences, and accommodations in my eyeballs... When I try to remember or reflect, the movements in question feels like a sort of withdrawal from the outer world. As far as I can detect, these feelings are due to an actual rolling outwards and upwards of the eyeballs."

In the early days of NLP, both Grinder and Bandler believed they identified a pattern of relationships between the sensory-based language people use in general conversation and corresponding eye movement. In 1976, Robert Dilts took this hypothesis to the next step. He conducted a study at Langley Porter Neuropsychiatric Institute in San Francisco to find out if this had relevance. Using electrodes, he tracked both eye movement and brain wave characteristics of people who when asked questions related to various senses (VAK) that involved both right-brain memory and left-brain mental construction. As a result of these studies, eye movement patterns or eye accessing cues were identified.

Eye Accessing Cues

When people access their memories, their eyes move in specific and observable directions. These movements are called **eye accessing cues** and they seem to correspond to the neural pathways in the brain that store and process sensory details. They are how people access stored information and everything there has a place. This is valuable information that can provide us with clues as to whether they are thinking in pictures, sounds, feelings, or talking to themselves. A skilled NLP practitioner will notice the sequencing of eye patterns. However, learning to read eye accessing cues will not make you a mind reader, but will give you relevant information to the way the other person is thinking. This is also referred to as a person's lead representational system.

NLP suggests such eye accessing cues are: (1) idiosyncratic and habitual for each person, (2) may form significant clues as to how a person is processing or representing a thought to themselves unconsciously.

This information can be useful in gaining rapport, achieving more effective communication, asking applicable questions, and gaining understanding. It allows you to communicate to people in their own language as you match it back. This is why we often call them eye accessing *clues*.

Let's take a look at the eye pattern chart. This chart is read as you look at another person's face straight on. This chart is referred to as **normally organized.** Some people are reverse organized and the eye pattern chart is flipped and opposite. We've found that some left-handed people are reverse organized (but not all) and a few right-handed people we've met have also been reverse organized. But, generally, the normally organized patterns are fairly consistent across all races, with the possible exception of the Basques in Spain, who seem to have some exceptions to the rule. However, never assume, ask questions and watch the eyes to find how the person stores information.

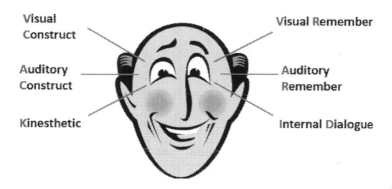

The eyes play a big part in how a person lives their lives. A whopping quarter of the brain is devoted to vision and our optic nerves are directly wired to the brain. In fact, our eyes are the only organ we can literally examine externally. A person's eyes tell a story as the eyes move involuntarily and in conjunction with whatever is being thought or felt.

Let us try it on. Ask yourself the following questions and notice what direction/s your eyes move as you think of the answers. (Note, this exercise is just to notice that your eyes are moving, normally we only notice and identify eye patterns in others.)

1. How many windows do you have in your home?
2. What would your car look like in 15 years if you never washed it?
3. What does your favorite song sound like?
4. What would your voice sound like if you were Donald Duck?
5. What does it feel like to take a warm bath or shower?
6. What does your voice sound like when you talk to yourself?

Each of the questions caused you to either access a memory or mentally construct some experience. If your eyes do not move, you may notice that, you may have looked in a direction for only a nanosecond or perhaps defocused looking out in front of yourself. This is generally considered either visual or auditory remembered as the memory is in your present awareness.

Now ask someone else these same questions using the eye-accessing chart. Face them directly and remember the chart is normally organized. It may be helpful to jot down your findings as you watch their eyes so you can review them later.

What happens when people's eyes move?

Note: The following eye movements are as you watch someone's eyes. When we refer to a location, this is your left or right as if the person is in front of you.

Visual Construct (Vc) – Up and to your left would be accessing an image they need to construct a picture of because they either have not seen it before, or because the picture has been stored in the past and not the immediate recall zone.

Visual Recall (Vr) – Up and to your right would elicit an image they seen or imagined before.

It is nearly impossible to tell if someone is lying from eye patterns alone. Be careful assuming that people are lying or making things up just because their eyes move to Visual Construct. It could be they just don't have the information readily available. For example, what did you wear two days ago? When you find the answer to this question, you may have to construct what clothes you have, use internal dialogue to ask yourself the question, you may have to remember what you did that day and even construct what you might have looked like in a certain outfit that day. So, your eyes may go more to construct although you're not making it up. To identify if someone is lying, you would need to calibrate the whole person – physiology, eyes, tonality, etc.

Auditory Construct (Ac) – Lateral and to your left would be accessing something they have not heard before, or they have to construct a sound or conversation.

Auditory Recall (Ar) – Lateral and to your right would be eliciting something they heard before. This could be a conversation or sound, and it could be of themselves or someone else.

Kinesthetic (K) – Eyes down and to your left would access a person's feelings internally (e.g. emotions) or externally (e.g. tactile feel of velvet or a cat's tongue).

Internal Dialogue (Id) – Eyes down and to your right would access the person's self talk or internal dialogue.

Practice makes understanding eye accessing cues easy. You can learn by observing people's eyes as you ask them questions in normal conversations; start noticing how different people use their eyes. Notice how some make big and obvious movements, while others make minimal little moves. Something that is available to everyone nowadays is television. Reality shows, talk shows, and unscripted interviews are great to use as a learning tool as they are usually spontaneous. Turn the volume down on the TV for a while and just identify where the person's eyes move to. This is a great way to become unconsciously skilled at making meaning of eye patterns.

With people you know and feel at ease with, ask verifying questions. For example, if you are talking to a friend about their weekend and you see their eyes shift up and to your right, you can ask, "What do you recall seeing?" When you see a particularly noticeable eye movement, ask them what they were doing internally. You are likely to find that where their eyes moved and what they were thinking is accurate for well over 90 percent of the people you meet. There are many practical uses of eye accessing cues.

Incorporating Eye Patterns into Life

- Upgrade your communication style. Using eye accessing enables us to communicate in a way that more effectively matches another person's current thinking style. This would enable you to respond by matching their eye movement with your words. When you do this, you will have more useful questions and replies.

Vr – Looking up to their right; it would be a clue to use more visual words and questions. Use visual aids; show them examples, slides, brochures, pictures, diagrams.

K – Looking down to the left; it is a clue to use feeling words and questions. Let them touch things or try them on or something they can thumb through.

Id – Looking down to the right; to use more logical, thinking, analytical words and questions. Use graphs, charts, and statistics and hard facts and figures.

Ar – Looking laterally to the right; use more auditory questions and examples. Explain and tell them about it. Use and refer to sounds, conversations and ask what they've heard.

- **Ask better questions.** One of Heidi's main reasons for wanting to master the elicitation and understanding of eye patterns is to ask better questions. As you will continue to learn, there are a lot of NLP tools to help us to make changes to patterns; sometimes a good question will bring you to the right tool to use. For example, one of her clients wanted to start his own business but was sabotaging his efforts. In their first coaching session, he made a statement: "I just don't know if I can really make it work"; as he said this statement, his eyes moved up and to her right – to Visual Recall. Heidi asked a question: "What are you remembering right now?" He then told her about a failed business of his uncle's and how his uncle struggled to create a successful business and keep his family together. This one question possibly saved a lot of coaching time – they were able to identify a major interference and then were able to do something about it.

- **Identify a strategy.** In NLP we also track eye patterns when we are eliciting someone's strategies. When we ask someone how they do a task, a pattern or even a thought process, they often don't consciously know. However, if we ask them to give us their step-by-step methods, we can find their strategy. Because the unconscious mind works in harmony with our thoughts, our eyes will move into various quadrants that verify our strategy. We will be looking at strategies more in depth on day 27.

Other Practical Examples:

You have a client you are trying to sell your product to. As you are talking about the benefits and features of the product, you notice the client looking up to your right (VR). When we see this eye moment, we can presuppose that they are seeing a remembered image in their mind. You could ask them if they have had/used a product like this before, or if they can remember where they will be using it, or if they need to see more literature. You could even lead them to a Visual Construction about your product by asking if they could imagine having/using the product.

You are having a conversation with your spouse. Your spouse is telling you where they want to go for a vacation. You notice their eyes go down and to your left (K). We can presuppose that your spouse is experiencing a feeling of some sort. You could respond with: "I know how much you want to enjoy where we go and it is important to find the right place where we feel comfortable."

You are talking to a potential new client. While you are explaining your services to him, you see his eyes go down and to your right (Id). We can presuppose that he is doing some self-talk. In this instance, you could use a logical tactic to give more information and detail about your services. Conversely, if his eyes had moved down and to your left (K), you might want to use a more emotional tact.

When we can identify and use a person's eye accessing cues, we can communicate easier at an unconscious level – if I'm talking in pictures when they have pictures in their mind, then their mind has to do less filtering of what is said. If I only go based on my model of the world, a lot more filtering has to happen. Using the vacation example from earlier, what if you would have said, "I can see how you would enjoy going there." It is not a "bad" way to communicate; however, you jumped to a visual while they are in K. As human beings we do change representation systems as we talk; however, miscommunication often happens when we disregard where someone else is coming from and tell them about ours.

To get this skill in your muscle we encourage you to start watching eye patterns of others and putting meaning to them by asking better questions, using them in your language patterns or responding based on the movement. This really is a great skill to have as a master communicator, and it makes a fantastic party trick!

Day 16 –
Perceptual Positions

A fundamental tool that we use in NLP involves considering an experience from multiple perspectives such as the perspective of self, other and a detached third person. This experience could be something that occurred in the past or something that will occur in the future. By moving between different perceptual positions, one can see a situation in new ways or with greater detachment, and thus gather more information and develop new choices of response.

There is never just one way to think about something; there are always multiple and meaningful perspectives, depending on how you look at it. Because of the systemic nature of human beings, a person who is in a situation cannot always see solutions that a person standing outside can. I (Laureli) had a client once who told me that he felt as though he had the world on his shoulders; I asked him to imagine what it would be like to have the world at his feet. Then to imagine standing on top of the world. Both of these illustrated to him that he could shift and move what he was carrying and that when he did it gave him more options.

In NLP we say *perception is projection*. What people perceive or focus on becomes what they project to themselves and the world. We go even further and say that projections become reality. It was Gregory Bateson's double description who supposed that a double or triple perspective or description is better than one. In the early days of NLP, John Grinder and Judith DeLozier referred to these perspectives as perceptual positions.

Perceptual Positions provide a balanced approach to thinking about an event or outcome. In situations where there is little or no insight, they present a way of developing new choices and understandings. This method is useful in gathering information and often a new choice becomes available without a deliberate intervention. In NLP, we know that a person can train themselves to move between perceptual positions to develop a greater awareness and new reactions. This is also a powerful tool and skill that is used in a variety of techniques within NLP.

We already use different viewpoints when we want to look at or experience something from a different perspective. When we imagine how other people see us, we automatically go into a perceptual position. At times when we are re-evaluating ourselves; we go into a different perceptual position. We do this when we are helping someone else to be able to see another side of something. We say things like, "Have you ever thought about it this way?" An old American Indian adage says, "Walk a mile in my moccasins and you will know my journey." This is a reminder to put yourself in someone else's place for a moment. Whenever you take a different viewpoint of someone, something and yourself, you are using perceptual positions.

The Blind Men and the Elephant

There are various versions of the story of the blind men and the elephant, and it goes something like this. Six blind men were discussing exactly what they believed an elephant to be, as each had heard how strange the creature was. They agreed to find an elephant and discover what the animal was really like.

Soon they found an elephant at a nearby market. The first blind man approached the beast and felt the animal's firm flat side. "It seems to me that the elephant is just like a wall," he said.

The second blind man reached out and touched one of the elephant's tusks. "No, this is round and smooth and sharp – the elephant is like a spear."

156

Curious, the third blind man stepped up to the elephant and touched its trunk. "Well, I don't agree with either of you; I feel a squirming writhing cold thing – surely the elephant is just like a snake."

The fourth blind man was now quite puzzled. So he reached out and felt the elephant's leg. "You are all talking complete nonsense," he said, "because clearly the elephant is just like a stump of a tree."

Completely confused, the fifth blind man stepped forward and grabbed one of the elephant's ears. "You must all be mad – an elephant is exactly like a fan."

Finally, the sixth man approached and, holding the beast's tail, disagreed again. "It's nothing like any of your descriptions – the elephant is just like a rope."

And all six blind men continued to argue, based on their own particular experiences, as to what they thought an elephant was like. It was an argument that they were never able to resolve. Each of them was concerned only with their own idea. None of them had the full picture, and none could see any of the other points of view. Each man saw the elephant as something quite different, and while in part each blind man was right, none was wholly correct.

We know that if each man would have walked around the elephant and felt all six parts, they may have had more concise conclusions. This is what we do when we take different perceptual positions.

There are three main perceptual positions:
1. **First position** or associated perspective of self. This is when you are in the experience having feelings about whatever you are thinking about or experiencing. This can be in the present moment, a past memory or future

thought. It does not need to be an embellished emotion; it only has to have feeling attached to it. When you are operating from the self, you use words such as I, my, me. You would be seeing, hearing, feeling what is happening and thinking; how does this affect me?

For example, think of a time when you were a happy-go-lucky little person, just playing without a care in the world. Go back to that time right now and see what you saw, hear what you heard and get the feelings of how that felt.

If you had a memory or even multiple memories come up and you had feelings that went with them, then this would be considered a first position or associated self perspective.

2. **Second position** is referred to as dissociated or distanced. It offers an extremely valuable model in deepening understanding of self and others. There are two ways of being in second position:

   a) Taking the other persons' position. In this position, you imagine looking at yourself through their eyes. It may be possible to find out what you look like and sound like from their point of view. In NLP, we often have people step into the position of someone else. This position gives a great deal of flexibility as you can appreciate how others feel about your behaviors and communication.

   There are many valuable revelations from this perspective. For instance, it can help you to formulate more effective questions; create an empathic point of view; calibrate how and when to respond or take action.

   Sometimes people are stuck in this second or other person position. This can result in a co-dependent relationship.

When people are co-dependent, they report feeling the feelings of another person intensely.

b) When you operate or look at yourself from a distance but without the emotions is the other way of being in second position. We can be dissociated from what is happening when we are having an experience and do not feel a part of it.

Take the example we gave when we asked you to think of a time when you were a happy-go-lucky little person. If you had the feelings that went along with that memory, then you were associated or in first position. If it is a memory only, without any feelings attached to it, you are in second position, dissociated or distanced from the memory. There is nothing wrong with either experience. In fact, most of our memories are dissociated unless we have an emotional tie to them.

3. **Third position** is also called Meta Position, double dissociated or observer. This gives you the ability to step back, detach and watch yourself and someone else interact. You are on the sidelines like a fly on a wall, which offers a way of double dissociating from the entire event or conversation. In the third position, you become an independent observer that allows you to be in the position of objectivity.

    You could also imagine yourself being out of your body and off to the side or up above the situation. When you are in third or meta position, you can see or imagine both yourself and the other person. We do this unconsciously, and it has been reported that in some times of emergency or distress people feel as though they are out of body or watching what is happening.

Knowing we can direct our self to this meta position is good for our unconscious mind, as it gives us a clean observer position to use as a resource. It also makes it easier to align the first position of self. It is a position of safety and comfort we can go to at any time. When we look from Meta or third position, we are watching both self and other interacting, from a position outside of either Self or Other.

Observer uses observer pronouns. Rather than saying "I" and "you," this voice will say "he," "she," and "they." "They are doing this, she this, he that." A great question to ask yourself would be, "How would this conversation or event look to someone who is totally uninvolved?"

Another type of perceptual positions involves looking at a situation from the viewpoint of multiple people involved. For example, a company revamp looks very different from the viewpoint of a CEO, a worker, a customer, and a supplier. It is much easier to be involved and/or informed when you can see things from multiple perspectives.

There are fourth and fifth perceptions that can be discovered, however in NLP we utilize mainly the first three. The further you distance yourself, the more detached and dissociated you become.

The founders of NLP modeled renowned family therapist Virginia Satir, who often had what became affectionately known as "parts parties" with her clients. She would guide a client to literally stand in everyone's shoes, until they understood each person's position and feelings in the matter.

Robert Dilts uses multiple perceptual positions in his Disney Creativity Strategy. This is based on his modeling of Walt Disney, where he has people examine a desired goal from the perception of the Dreamer, the Realist, and the Critic. He has people step in each of these areas in first person or associated; and second person or dissociated, and sometimes in third position or meta.

Connirae Andreas and Tamara Andreas teach a process called Aligning Perceptual Positions. This process enables a client to use their ability to see, hear and feel things from each of the three perceptual positions and eliminate any overlap from other positions. This helps people re-align back to themselves especially if they had become co-dependent.

Dr. Milton Erickson would use hypnotic language to get a client into second and third positions, so they could observe, reflect and make inner changes unconsciously. Some people communicate on a surface level; however, their body language and reactions speak volumes. Often having someone get into one or more of the perceptual positions helps to understand their model of the world. Therefore, we can assist them and even ask questions that are more relevant.

NLP was founded on modeling excellence. When we model someone, we do so to enhance our performance or to learn how to do something relatively quickly or for self-improvement. Modeling enables people to elicit what someone is doing and how they approach the task. One method we employ is perceptual positioning. This enables us to transfer qualities and strengths to an individual, team, or entire organization. Most professional athletes and sports people use modeling and perceptual positioning exercises.

For instance, Wyatt Woodsmall has used his NLP modeling skills to help the USA Olympic Diving team win over six medals since 1994. One of the things he introduced was perceptual positions. He has the athletics imagine themselves doing their routine associated, seeing, hearing and feeling what they are doing; then he has them imagine watching themselves complete the routine to refine it. This can be done mentally or by watching a video of them from a real-time practice session. This acts as a second position. He then has them go to third position to view them watching themselves watch themselves. This takes out the emotion of the routine and allows them to refine their performance.

These are only a few examples of how perceptual positions are used. We would like to share an NLP Process using Perceptual Positions with you.

We use this process with many of our students, clients and ourselves when needed. A few years ago when we were training a group of high school educators in Singapore, the Deputy Head Master had an amazing experience. He had a male student that was always in his office for discipline. He said when he used the second position with the boy he made an astounding discovery. He realized that the boy saw him as a bully who was so inflexible and intolerant that whatever he (the boy) did he would always be in trouble. When he used the third position, he could see how they both were having miscommunication and getting emotionally upset which aggravated the situation. He said the exercise gave him invaluable insight. The teacher decided to change his voice tone and how he held his body and to allow the boy to talk. Doing this he believed would give them space so they could resolve their issues. He said it was a very emotional realization for him and he would be forever grateful for this technique.

We invite you to begin to notice when you automatically use perceptual positions. Perhaps you can begin using them with purpose and realize how powerful they influence our lives.

Perceptual Position Exercise

Pick a situation that involves another person in which you would like to gain more clarity. You can either read this first and then do the exercise or have someone lead you through it.

1. Get into a comfortable and relaxed position and close your eyes. When you are ready, go back to an event that reflects this situation and imagine looking through your own eyes, seeing what you saw, hearing what you heard and feeling what you felt during that interaction. Let yourself feel whatever you felt. Here you are experiencing the event from first position. When you are finished, open your eyes and move and shift your body to break this state.

2. Close your eyes again and now imagine you can float or step into the other person. Take on their physiology; in other words sit or stand how they would, breathe how they would, hold your head, jaw, mouth as they would. See, hear and feel what they did and to the best of your ability allow yourself to experience how they felt to be in that conversation with you. What tone of voice are they using, what about their gestures and words. Now how do they see, hear and feel about you? Does this give you some insight into how and why they reacted the way they did? From this perspective what advice would you give yourself? Now, when you are ready, open your eyes and move or shift your body to break this state.

3. From this perspective, did you learn anything about the other person that could help you handle this situation better or differently? In addition, what did you learn about yourself?

4. Make yourself comfortable and close your eyes and this time imagine you can watch the situation as if you were a fly on the wall. Making sure you can see it as if it were there in front of you. From this perspective what can you notice? What advice or words of wisdom would you give yourself so this situation could be handled differently or with results that are more positive? What did you learn?

What resources and / or behaviors could you incorporate in order to have clarity and a better resolution?

5. Now taking all these insights and information, imagine seeing yourself and the person communicating and responding in the new, more resourceful manner.

    When you are ready, open your eyes and move or shift your body and come back to now.

Day 17 –
Rapport

Have you ever had the feeling that you knew someone very well, although you just met them? This is **rapport**. According to the dictionary, rapport is a sympathetic relationship or emotional affinity. Interestingly, the origin of the word rapport comes from French *rapporter* which means to bring back.

Having rapport is a sign that you can efficiently communicate with another person. This does not, however, mean that you will necessarily like everyone you have rapport with, nor does it mean that you agree with them; but it does open lines for communication. Rapport is one of the most important NLP skills used to build a relationship.

From an NLP perspective, the level of quality communication you have with a person greatly depends on the quality of rapport you have with them. When two people have rapport, it opens up channels of communication and more can be said with less words, a greater understanding of each other takes place and an affinity to be like each other happens.

Dr. Milton Erickson was a master at developing rapport with his clients, and there is a good chance he would not have called it rapport. Erickson, being a hypnotherapist, entered into a state he called a therapeutic trance when leading his clients into a trance state. His breathing would change, his pupils would dilate, and he showed all of the signs of going into a trance himself. His students noticed this and asked him if he was entering a trance state when leading his clients and Erickson replied, "Invariably." To this the student asked, "Who is hypnotizing whom in that case?" to which Erickson replied, "Invariably," suggesting that the state of rapport is a loop of mutual harmony and interaction. Rapport is more like a dance between two or more people than a cause-and-effect relationship.

If you are over the age of three months, you are already very skilled at rapport. You know how to build rapport, use rapport and break rapport. But, how do you do it? Right now, unless you have learned the NLP skills of rapport already, you are unconsciously skilled at rapport. When we ask this question to our students, they invariably tell us that they do things like: talk about the weather, get someone engaged in a conversation, agree with someone about what they are saying. All of these things may lead to rapport; and they may not as well.

The NLP skills of rapport are very simple and were developed by modeling people who were establishing naturally occurring rapport. That is, rapport which was not contrived or developed using any specific skills or techniques. Time and time again, it was seen that people *become like each other* when rapport takes place. Next time you are in a food court or on a bus or in a movie theater, watch the people around you. People near each other will sit like each other, talk like each other, walk like each other and move like each other. It seems that *when we are like each other, we like each other.*

Let's dissect exactly how to get into rapport using the NLP skills that work so well. While you are learning this information, keep one important thing in mind: you will only use these skills of rapport if you *don't* have rapport with someone already. Because we are all naturally talented at building rapport, we only have to consciously build rapport when what we are normally unconsciously doing isn't present. So, if you feel a lack or rapport that is the time to use your new NLP rapport building skills.

The first step of having rapport with someone else is to *have the intention* of building rapport. By having rapport with another person, or a group of people – you are more likely to be able to respect their model of the world, gain agreement, sell to them, converse, and understand each other better. And it needn't be a hard task either. The next steps of building rapport include the skills of **matching** and **mirroring** the other person, or people. Matching and mirroring someone else communicates at the unconscious level, and when performed somewhat covertly, it will become second nature to you and you will be able to build rapport with anyone, anywhere. By matching and mirroring someone, you become like them, and as we mentioned earlier, we tend to like people who are like us.

Matching is when you do the same as someone. For example, if we are sitting opposite each other and I lean my chin on my right hand, you can do this exact same move and we are matching each other. You can also match a person's predicates (visual, auditory, kinesthetic), key words, voice tone, volume, pitch, speed, accent, word choice, metaphors, experiences, and nonverbal patterns like facial expressions, physical movements, and posture. You can even match someone's breathing patterns, eye blinking rates, muscle tone, and swallowing if you choose to do so.

Mirroring is when you are doing the opposite of something someone is doing; so it looks like we are in a mirror. Mirroring is most often used with physical movements. For example, if I am sitting by someone and they have their right leg crossed over their left, I may do the opposite and mirror their physiology, crossing my left leg over my right. Mirroring is often less obtrusive or noticeable than matching when it comes to physiology.

Normally, when you are building rapport, you will choose 2-3 things only to match or mirror. For example, you may choose to match someone's predicates and posture while mirroring how they are sitting. There are a few tips that unfortunately a lot of people miss when consciously building rapport:

1. Match and mirror discreetly. Choose only a few subtle things to match or mirror, move only when you are

speaking. Subtlety is the key to elegant rapport building. For example, if you are talking to someone and they cross their arms, when it is your turn to talk, cross your arms when you speak. If they move again, you may choose to alter your position again when it is again your turn to speak. However, if only one of you is speaking, alter your position 15-20 seconds after they move. This way you won't come across as "mimicking," in fact, they shouldn't be able to notice at all.

2. If your communication partner does something that is not comfortable for you, don't match or mirror it. If you do, it will be seen as a very contrived movement.

3. Once you know you have established rapport – you can stop matching and mirroring. Only if the rapport diminishes do you need to start matching and mirroring again.

You can build rapport with more than one person at a time. If, for example, you are in a meeting with three other people, you may want to match one of their predicates, another person's posture, and the third person's physical movements. While it takes practice, it can be done very easily!

Once you are in rapport with someone, the conversations usually flow easier and it is easier to work together. Remember one of the presuppositions of *NLP is Resistance in communication is a sign of a lack of rapport*. Next time there is any friction between you and someone else, ask yourself if you have rapport, and if not – spend 30 seconds to 2 minutes matching and mirroring and you should establish rapport. The more you practice establishing rapport, the easier it will become for you to do these things unconsciously and very quickly!

In addition, when you have established rapport with a person, you can **pace and lead** them to another behavior. For example, if you are talking to a "quiet talker," match that person's volume and one other thing. Once you have established rapport, you can begin to speak a bit louder each time it is your turn to speak – and before you know it, both of you are speaking at a "normal" volume. This is called pacing and leading.

A good rule of thumb for pacing and leading is to pace, pace, pace and then lead. Think about pacing like this: when you see two people jogging together, how many footsteps do you hear? Only one person's because they are stepping at the same time. When one person speeds up the other person follows. If you want to lead someone to a different behavior or state, you will need to make sure that you pace the person adequately at all times and lead them gradually to the destination.

A few years ago, in a client session I (Heidi) had a very depressed young man come to see me for NLP Therapy. He sat down in the chair opposite me, elbows on his knees, and he spoke slowly to the ground. When it was my turn to speak, I took on his same posture, and I too spoke slowly to the ground. After a few minutes, once I could feel the connection of rapport, when I spoke I slowly raised myself up each time I spoke and started to look at him. After a few more minutes of this, we were both sitting normally in our chairs and looking at each other as we spoke. Not only did I build rapport with him, I also established a feeling of trust between us, simply by respecting his model of the world, matching him and eventually pacing and leading him to where I wanted him to be.

f you have children, pacing and leading is great at the beginning of the day to help get your kids motivated and ready for the day and also great at the end of the day to help get your kids quiet and ready for bed. At the end of the day, for example, when the sky is getting dark and energy levels are still high, you can match your children's energy level and build rapport at that level. Talk in their tempo and volume and then gradually start talking slower and softer. Stay at one level until your child comes to the same tempo and volume as you and then again drop your tempo and volume and stay here until you lead him to this new level. Keep pacing and leading until the new state is quiet, relaxed and ready for bed. A friend of ours did this so much with her children that she was told by her eldest that she knows when it's bedtime now because her mommy uses her bedtime voice.

If someone has a behavior, emotion, or movement which might not be appropriate to match or mirror directly, you can use a technique called **cross over mirroring**. This simply involves matching a person's movement with a different type of movement. For example, I could sway my head left to right in time with a person's breathing pattern. Or, I could tap my foot to the same tempo as a person who is clicking a pen or tapping a desk. Once I have established rapport with my cross-over technique, I can then pace and lead the person to a new behavior if desired. This can be extremely useful on airplanes. Recently, I was on an airplane sitting next to a person who had nervous behavior. Most irritating (and I say that because it was) was her very quick, very sharp jiggling of her knee. I could see her knee out of the corner of my eye and it seemed that my heart rate was starting to match it. Since that was not my desired state, I decided to take matters into my own hands. I started to build rapport with this woman. I sat in her posture and breathed in and out when she did. After a few moments I felt a sense of unconscious connection and then I started to tap my hand on my knee in the same rhythm as her knee jiggling. At the same time, I continued to breathe as she was breathing. Then, I slowed down my tapping and after a few seconds, she followed. I kept this new tempo for a while before slowing down again. And, she followed. We kept up this dance for a few minutes, and then finally I stopped tapping my hand and she stopped jiggling her knee. We had silence, visually and auditorily.

At times, it is necessary to **mismatch**, to establish the end of something or to break rapport with someone. Note that it is necessary to have rapport in the first place in order to break rapport. Mismatching is useful to signify the end of a meeting, redirect a conversation or interrupt a non-useful thought pattern. Sometimes we have found that highly kinesthetic people have a hard time mismatching, because it might "hurt someone's feelings." Perhaps you know someone that just can't end a conversation, or that gets followed around by someone they would rather not be followed around by simply because they can't break rapport. On the other hand, sometimes Internal Dialogue people are known for their mismatching skills – often playing the "devil's advocate." While this can be useful in some situations, if rapport is not first established, it may come across as very negative and pessimistic.

Rapport Exercise
In an effort to gain some skills and knowledge of how it feels to build rapport consciously with someone, we offer the following exercise to do a few times each day over the next couple of weeks:

1. Sit down near someone that you either don't know or don't know very well.
2. Look around you, stare at the floor – do anything you can to not make contact with the person.
3. After about 30 seconds, stop and take notice of what you might be feeling or sensing (if nothing, that is OK).
4. Now, choose 2-3 things to match or mirror.
5. Match and mirror for 1-2 minutes or until you sense that connection and feeling of rapport. There is no need to even talk.

Continue to do this exercise until you can identify what your sensations are when you have rapport, this will help you to know in the future when you don't have rapport and when using your NLP rapport skills would be useful. As your skills of rapport improve, it may take as few as 10-20 seconds to establish rapport.

Day 18 –
Understanding Submodalities

Before NLP, I (Laureli) was like so many people who just lived their life each day handling whatever happened to the best of my ability. I planned for my future, said my affirmations, made my decisions, but I did not know how to manage my own thoughts and states. Learning how the mind, brain, and body function allows us to change how we think, make decisions and express ourselves. One of the NLP presuppositions that support this is when you know better you can do better. In NLP a key component of taking charge of how you feel, what you think about how you act, is known as **Submodalities.**

Earlier we talked about the four representational systems; visual, auditory, kinesthetic and internal dialogue. As you recall, one of the ways we take in information from the external world is through our representational systems; submodalities are the finer distinctions and details of these modalities. These distinctions are often referred to as the architects of the mind. They are the way we code and make up the structure of our internal experience. Much like how a computer codes information, our brain does the same thing. It is something that happens automatically and outside of our conscious awareness. Submodalities give experiences their uniqueness and have felt-sense qualities that can describe how our emotional state relates to our memories.

Every thought we have, whether a recalled or imagined one, is formed out of these fine distinctions. They are the code of pictures, sounds, feelings, tastes, and smells. For instance, when we are thinking:
- *Visual – the pictures or images have some sort of color or hue, size, contrast, and location.*

- *Auditory – the sounds have volume, tone, location, rhythm, and are heard either internally or externally.*
- *Kinesthetic – the feelings we have intensity, location, duration, weight, movement and pressure.*

Generally, when working with submodalities we use the visual, auditory and kinesthetic modalities; however, some thoughts are intensified with smell and taste.

Once you understand how you create your internal world, you can realize you can change it. Submodalities determine the way you feel about your experiences as they represent your map of the world.

Here is an experience that I think will be a good example of one of the ways submodalities automatically code themselves: I had just moved into my first apartment. My mother came over to help me clean it as the previous tenants had left it a mess. The second bedroom was used for their pet rabbits. My mom brought tuna noodle casserole for lunch, which was one of my favorite meals. While we were cleaning, the casserole was in the oven cooking and sending the nice smell throughout the apartment. I was diligently scrubbing down the walls which had the smell of rabbits. When it was time to eat, I found it totally impossible to eat because the smell of the casserole had mixed with the smell of the rabbit. For a long time after, I could not even think about the casserole without getting the mixed smell coming through. This is because the submodalities of both smells happening at the same time, they got coded or wired together. Only when I learned about NLP did I use a submodality process to change tuna noodle casserole back to a likeable meal.

Submodality elicitation and change work allows you to take charge of your life.

The quality of your life is the outcome of your thoughts.
Your thoughts sometimes have irrational feelings, perceptions, hang-ups, misconceptions, and uncertainty that cause random mood swings. What causes this? It is a result of your programming. How you code your thoughts and ultimately your experiences determines how well you handle life. Understanding and learning how to communicate with our unconscious mind to make internal changes lets us take charge of our lives. As Aldous Huxley said, "Experience is not what happens to you, it's what we do with what happens to you."

In NLP we can use submodalities to enhance the qualities of thoughts and memories to increase the intensity and we can reduce the qualities of things that might block us, therefore diminishing them in our mind. We may want to make a goal bigger, brighter and more colorful, while a limiting thought or undesired state may be better if it is dim, further away and smaller. However, as in any technique or process, we always check for ecology and only make changes if it increases choices and wholeness. In order to learn about submodalities, we will be experimenting with a few examples. You can always change them back to how they were previously, which shows you the flexibility and ease of eliciting and changing submodalities.

For example, close your eyes and think about something that you really dislike doing, maybe even *hate* doing. Get an image or representation (this could be a picture, sound, or feeling) in your mind. When you have this representation, notice the following qualities:

- Is it a black-and-white or color representation?
- Is it near or far?
- Is it bright or dim?
- Where is it on the screen of your mind? Upper left, upper right, lower left, lower right, or center.
- Is it moving or is it still?

Now clear your mind and think of something that you really enjoy doing, even *love* doing. Get a representation in your mind and quickly notice the qualities of this representation:

- Is it a black-and-white or color representation?
- Is it near or far?
- Is it bright or dim?
- Where is it on the screen of your mind? Upper left, upper right, lower left, lower right, or center.
- Is it moving or is it still?

Most likely there are some differences between these two representations. After all, one is coded as something you like doing and the other is coded as something you dislike doing. As you are realizing by now, your mind is an amazing tool; not only can we differentiate an image based on the submodalities of it, but you can also hold several thoughts or images at any one time. So, let's really compare these images. In your mind, bring both pictures up at the same time and notice all of the differences. There is a good chance that not only do they *look different*, but they also *feel different*. And we've only specifically looked at the visual submodalities.

As an experiment, move the representation of the thing you don't like doing to the same place as the thing you love to do. What happens? What most people tell us is that it feels weird, odd or just plain wrong to have that thing you don't like doing in the love-to-do-it place. That just isn't how it is supposed to be!

There is no right or wrong, there is also nothing that is considered normal. In fact, everyone codes their experiences exactly where they belong for them. Once you have completed this, you can return them if you like to their original position.

Understanding the finer qualities of Submodalities

In order to better work with submodalities, we offer you the following guidelines:

- When working directly with submodalities, closing your eyes is useful as it shuts out the external real world and allows you to get in touch with your unconscious mind easier. Remember we are doing inner work and working with the unconscious mind which is abstract and symbolic. So, whatever you imagine is just right.

- When eliciting submodalities from a checklist, it is important to get a response quickly. Otherwise, the conscious mind may try to make sense of it and block the information from the unconscious. It may be useful to preframe with another person that you are going to ask some questions and you want them to give whatever answer comes up without thinking or thought. If people pause too long, it is usually because they are trying to think versus let their unconscious give them a reply. Practice makes it easier.

- Again, the unconscious mind is very symbolic; some people do not get images or pictures. They may get blobs of color or masses moving around, which can be quite common. This is why we ask you to get an image or representation. The unconscious mind will present whatever you are thinking about. Be mindful that the unconscious mind often will give you an answer, while at the same time your conscious mind might be thinking, "Am I making it up?" or "I don't know." This is common for the conscious thinking mind to try to take charge. A big part of doing any of the NLP processes is to learn to trust your unconscious mind and accept the answers that spontaneously come to you, while ignoring the invading conscious mind thoughts that try to make everything make sense.

- An associated or dissociated submodality may tell you if there is any emotion attached to the thought or feeling or not. If a troubling thought or emotion is associated, you can imagine stepping or floating out of the image and let yourself observe it. This would dissociate the image and make it less intense. Doing this allows you to work with a limiting thought and belief easier, as associated emotions can get in the way of doing the work.

- The location of the representation is divided into quadrants on the screen of your mind: upper left, upper right, lower left, lower right, or center of the screen of your mind. The location of a representation can make a big difference to how something is coded. Even subtle differences such as if an image is in the center forward, center left, center right or center back on the screen of your mind can make a big difference as they represent four different locations.

  Some people store things and/or people that they do and do not care about in special areas on the screen of their mind. Sometime they may indicate center for many images. It can be useful for some people to simply use their hand and point to where their image is stored. This can be much easier than requiring the conscious mind to know left from right.

- The submodalities that make the most dramatic change when moved or altered are known in NLP terminology as the submodality **drivers**. I like the analogy that when a person is driving a car and makes a turn, the passengers automatically follow. There are three main drivers that often make the biggest difference: black and white or color; location; associated or dissociated.

When you change a submodality, it changes other submodalities, which in turn change your state and then your behavior. For instance, one of my clients could not get her ex boyfriend out of her mind. It had been two years and she wanted to move on. I had her get an image of him and then I elicited the submodalities. They were:

- ○ Color
- ○ Near
- ○ Bright
- ○ Location – center, right in front of her face
- ○ Medium size
- ○ Associated

I had her make the image black and white and to push it back so it was further away. At this point, she told me it automatically became smaller. I had her move the location of the image the left of center, and asked her what happened to the image. She told me that it no longer had any emotion and it seemed to be getting smaller and smaller.

This is just one example. People have all sorts of experiences, however it illustrates that when we move one or more submodalities the others will follow. The key is to have them move alter a few submodalities and then check on what they notice or feel and continue to make alterations as you go.

- By changing the submodalities of a memory or thought, we change the effect they have on us. For example, for most people, increasing the size, brightness, making it nearer and in the center will increase the feelings of the memory either good or bad. If we wanted to decrease the intensity of a thought or memory, we could make it black and white; farther away from the person, smaller dimmer. Normally, the less intense the connection, the further away the image, which often diminishes in color to black and white or sepia. This is where you can move submodalities around and experiment to find the right spot. Remember, there are no right and wrong submodalities, just submodalities that fit best for the desired state. Here is a thought which will give some people reading this permission to play with submodalities: you cannot hurt someone by changing their submodalities. The worst case scenario is that something doesn't feel right and the mind will change the image back to how it is normally coded. Go ahead and play with submodalities, be curious about what can happen!

Let's use a simple exercise. You can either guide yourself or use this to guide someone else.

1. Think back to a time when you were on a relaxing vacation and get an image or representation of that time. Using the submodality checklist (today's final page) elicit the visual submodalities:
   - Is the image black & white or color?
   - Is it near or far?
   - Is it bright or dim?
   - Is the location upper left, upper right, lower left, lower right, or in the center? Point to it now.
   - What size is the image?
   - Are you associated (any feelings involved) or dissociated (observing)?
   - Is it focused or defocused?
   - Is it framed or panoramic?
   - Is it moving or still?

2. Now move and change some of the distinctions. If the image is color, turn it to black and white, and if it is already black and white, make it color. What happens? Now turn up the brightness. Does it alter how you feel about it? Then gradually make the image dimmer until you can barely make it out.

    Many people find there is a select brightness, at which their feelings intensify, and when it is too light or dark they do not have any feelings for it at all.

    If the image is moving, make it still or frozen, like a photograph. If it's already still, give it movement. How does that change things? Move your mental image further away, then closer, to the side, and up and down. How do you feel when it's in those different locations?

    Now we will tune into the auditory elements. What sounds are you aware of – voices, music, or any type of noise? How many different sounds are there? Are the sounds close or further away? Which direction do the sounds come from? Do they sound clear or are any of them muffled? If there are voices, are they high or low? Are they quick or slow?

    Turn up the volume and get a sense of the difference it makes to your experience. Now turn it down to a whisper. If there are a number of voices or sounds, adjust the tone of each one, much like you would if you were using a tuner. Move the sounds around into different locations. Try changing the speed. What effect does each of these changes have on the way you feel about it?

    Now, get in touch with any feelings you had at the time. Where in your body do you feel them? How would you describe the sensations? What happens if you move them around or change their intensity?

You can do this with any memory, "good" or "bad." You can strengthen those which you want and diminish those that cause you problems. We can also use the same process when planning future goals. By enhancing the submodalities, you can make your goals and outcomes more compelling.

Other Uses for Submodalities

Literally, everything has a submodality or finer distinction. Have you seen the movie Pleasantville? Everyone lived in a black and white world. It was void of emotions and was very dull and certain. One day a boy had a bit of emotion and as soon as he did he started seeing color and eventually other people started to as well. Once this happened the whole community started to come alive. This is the function of submodalities.

We don't all live in Pleasantville, yet submodalities are useful in so many real-life aspects, here are a few:
- Changing unwanted habits and behaviors such as smoking, biting nails, swearing, procrastination, boredom
- Creating and enhancing behaviors such as exercising, motivation, any sport
- Enhancing goals
- Changing and / or enhancing how you react to people and situations

Often people ask how often they need to repeat a process. We always say that once should be sufficient. The rule of thumb is that the last way the unconscious mind is left is how it will stay. It would be like vacuuming up dirt and then revacuuming repeatedly. Sometimes it takes a few different processes or techniques to help clear and solidify the changes; however, it is important to trust the unconscious mind.

SUBMODALITITES CHECKLIST

	1	2	3	4
Visual				
Black & White or Color?				
Near or Far?				
Bright or Dim?				
Location?				
Size of Picture?				
Associated / Dissociated?				
Focused or Defocused?				
Framed or Panoramic?				
Movie or Still?				
Auditory				
Location				
Direction				
Internal or External?				
Loud or Soft?				
Fast or Slow?				
High or Low? (Pitch)				
Kinesthetic				
Location				
Size				
Shape				
Intensity				
Steady				
Movement/ Duration				
Vibration				
Pressure/Heat?				
Weight				

Are there any sounds that are important? (bracket beside Auditory section)

Are there any feelings that are important? (bracket beside Kinesthetic section)

Remember, there is a need for speed when eliciting submodalities. If you elicit at too slow of a pace, you are giving the unconscious mind too much time to think about them.

Day 19 –
Using Submodalities

As we talked about yesterday, when you use submodalities you are training the mind to instantly redirect your thinking. This gives you the ability to develop and maintain resourceful states and manage your responses. The importance of eliciting submodalities is that it gives the representation more concrete substance versus an abstract feeling or state. It is easier to work with concrete images, as abstract ones sometimes are harder to hold on to. Whatever they are, they will be full of the individual building blocks that are unique to the person you are working with.

Let's elicit some submodalities for practice.
- Think about any holiday that is important to you such as Christmas. What is your representation for it? Are there any sounds or feelings with this representation?
- Now, think of going to the dentist. What is your representation for this? What do you see, hear and feel?

When eliciting an experience you may be able to recall it in more detail. You could help someone to focus on more and more aspects of the representation by asking what you specifically see, hear, smell, taste and feel during the experience. When we elicit the submodalities, we are getting the finer distinctions of your representation.

- Now, think about something or someone that you are in conflict with. Where do you feel the conflict? (strange question, we know!) Is it in your head, torso, stomach, or somewhere else? What does the feeling look like? How big is it? What color is it? Is it moving or still; is it heavy or light; is it transparent or solid? Generally you will get an image that represents the person or conflict and it probably has a feeling with it as well.

Working with submodalities

Submodalities are useful to replace a negative habit, belief, behavior, or response with a more productive and resourceful one. They are also useful to make a goal or outcome more compelling. Using submodalities is quick and very easy and can be done on yourself or with others. Today, we will share some simple ways that you can use submodalities for yourself as well as others.

If people have difficulty in visualizing, you could use a technique called overlapping. This is where you lead them from one representation system to another; you follow whatever representation they give you and then get the visual submodalities of it. For example, if you wanted to elicit someone's working conditions and they can get a feeling but not an image, you could invite the person to tell you where they feel the feeling and then elicit some of the kinesthetic submodalities: size, shape, color, movement, temperature, weight, texture, etc. These kinesthetic submodalities can lead the person to getting a visual image even if it is a blob or mass or energy. When eliciting any emotion, behavior, thought, or habit, understand that everyone has their own representation; there is not a right or wrong.

Another simple method to help people see an image is to ask the person to pretend or imagine they can see an image and to trust their unconscious mind to tell them what they see. This will often work just as effectively, and often quicker. However, if people are being too conscious and doubting what they "see," use kinesthetic submodalities.

When working with submodalities we sometimes compare them and **Map Across** the differences. For example, we can map across the submodalities of a person that we like and one that we don't. When we compare the differences we can decide which particular submodalities we want to bring over or map across. When we map across we are recoding one submodality with the coding of another. To put it even simpler, we are identifying a template of a desired state and moving something across to match it.

In NLP, when we are working with ourselves and others in any change work, we always want to elicit both a present state and a desired state. This is because NLP is outcome and solution based. We can lessen the effect of any unwanted state and intensify a desired state.

NLP Submodality Techniques

There are a number of NLP techniques which use submodalities, either directly or indirectly. Today we will be looking at a few of them, and over the next few weeks you will see more submodalities show up in various other techniques.

Swish Pattern

The Swish Pattern is one of the very early NLP techniques, first demonstrated in a workshop in 1981, presented by Richard Bandler and Robert Dilts. They were modeling what people do in their minds already and used that information to move and change it. Whether you realize it or not, you already do the Swish Pattern. This process enables you to consciously create the changes you want by quickly dissolving the feelings attached to unwanted thoughts, habits, or behaviors as it reassociates these and redirectionalizes how we think about them.

What happens with behavioral and thinking habits is that the mind focuses on something and moves in that direction. As we say, energy flows where attention goes. This is how we acquire unwanted thoughts and habits. We can use the NLP Swish Pattern to redirect our unconscious mind away from the unwanted focus, towards a new, wanted directional focus. One of the great benefits of the Swish Pattern is that it creates generative change. Once you know how to use the Swish Pattern, you can create or design any number of ways to use it that would suit whomever you are working with.

The Swish Pattern is best used to change unwanted habits and behaviors. Some examples include: smoking, procrastination, swearing, biting nails, boredom, nervousness, worry, being untidy, binging, drinking, etc.

We worked with a woman who really wanted to go back to University, but she believed it would be hard and very difficult as she always thought of herself as a slow learner. She had a lot of evidence to support this belief. Her desire was to learn and retain information with ease and enjoyment. We used the Swish Pattern to change her Present State of Slow Learner to her Desired State of learn and retain information with ease and enjoyment.

After using the Swish Pattern with my client, she could only see herself attending class and easily absorbing the information. She said she could not access the old belief and in fact thought it was quite silly she used to think it at all.

The Swish Pattern is also useful for people who want to get into any type of routine or create a positive habit. We worked with a guy who used to get up every morning and go for a run before he got ready for work. He said he had done this for about four year's rain or shine and had been in great physical shape. Somehow his pattern got interrupted. He had told himself it would only be for a week or two and then he'd resume; two years later he still could not motivate himself to run in the morning. The Swish Pattern was perfect for him as all he had to do was imagine his desired state of getting up and running and how good it felt, then dissociate it and shrink it to a lower corner. Then "swish" the desired state over his current unwanted one. It only took a few swishes until he could not get the old image back. From the next morning onward, he says he gets up without any thinking or thought and does his run.

Like all NLP techniques, the Swish Pattern is best learned "live" in a classroom where you are able to interact with your trainer and with other participants; and where you learn the background steps before you get to actually use the Swish Pattern. However, you can still get good results if you carefully follow the steps on the next page.

The Swish Pattern

1. Get a representation or image of the desired state. With their eyes closed, have them see, hear, and feel what they feel. Then have them make it more intense and compelling. For instance, make it really colorful and bright and near and big, but not too big, and put it in the exact right place on the screen of the mind where it is most compelling. Have them make it feel really good and using any of the other words they used to describe their desired state.

2. Turn the image into a photograph or something they can look at. This makes the image dissociated. It is quite important that it is dissociated at this point. Now, have them shrink the image and place it in a lower corner of the screen of their mind and open their eyes.

3. Close the eyes and get an image of the unwanted state. Have them imagine being in that state now; seeing what they see, hearing what they hear, and feeling what they feel. This gets them into an associated state.

4. Have them notice the shrunken image in the lower corner. Now on the count of three you want them to bring the desired image up and right over the top of this one, as you say the word "Swish."

5. As soon as the image is big, quickly shrink it back into the corner. Tell them you are going to do this a number of times very quickly and as soon as the picture comes over the old one have them shrink it back down again. Do this until they can no longer get the old picture back. This can take from as little as one time to as many as 10.

6. Test and Future Pace: Ask, "Now when you think about that old state you used to have, what do you notice?"

Submodality Distortion Technique

Besides doing a swish pattern for smokers, we often elicit them smoking and then change their submodalities of how it smells and tastes. Here is a sample of what you could do.

1. Get an image of smoking so you can see yourself and the cigarette. Let yourself feel how it feels to smoke. See the smoke, see the cigarette and smell how it smells and taste how it tastes.
2. Imagine seeing a smelly cigarette with smoke coming from it just burning away. You can smell its disgusting smell and see the haze of smoke all around it. See the ashtray full of old, smelly butts, stacked high. Let yourself take a smell of that now, let it sit in your nose and mouth because that's what it's like. Every time you think of a cigarette or smoking you get that smell and taste and nothing will take it away.

The Compulsion Blowout Technique

A compulsion blowout is a submodality pattern for intense behaviors and responses you feel compelled or forced to do. This is used only for compulsions that interfere with your life or you feel you do not have a choice in the behavior. It is sometimes referred to as the Threshold Technique. Take care with this technique, as you should be considering the positive intention of the behavior and addressing it as well.

Compulsions usually have four aspects:

- The representation can be visual, auditory or kinesthetic.
- There is some type of distortion in the submodality of the representation; you consciously do not know this. For example, chocolate compulsion; the chocolate is larger than normal and not realistic.
- The feeling of compulsion is of having no choice.
- There is a desire that you have to do something.

This technique again is a very simple one. Have you ever over done something until you just could not do it again? Has there ever been something like a song that was played over and over again until you just couldn't stand it anymore? This is what the blowout technique does. It alters your submodalities so much that you can no longer represent the image or object in the same way. It breaks the connection, so be sure you want to get rid of your compulsion before you use this technique.

Compulsion Blowout Technique

The following is an example of using this technique for someone who compulsively eats chocolate. You would simply follow these steps for whatever topic you are using for the Compulsion Blowout. It is always appropriate to do an ecology check before you do the process. What will happen when you no longer have the compulsion? Does it satisfy something else? What positive behavior can you put in its place?

1. Elicit how you picture the chocolate and what compels you and exactly what attracts you to it. Is it the size, nearness, color, or brightness of the image, or the imagined smell, taste or texture of it? What is distorted about this image?

2. What makes you feel attracted to the chocolate? Now imagine increasing or decreasing it and seeing whether that makes the attraction more or less.

3. Visualize the chocolate and very quickly increase the trigger that makes you crave it until it becomes ridiculously intense. Imagine being completely full of it, so much that it is all over you. Repeat this rapidly over and over until you feel something pop or change. For example, if you were visualizing chocolate by imagining its taste, you could rapidly increase that chocolaty flavor from a mild to overwhelmingly powerful in a matter of a few seconds. Quickly repeat the visualization several times. You will feel a change in yourself as you go over your threshold and the craving will be gone.

These are just a few NLP techniques which use submodalities as a primary focus. Other such processes include techniques such as: Pragmagraphic Swish Pattern, Designer Swish Pattern, Self-Concept, Submodality Generalization Strategy, and Time Line elicitation.

One of Heidi's favorite Submodality techniques is Self-Concept, which is about realigning identity, created by Steve Andreas. We couldn't do the process justice in this short chapter, but you can find more information about it in the book Transforming Yourself: Becoming Who You Want To Be by Steve Andreas or in the DVD Building Self Concept. We also recommend Change Your Mind and Keep the Change: Advanced NLP Submodalities Interventions, written by Steve Andreas and Connirae Andreas.

Earlier we shared Bandlers' view that NLP is an attitude and a methodology, which leave behind a trail of techniques. As with submodalities, they are used as one of the many things that we apply to make changes and rewire our neurology. We use submodalities in a number of NLP techniques such as anchoring, parts integration, in fact any technique that requires us to make the symbol or interference more concrete or where we are gathering information.

Day 20 –
Anchors

As the actor Tim Robbins strolled up to the podium to present an Oscar at the Academy Awards ceremony a few years ago, NLP'ers may have observed him tapping himself on one shoulder and then pulling his ear three times. Although such subtle movements were probably undetected by millions of viewers, in doing so, Robbins was joining a long tradition of celebrities and other people who have learnt how to use physical triggers to alter their emotional state. This technique is known as **anchoring.**

What is an Anchor?

Simply put, an anchor is any type of stimulus that creates a response. The sound of the ocean, the smell of baking bread, a photo on your desk, the sunrise, a piece of jewelry, your favorite jeans. Anything that creates a response.

Anchors come in many shapes and sizes – visual, auditory, kinesthetic, smells, tastes – when they create a response, they are anchors. Anchors are all around us. Some have been consciously created, most however, unconsciously.

Most people have heard the term "knee-jerk reaction"; the phrase comes from study and research by William Twitmeyer in 1902. He found that when you tap the fleshy part of the knee cap the leg will jump and straighten out. He also realized that after 50 to 100 times of repeating this process, just holding the hammer and suggesting he was about to hit their knee produced the same effect.

In 1904, Ivan Pavlov conducted a study that he called the Stimulus Response. In his study, he would show a dog some meat and then ring a tuning fork and the dog would salivate. After doing this a few times, the dogs were conditioned so when he rang the bell without showing the meat the dogs would still salivate. Thus was born, classical conditioning.

Have you ever smelled food and immediately became hungry? Have you ever heard a song that took you back in time, or smelled perfume that reminded you of someone? What happens when you look at pictures from an old photo album?

The responses we have are unlimited to how many anchors we are linked to. Some psychologists think that our behaviors are a series of anchors that come from a chain of conditioned responses; and they are probably correct. Everything that goes through our minds is a response that has been anchored in some way. Therefore anchoring is a major facet of everything we do.

As we've said, anchors are all around us. Here are just a few *naturally occurring* anchors that some people have. We invite you to take a look around your home, office, car, and life to see what anchors you already have. As you will see, not all anchors are positive. Anchors that produce a positive response we often refer to as **resourceful anchors**; conversely, anchors that produce a negative response we refer to as **unresourceful anchors**. Later in this chapter we'll look at how to consciously create an anchor, and tomorrow we'll look at even more anchoring tools, including a tool to change or remove a negative anchor.

	Stimulus/Anchor	**Response/State**
Visual Anchors	• Sunset	• Relaxation
	• Your child	• Happiness/ Love
	• A fast car	
	• Red traffic light	• Freedom
	• Your house	• Stop
		• Security

Auditory Anchors
- A fast song
- Birds chirping
- Ocean waves
- Sound of parents voice
- Dog barking

- Motivation
- Relaxation
- Calm
- Fear
- Annoying

Kinesthetic Anchors
- Laying in bed
- Movement/ Exercise
- Massage
- Favorite jeans
- Motion of a car

- Sleep
- Motivation/ Awake
- Relaxation
- Comfort
- Sleepy

How Do Anchors Develop?

Our neurology automatically creates anchors by linking a stimulus with a specific response. Once an anchor is set, firing the anchor automatically triggers the response. If someone has a fear of cockroaches, if they see (or even imagine) a cockroach, the brain will secrete a cascade of chemicals and hormomnes such as adrenaline, cortisol and norepineephrine automatically, creating a rapid sense of fear. This happens instantaneously because an anchor has been triggered. No conscious thought, just boom – fear.

Cockroaches are an example of a negative anchor, however, anchors are especially useful for triggering positive emotional and resourceful states at will. Most anchors are created accidentally and remain below conscious awareness, as they have not been created with purpose. In fact, we often think that our mood has nothing to do with us and that our moods occur by chance; yet as NLPers know, there is no such thing as coincidence. There are however many anchors in life we may be unaware of!

Let's look a this example: what if every night you have a snack while watching television. There is a good chance that every time you watch television you feel hungry. Speaking of television, commercials are full of anchors to get people to buy their products. Have you ever been shopping and purchased something that you saw an ad for. This could be a response to an anchor that was installed unconsciously.

An interesting study by Dr Ellen Langer, in 1981, showed how people can be anchored. She was hoping to find that fixed ideas that are internalized in childhood affects how people age. In her study, two groups of 75 to 80-year-old men went to an isolated monastery for five days. The monastery was set up with 1950's memorabilia and mementos, such as music, magazines, black and white TV, old style radio, posters, and pictures.

The first group were told to stay mentally in the present but to reminisce and think about that time. They were to write an autobiography, to discuss the past.

The second group, who arrived a week later, were asked to pretend they were younger men and live as if it were the 1959. They were to dress and talk and act as if they were 22 years younger. They watched 1959 movies and listened to music on the radio and records. They wrote an autobiography up to 1959 describing that time as now.

Before and after the five days, both groups were studied on a number of criteria associated with aging. The first group stayed constant or some actually deteriorated on the criteria. The second group dramatically improved on physical health measures such as joint flexibility, vision, and muscle breadth, as well as on IQ tests. The difference being that they were anchored back mentally and physically to being 50 years old.

How to Use Anchors
Now that you know what anchors are, you can consciously decide how to use them. In NLP training, you will learn how to create anchors to elicit and reinforce positive behaviors and

habits, and how to collapse or change unwanted anchors. Even without specific NLP techniques, you can use anchors to:

- **Manage your State.** You can create an anchor to be triggered by a consciously chosen stimulus (for example, a word you say to yourself of the touch of your hand to the back of your neck). This will give you instant access to a resourceful state at will.

- **Set the mood**. Many artful marketers, filmmakers, teachers, clergy, lawyers, sports people use anchors to set the mood of situations. This can be done using music, sounds, rituals, voice tones, visual cues, or anything that evokes a response. We know people who still cringe when they hear the music from *Jaws.*

Types of Anchoring Processes

There are so many ways that we can use anchors we will be discussing on a few of them here. The following information is an overview of some of the most common types of anchoring processes in NLP, or ways to use anchors. We will look at some of these processes tomorrow.

Spatial anchors are associated with a particular physical location. Many NLP processes utilize spatial anchors. Often whatever is being anchored is set on a floor or space or place for a person to walk into or stand in. This can be a powerful way for people to experience an anchor. Spatial anchors are also useful to allow someone to step out of a traumatic event into either a second or a third perceptual position, to lessen the effect as they observe it only. We can also use spatial anchors to anchor words in a conversation. For example, if you were speaking to someone and each time they mentioned *work*, they would gesture to their left, you cold also gesture to their left when you talk about their work. This is using anchors in a very unconscious manner while communicating.

Resource anchors add more intensity and power to a state. A resource anchor is a specifically created anchor; normally an image, touch, movement or sound, which when fired will produce a positive resourceful state. Some common resourceful states to anchor are motivation, determination, peaceful, calm, and energized. If one stimulus (for example, a ring I wear) is laced with a number of different states to be elicited all at once, this is known as a **stacked resource anchor.**

Integrating anchors is an NLP technique that uses anchors to help move from a present unwanted state to a desired resourceful state. It establishes a more resourceful way to feel and operate. It is especially useful when there is a large discrepancy between the two states. For example, triggering a powerful resourceful state and integrating it into a stuck state. This gives more choice and resources.

Collapse anchor is a powerful NLP technique that is useful to clear or change negative anchors. Fears, phobias and unresourceful emotions and behaviors can be changed with this process. Ultimately, this process helps us to collapse an unwanted anchor and replace it with either a neutral state or a more positive one.

We had a student who used to be a Navy Aircraft Director. When he learned about anchors in his NLP Practitioner training he said he had several examples. Aircraft directors have specific movements that communicate to the pilot what to do next. The noise from the aircraft is deafening,

therefore most of the communication comes from visual signals, which he now realizes are anchors.

When he gives the all-clear-to-go signal he crouches down and points forward. Not only is this an anchor for the pilot, he also has a positive association with this movement that takes him to a state of confidence and well-being. He told us that even thinking about giving the all-clear-to-go signal takes him back to the sound of the roar of the jets, the powerful wind that reverberated and it takes him to a powerful and positive state. All he had to do was to think about it.

The Four Keys to Anchoring

While most anchors happen naturally, we can also consciously set an anchor. It can be as overt as blowing a whistle to signal the end of a break or as subtle as standing in a certain place to answer questions.

a) **Intensity or purity of experience.** The best states to anchor are naturally occurring states. Next best are past, vivid, highly-associated states. Least preferable are constructed states.

b) **Timing.** The peak of a state lasts only a short amount of time. Approximately 5-15 seconds. When we want to purposefully create an anchor, it will work only if applied just before and until the height of the emotions.

c) **Uniqueness of the anchor.** How will you store the anchor? If kinesthetic or a touch anchor, make sure it is in a place that is not commonly used such as palms of hands. Put it in a unique place such as an elbow, ear lobe, and knee. With any other anchors, make sure that however it is stored, it is unique to the anchor.

d) **Accuracy of replication of anchor.** When you want to trigger the anchor, make sure you can replicate the original anchor stored. For instance, if a touch anchor was set with a firm touch, then replicate with the same firmness.

Creating Anchors

Here is an example of how to set a touch or kinesthetic anchor. We are using calm and relaxed for this example.

1. Think of a past vivid experience when you were calm and relaxed. Get yourself into a calm, relaxed state now. Imagine seeing yourself calm, peaceful and relaxed.

2. At the peak of your state, at the most intense feelings of calm and relaxed, set your anchor. For example, apply a firm touch to your left elbow and hold it 5 to 15 seconds, or as long as it is at the peak.

3. Break your state by standing up or moving around. Then repeat the process again, and after a few repetitions the state will be anchored.

4. Activate or fire the anchor. This is how you test and use the anchor by applying the same touch to your elbow and noticing what happens. Each time you touch your left elbow in the same place you will be in a state of calmness.

5. Check and fire the anchor often especially in the beginning. Every time the stimulus is applied, the emotional response will be triggered. The more you use an anchor, the stronger it will become.

Anthony Robbins has a physical anchor that he uses hundreds of times when he is on stage. The interesting thing is that when he anchors himself he also anchors the audience.

Tips for Using Anchors

- The anchor should be fired in exactly the same way every time you link them to the resourceful experience.
- Anchor at the peak of the experience, as it contains the resourceful state.
- If you do not experience the state when future pacing and especially if you experience anxiety, then stop applying the anchor. Otherwise, you will anchor the negative state.
- You can strengthen an anchor by repeating the above process over several days. You can also add a state that fits any time something good happens.
- Be mindful when others are in any negative emotional state how you touch them to avoid any negative anchoring.
- We can be unconsciously anchoring other people with a look, tone, or movement. I am sure when you were a child you could tell by your parents' face or voice if you were in trouble.

Anchors can come in never-ending possible forms: verbal phrases, sensations, certain sights and sounds, or internally, such as words one says to oneself, or memories and states one is in. A simple high-five is an anchor.

The New Zealand All Black football team starts every game with the traditional Māori dance called the Haka. This ritual not only gets the All Black payers in a heightened state, it also puts their opponents in a state of concern and riles up the spectators.

When we are aware of anchors that are set in us and that we set in others, it makes us more responsible. Some people only need to "see" someone or something that triggers a negative anchor. I know a person that every time George W. Bush came on television he would go into a rampage and get in a bad mood. If you find you have any negative reactions, you now know you can choose do something about them.

Tomorrow we will be investigating some useful ways to use, set, change and incorporate anchors into your daily life.

Day 21 –
Using Anchors

Nokia did a study using their GPS tracking system to track 100 people for a month. They found that 90% of people are in the same place everyday at same time. Humans are creatures of habit so this should be no surprise. We like to think we are in control as we surround ourselves with structure and routine, therefore it supports the philosophy that we operate from a set of conditioned responses.

If you have been looking around your life since yesterday's chapter, you would have undoubtedly noticed many anchors around you. People, objects, food, sounds, smells, there are too many to count. We can use the anchors around us to deliberately get ourselves into a certain state, we can create new anchors, collapse negative anchors, and we can use the anchors that other people present to us to communicate at an unconscious level and even pace people to respond to the anchors we use.

If you have a song that motivates you, you can play that song in the morning as a deliberate way to motivate yourself. If you have a chair at home that relaxes you, you can deliberately sit in the chair to create the state of relaxation. In normal life anchors are often triggered by happenstance, however now that you are more aware of anchors you can use them more consciously and deliberately.

On the other hand, if I don't have something that gets me into a certain state, I can create something. Let's say that I suffer from two-thirty'itis, that is, I get sleepy at two-thirty in the afternoon. I find something that is within my vicinity at two-thirty and use that to create an anchor using the exercise in yesterday's chapter.

Our office is located in the central part of Sydney. Out of our windows we can see the glorious old Queen Victoria Building. We could use that building as a visual anchor to trigger a state of motivation, alertness, and awakeness. Then, anytime I look out the window with the intention of having this state, it just happens because I've set it as an anchor. Later in this chapter we will look at the technique Circle of Excellence to create an anchor you can transport with you anywhere.

If you have a negative anchor, that is, a stimulus that produces a negative response such as lightning, the dark, loud voices, or a certain smell, we can change how we respond to these stimuli by collapsing an anchor. One of the NLP Presuppositions says that *you are in charge of your mind therefore your results.* Anchors can help us to be more in charge of our results. In a while we will look at the process of collapsing anchors.

Being able to communicate at the unconscious level is also a simple way to use anchors on a day-to-day manner. You can mirror the gestures, facial expressions, and tonality of other people to create anchors that allow less words to be used to say the same thing. For example, if you are talking to someone who is discussing their feelings about their mother-in-law, and every time he mentions his mother-in-law he gestures to his right, you can reference that same spatial location when you mention his mother-in-law, and after a few times making that gesture, you no longer need to verbally mention her, you can just reference that space. This is a great technique to use all the time. In a business meeting, with a friend, with your children. The movements we use have meaning, therefore we can use those movements for purpose.

Also, we can pace someone to respond to an anchor we use. At the end of her client sessions, Heidi puts down her pen, sits up straight and takes a deep breath. Every time a session ends, this is what you would observe. After about the second session, her clients unconsciously know "it's time to go." She doesn't have to say anything more, her movement is the anchor for the end. If your parents have a certain way they used to look at you to let you know you were in trouble, this is an example of this type of anchor. What anchors could you set to let people know when a meeting is done with you? Or when you want them to be quiet, pay attention or relax? The possibilities are quite endless.

Working with Negative Anchors

Emotional freedom happens when we are aware of and respond to our anchors as we choose. Since most of our anchors are below our conscious awareness, it takes conscious effort to notice what the triggers are so we can adjust our unwanted anchors.

Anchors sometimes get set by negative reinforcement. You touch a hot stove, it hurts, so you don't do that again. Learning to ride a bike comes from knowing how to stay balanced and upright; however, it probably came at the cost of pushing through any spills or negative incidents. We do have some anchors that hold us back from doing things we want to do because of an adverse effect we had, and we revert to an unwanted anchored state.

One of our clients at age twelve had to stand and speak in front of a class. He said he became so self-conscious and embarrassed, that he went blank and got tongue tied. Thus, an unwanted anchor was created. From then on, when he was required to talk in front of more than ten people he experienced the exact same response. Now a part of his role at work is to make presentations. He knows the subject well, however, he goes through so much emotional and mental turmoil that it impairs his presentation.

Interestingly, when people are stuck in unwanted anchored states, they sometimes revert to the age they were when the anchor was created. NLP has some great techniques for helping people out of these kinds of states. In this chapter we will be discussing and showing you how some of them work.

Collapsing Anchors

Collapsing Anchors is a technique used to eliminate an existing negative anchor by collapsing it into a positive resourceful anchor. It is based on the assumption that people will usually select an outcome that is positive and resourceful versus negative and unresourceful. Some common states to collapse are test anxiety, not liking compliments, not liking to be alone, afraid of the dark, fear of loud noises, and almost anything that has an unwanted response.

The simplicity of collapsing anchors is that you replace it with a more resourceful state. It could be the opposite of the unwanted state or perhaps replacing it with a positive state such as confident, relaxed, calm, happy, and determined. Instead of analyzing the unresourceful anchored response, we release it naturally with a new resourceful anchored state. We do want to replace the unwanted state with something - if you take something away from a toddler without doing an exchange, you will find a howling and sometimes inconsolable child. The unconscious mind is similar and it responds to a swap just as easily. They say the mind abhors a vacuum.

In NLP we always look at the ecology of the whole situation and system to make sure we are creating solutions for tomorrow that do not become tomorrow's problem.

Setting Up the Technique

Most techniques require some pre-framing and conscious thought, therefore taking the time to find exactly what the unwanted anchor is and what to use to collapse happens first.

1. Identify the negative anchor and calibrate how it affects the person.

2. Determine the positive resourceful state they would rather have. Whomever you are working with should be

the one to decide what works for them. You can make suggestions, but it has to fit into their model of the world.

3. When leading a person through a collapse anchor technique, we often touch them to set it. The anchors need to be in two different locations on the body. The use of knuckles, knees, or shoulders works well as people have two of each.

Remember the keys to anchoring are:
- Intensity or purity of experience; lead them to reach an intense memory of each elicited state.
- Timing; anchor them when they are at the peak of each experience.
- Uniqueness of the anchor; use something or a place that is unique.
- Accuracy of replication of anchor; for a touch anchor, be able to replicate the same intensity of touch in the exact same place. For instance, if I use a shoulder, I normally press on a shirt seam or something that I can locate easily.

Collapsing Anchors Process

1. Elicit the negative anchor and create a physical touch anchor on the left shoulder. Remember to calibrate their breathing, facial features, body posture and have them tell you when they are at the peak.

2. Elicit the positive anchor and create a physical touch anchor on the right shoulder.

3. Break the state by having them open their eyes and test each anchor separately. Ask what they notice as each anchor is fired. Each state should invoke a similar response that is anchored. If not, you may want to anchor the state again, making sure you anchor it at the peak.

4. Close eyes and touch both anchors at the same time – hold them both for 5-10 seconds. Most people will have some sort of physiological response. It could be a shutter, squirm, so calibrate.

5. After no more than 10 seconds, release the negative anchor only and continue holding the resourceful anchor for another 5 to 10 seconds. Then release and calibrate their breathing, facial features, body posture for signs of a difference.

6. Ask, "Now what do you notice when you think of that old unwanted response you used to have?"

7. What happens is the desired anchor collapses the unwanted anchor. Some people report having an electrical buzz go through them. We have had people who do not recall anything except confusion. In addition, in many ways this is what we are looking for, even asymmetric muscle movements in the face is normal. When an old unwanted anchor is scrambled and short-circuited it no longer works. Remember the last way the unconscious mind is left is how it will respond.

8. If the desired result is not achieved, you may find that stacking a few anchors on the desired state side will give it more intensity. If you do that, then repeat steps 3 through 5. It also might be possible that a belief or something else need addressed first. There are also processes specifically for sounds and feelings that may work as well or better depending on the situation. We will be exploring more options in the coming days.

NLP was founded on modeling excellence. Knowing how to change your state in a moment's notice is a great skill to have. Remember your unconscious mind does not know the difference between a real memory or an imagined one. All you have to do is recall and capture any feeling that you want to incorporate into your life and anchor it so you can fire it when you need it.

The actor Gregory Peck recalled when he was filming a movie where he played General Douglas McArthur. Normally, he was an easygoing, placid person who did not like confrontation and would reflect for a period of time before making decisions. During filming, his wife asked if he would come on his lunch break and look at a house she was hoping to purchase. Still in full uniform of the General, he arrived and, for some reason, was still in character. He looked at the house, barked some orders to the real estate agent and aggressively made a decision to buy the house. Only later when he was back on the set did he reflect on how he behaved. He said that from that day onwards if he needed to be more aggressive, he would remember how that felt and get himself into the General's character.

Circle of Excellence

The Circle of Excellence is a fundamental NLP anchoring process that was designed by John Grinder and Judith DeLozier. It is like a stacked resource anchor that helps people to discover things about their own internal behaviors to enhance themselves. It uses spatial anchoring to set the anchor and to access the state again to use it anywhere and anytime you wish.

This process will allow you to access your best state any time you need it. There may be times when you would like to *walk* into a powerful and resourceful state at will, this is a great process for that. Because the Circle of Excellence is filled with positive and beneficial states, is also useful to eliminate some habitual states such as the fear of public speaking.

A client of ours was in the management side of a major bank. Normally, she does not go into the public banking sector as a part of her job. One day, however, she was attending a meeting at a local branch, waiting in the lobby for someone to come greet her and an armed robbery take place. Her reaction was fairly common, she froze and then shock set in. Over a few days, she became teary and unable to think straight, she explained that she felt *out of body*. Soon she was on sick leave seeing a psychologist. After 6 months of still suffering what was deemed post traumatic stress disorder, she came to us. We did a few NLP processes and she soon started to recover and get her old self back. When she felt she was ready to return to work, we knew that if she had her own internal resource anchor it would assist her. Circle of Excellence was the process we installed and she said helped her return to work easily and comfortably.

Here are the steps to creating a Circle of Excellence. Once you establish your own, it will be with you wherever you go. In order to activate it at will to a high level of association, practice using your Circle each day.

Circle of Excellence Process

1. Choose a resourceful state or a few states you would like to experience whenever you wanted it.

2. Identify and recall a specific time in which you fully experienced this state. If you cannot find an experience, use a highly imagined one.

3. Imagine a circle on the floor in front of you. Something large enough to walk into. If you wish, you can select a specific color in the circle.

4. When you are ready step into the circle and relive the experience by associating to the desired state as though you are there now. Seeing through your own eyes, hearing through you own ears and feeling the sensations of this state. Let all the memories of that time, real or imagined, come and flood your mind and body. Hold your body,

your face, head, arms, the way you would in this state. Notice how you breathe, move, and speak.

5. Enhance the state by amplifying the submodalities. Make it more colorful, brighter, bigger, closer, make it compelling and intensify it so it can't get any better.

6. Then step back out of the circle and shake it off.

7. Quickly step back into the circle. Let yourself immediately get back into the state.

8. Step back out of the circle and shake it off.

9. Quickly step back into the circle notice how easy it is to get into this state.

10. Step back out of the circle and shake it off.

11. Repeat step 9 and 10 a few times until you can access the state within 1 or less seconds.

12. Test the results. Think of a situation in which you would like to have this state. Let yourself imagine it now and then, quickly step into the circle. What did you notice?

There are many things you have learned up to this point, from reading this book that allows you to use NLP techniques such as anchoring with skill. For instance:

- Sensory acuity and calibration skills help to be aware of the changes people have as they go through different states.
- Rapport enables you to engage and get comfortable with others, in order to understand them and perhaps lead them through a process.

- Understanding how the unconscious mind works helps you to navigate your mind better.
- State elicitation allows a person to remember or imagine past states.
- Submodalities amplify or intensify memories and states.

A movie from a few years ago displayed the use of anchors very well. Kevin Costner an aging, once powerful, but now mediocre pitcher is on the mound for the last time, pitching at Yankee Stadium. The hostile crowd is hurling insults in what becomes a dissonance of belligerent noise. The memorable lines in the movie are a resource anchor. As he stands on the mound and stares at the batter, he repeats to himself, "Clear the Mechanism," a refrain that has become through the years his trick for clearing his mind and achieving ultimate concentration. The film then lets us inside the famous pitcher's head as the noise is muffled, the volume being turned down, until it is as if he and the batter are on a deserted island, alone in total silence. The cameras let us see the raging crowd, but we no longer can hear them.

We always suggest having a powerful NLP anchor ready whenever you need it. They are helpful before a key meeting or if you feel uncomfortable or whenever you feel your state slip. The secret is to use it and for it to be subtle. You could say a word or phrase to yourself quietly in your head or just imagine that image that evokes the desired state.

We invite you to create a few anchors around your home and work that elicits resourceful states when you use them. It is important to note that intention is the key. An anchor works when you have the intention for it to work. So, when I look at the Queen Victoria Building in the afternoon with the intention to be more awake and alert, that is what will happen. If however, I just happen to glance out the window, there isn't likely to be a surge of energy running through me!

Anchors have so many uses in life, and there are already so many anchors around us. Identify those that work well for you and use them more. And identify those that produce or elicit an unwanted state, and choose to do something about those too. You are after all in charge of your mind and your results.

Day 22 –
Congruence and Parts

Congruence. It is a word that NLP seems to love. It is a state which people tend to gravitate toward and it can be relevant in every aspect of life. Until we know more about congruence, most people never think in terms of "I'm congruent with that," yet our body and our mind will let us know in no uncertain terms when we are incongruent. You know, that feeling of unease, a churning of your stomach over a decision to make, the internal battle that happens when you know something isn't right, the little voice in your mind that tells you to keep looking – and the other little voice that tells you to stop looking. That is incongruence.

One of the Prime Directives of the Unconscious Mind (functions) tells us that the unconscious mind works best as a whole integrated unit – that is, congruently. Therefore, many of the NLP processes and techniques are helping a person find congruency in their emotions, behaviors, and beliefs.

So, what is congruence? Well, do you know that feeling when you are whole, complete, in alignment, at a "yes" point, equal and in agreement with yourself or with others? This is congruence. The dictionary defines congruence as a state of agreement or being the same. Virginia Satir defined congruence as the balance between one's self and others or a context. A few days ago when we spoke about rapport with 'things' (time, money, etc.), what we were actually talking about was being congruent with things. So rapport and congruence can be very similar in many ways. After all, when building rapport with another person our aim is to get to a state of being the same.

From a personal standpoint, understanding and knowing how to reach your state of congruence is important. Being congruent means that you own whatever state you are in, whatever behavior you are having, whatever thoughts you think. Being congruent puts you at cause in your life. Conversely, when you are incongruent, you are at the effect of what is going on in your life because you can never be fully "whole" if you are also incongruent.

When a person is internally congruent about something, they are in total agreement with themselves. They are at a state of absolute yes or absolute no. You can be in congruence and be at no. Let me show you: would you actually sell one of your children? Do you have it in you to rob a bank? Do you want to do time in jail? Do you want to be homeless by choice? We have a good idea that most people reading this answered "No" to each of these questions. And not a no that says, well, maybe at some time, if it were possible (that is incongruent by the way), but a foot stomping, grounded NO!

As coaches and trainers of NLP, we are always on the lookout for congruence and incongruence. When we are training and see heads nod, eyes light up, deep breaths being taken; when we hear "aahhh" we know there is congruence with what is being taught. On the other hand, when we see furrowed brows, confused looks, tight jaws, tense shoulders, breaths held, we know there is some kind of incongruence going on. This may mean that the information doesn't fit well, that there is a question or confusion or a misunderstanding. We'll often ask this person a question and see if we can get them to a state of congruence. We know that for some people congruence comes later, once they've been able to really try something on and have time to think about it. After all, confusion is the doorway to understanding.

Tomorrow we will be looking at a few NLP processes that will assist you to create a state of congruency when there is an internal battle taking place. Today, we want to share with you tools to help you be aware of when you are incongruent; remember from state management a few days ago, the first step to managing your state is being aware of your current state.

If you can identify when you are incongruent, or when someone else is incongruent, you can use this information to get back to congruency. Let's look at some real-life examples of when it's useful to identify if you're congruent or incongruent.

If you are having an argument with your partner, are you congruent or incongruent? This, of course, is a trick question. You can be either. The real question is, are you in agreement with yourself about the stand you are taking (congruent) or are you wavering (incongruent)?

If you go to a job interview and you are feeling confident about getting the job, but you are nervous and fidgety, will you come across as congruent or incongruent?

If you are studying for an upcoming test and you are worried about not doing well or have a fear of forgetting the information you're being tested on, will this incongruence assist you or hinder your likelihood of doing well on the test?

How about this one, and this will be big for some people; how do you deal with uncertainty? Are you OK with not knowing what the future holds or are you incongruent about that uncertainty. We have found that when people can be congruent about uncertainty they can actually move through uncertainty easier. Let me give you an example of a past client. Scott owned and ran a small website design company. He was very good at what he did and his customers were very pleased with his service. Scott, however, was very uncertain about many things: where his next clients would come from, when he would be paid, if he'd have enough income to pay his mortgage, etc. His high levels of uncertainty hindered the growth of his company because he was so incongruent with uncertainty. Most of his "spare time" at work was spent worrying about his uncertainties, of adding up his debts and contemplating what would happen if he couldn't pay the mortgage. His incongruence was stopping him from spending time getting new clients and doing their work so he could be paid.

One of the first things we did with Scott was to help him to find a state of congruence with uncertainty. We have found that when people are congruent with uncertainty, which opens up mind space for inspiration, creativity, and motivation, they are able to more easily move toward what they want. In Scott's case, when he was able to become OK with uncertainty, the unknown future was not as big, scary or daunting. In fact, being congruent with uncertainty allowed him to have more motivation to make great things happen, he found that if he had certainty (which is what he was looking for before), then he wouldn't have the drive or passion that came from sourcing new clients, learning new skills and surpassing his clients expectations. In fact, not knowing where his next client was going to come from added an element of excitement and creativity that he had not known before in his company. Are you congruent or incongruent with uncertainty?

How You Do Incongruence

Let's take a look at your recipe for incongruence. Think about something you are incongruent about. This simply means something that you are currently unsure about. It might be something big like moving homes, or something small like what you are doing this weekend (if you don't know), or what the weather will be like next week. Interestingly, your internal recipe for big and small incongruence will be just about the same. If you are incongruent about if you should move home or not, you will most likely have the same internal sensations and incongruence if someone asked you to predict next week's weather with a sense of certainty. You can test this out in a moment.

OK – again, think of something you are incongruent about. And then allow yourself to really see, hear and feel what is going on inside of you as you think about that. Even right now, take a moment to close your eyes and gauge what is going on inside, then you can open your eyes and continue reading.

Now, answer these questions:
1. What internal feelings or sensations do you notice? (*i.e. a tightness in your stomach, your neck muscles tense, etc.)*

2. What do you say to yourself when you think of this?

Test this out with a few things you may be incongruent about and see how similar this sensation or state is. Then, remember it consciously. This is your state of incongruence. Remember, the unconscious mind functions best as a whole, integrated unit; and when you know better you can do better. Once you are aware of this state, you can become aware of it in real life and then you can do something about it; namely, you can become congruent if you choose to.

We can use this information about identifying congruence with other people too. If you are talking to a colleague about something and he is saying yes while shaking his head no, this is a sure sign of incongruence. Developing your sensory acuity skills, like we discussed on Day five, will help you to spot incongruence in others. To spot incongruence you can look for physiology changes like muscle tension, breathing, shift of body posture, hand clenching or wringing, leg or foot tapping, and eye narrowing, to name a few. Additionally, you will often be able to hear a change of tonality, tempo, volume, and pitch of a person's voice when they are incongruent. As you notice these characteristics, you can identify the source of incongruence by asking a question. When you know what is going on inside a person's mind by identifying this, you then have more knowledge and leverage to get this person to a state of congruence.

If you are selling a product or service to someone, it would be a lot easier to do if they were congruent with it. The same goes if you want your children to do their homework, clean their room or eat their vegetables. For yourself, if you are making a decision, it would best be made from a state of congruence.

You already know how you do congruence. You might not know it consciously yet, but you soon will. Now that you know your recipe for incongruence, do the same exercise, but this time for something that you are totally congruent about, something that you have absolute certainty in regard to; even something as simple as I am a woman (or man) can be used. Once you do this, you will know how to manage your state and be able to step into a state of congruence when you recognize incongruence.

Putting a few skills together, now that you also are aware of how to create an anchor, maybe you'd like to think about creating an anchor that will help to instantly help you back to a state of congruence.

No matter what you do to help yourself get into a congruent state, the most important aspect of this chapter is that you now know more about what it means to be congruent and incongruent. Knowing this information will hopefully give you even more tools for managing your state and stepping into your own personal power when and where you choose to.

Day 23 –
Parts Processes

Alice was a client of ours. She came to see us for NLP Therapy to help her with her "sabotaging behaviors about relationships." Alice's pattern with relationships was a fairly common one. She would get into a relationship and after a few months when it was going well she would start to put a wall up, push her partner away and slowly remove herself from the relationship until it was over. When she came to see us, she had met what she described as the perfect man, everything she had been ever looking for. Yet, she could feel this pattern starting to take hold. She was doing behaviors like avoiding his phone calls, being sarcastic, blaming him for little things.

Gary was also one of our clients. Gary suffered from overindulging in alcohol. We could call it an addiction to alcohol or possibly alcoholism, but he hadn't called it that, he called it overindulging in alcohol. This was a behavior that he did not want to have, yet it happened almost every day. He would get home from work, semi convinced that tonight was going to be different. Then he and his wife would start talking, Gary started to get stressed and needed a release. This release would start with one beer and a vow to himself that it would only be one. The next thing he would know is that it was morning and he was waking up with a hangover again.

We also worked with Oliver. Oliver was a ten-year-old boy who was brought to see us by his parents because he was having a hard time at school, in particular with mathematics. He was great at sports, but very bad at math; and he wanted to get help and do better in school. He felt dumb and not as good as many of his friends who did well in school, and Oliver compensated by being great at sports. His internal voice told him that he couldn't be a sports star and be good at school. It was literally an internal struggle for Oliver.

The simple fact is, the majority of people who walk into our private practice have some sort of conflict going on inside of them, a part of them wants to do something (emotion, behavior, thought) different, yet they aren't doing it. When a person's emotional or behavioral desired state does not equal their present state, this is a sign of incongruence.

Yesterday we talked about congruence, the state of agreement within one's self. As we found, when a person is congruent they are more likely to move in one direction versus when they are incongruent and being torn in two or more directions. Incongruence can be found in an individual person, in a family, couple, team, company, leadership team, school faculty, or any group. Whether the system is an individual or a group, if any part of the system is not aligned with the rest, there is incongruence. These parts need to be effectively negotiated in order to work together and bring about congruence once again.

One of the NLP Presuppositions is, *the most important information about a person is that person's behavior.* Observing a person's behavior will help you to identify and describe the conflict within a person. When a person says one thing and does another, or when the message sent from a person doesn't say what they mean, they are incongruent. NLP looks at all messages a person sends, consciously and unconsciously, as real and valid. For example, if you are talking to a friend who is having an argument with their partner and during the conversation your friend tightens their jaw and clenches their fist while saying, "I'm OK, really," this is a mixed message and a sign of incongruence.

When we are able to help a person identify this incongruence and then negotiate between two or more parts of the system, we can reinstate congruence and wholeness in a person, team, family, or group. Today we will be looking at a few NLP processes that are intended to bring harmony to an individual person and also to a group of people. First, let's get a better understanding about **Parts**.

According to Robert Dilts, the term "parts" is a metaphorical way of talking about the various beliefs, states, ideas, and abilities, which make up an individual's consciousness. These aspects of consciousness are parts of various sub-systems and can work quite independently from each other. As an illustration of parts in different sub-systems, let's look at two specific areas of Heidi's life: home and work. In the sub-system of home, Heidi is sometimes (often) untidy and very laid back about where things belong. However, another part of her likes structure and tidiness, specifically in the sub-system of a training room. We are looking at the same content of tidiness and organization, yet in different contexts (home and training room). Although the content is the same, the context allows each of these parts to exist due to different beliefs, states, and ideas about tidiness and organization. This illustrates two parts, but these parts are not incongruent with each other because they are not about the same thing, nor do they represent incongruence within Heidi. People can and do have different behaviors, beliefs, ideas, and states in different places. If a person is incongruent about these differences, that would be the incongruence, not the behavior itself.

The concept of parts and incongruence were first introduced in NLP by Grinder and Bandler in their book The Structure of Magic Volume II (1976). The work with incongruence and parts was inspired mainly by the work of Virginia Satir. Satir was a family therapist and one of the main people modeled to create NLP. At the center of Satir's work, she coached people to negotiate and interact with their internal parts. She developed a technique of holding a "parts party" with a family where one family member would assign other people to "stand in" for various parts of him or herself. Each person would take on the characteristics of the "part" they were assigned (e.g., anger, depression, stoic, etc.). This technique was used as a model to better understand aspects of these parts and various family members.

They even distinguished between simultaneous and sequential incongruence.

Simultaneous incongruence occurs when a person is expressing more than one message at the same time. For example, saying "Yes" while shaking their head "No," or saying, "I'm certain that I'll get this project completed on time" while having furrowed eye brows and a questioning tonality.

Sequential incongruence occurs when a person congruently expresses one message and then congruently expresses a second message at another time. Our client Gary's behavior, overindulging in alcohol is an example of this type of incongruence.

Grinder and Bandler proposed that in order to work with simultaneous incongruence, its polarities (e.g. Yes versus No) should be sorted into sequential incongruence before the parts message can be fully expressed. This is done by identifying and acknowledging the simultaneous incongruence. In the above example about getting the project completed, you could bring the incongruence to the speakers' attention and ask a question like, "I noticed that as you said that you'll get this project completed on time your eye brows were furrowed and your tonality was questioning. Do you have any doubt about getting the project completed?" We can then work with and address sequential parts. When we do this, we can communicate with each part without the other interfering or interrupting its counterpart. Ultimately, the intention of addressing each part is to negotiate a contract between them or to bring them together to create one congruent part.

Identifying Parts

In order to work with parts, we first need to be able to identify them. People will often simply tell you they have parts through their words: "A part of me is ready for a change in my relationship." This is a very blatant and overt acknowledgement of a part, and if it serves as an interference in a person's life, it is an incongruent part. That is, if the person with this part is feeling or behaving with incongruence. It is possible, however, that the part of this person that is ready for a change is congruent in itself and not incongruent with another part. People will also tell you with their physiology and body language if they have parts, they may use their hands, head, or gestures, as in, "On one hand I'd like to be in a relationship, but on the other hand I enjoy my independence." This comparison identifies not only parts, but incongruent parts.

A person's behavior will also tell you a lot about incongruent parts they have. Satir often identified parts based on categories of behavior now referred to as **Satir Categories** or Satir Gestures. According to Satir, when a person moved into one of these categories, they were demonstrating an incongruent part. The Satir Categories are: Blamer, Placater, Computer, Distracter, and Leveler.

> *Blamer* – the blamer finds faults and finds people or things to blame for problems, never accepting responsibility themselves. Blamers are more likely than the others to initiate conflict. The Blamer hides their feelings behind a tough mask.

> *Placater* – the placater is out to please, is non-assertive, approval seeking, and tends to avoid conflict. Their main concern is how people perceive them.

> *Computer* – the computer has behavior that is very correct and proper, and shows no emotion yet masks feelings

of vulnerability. Computers often appear cold and unfeeling; yet they can be a mass mixture of emotions on the inside, while appearing calm on the outside.

Distracter – the distracter seeks attention to compensate for their feelings. Rather than use positive action, they often resort to bursts of negative emotions like anger or guilt to either avoid a situation or manipulate how others feel and react. The distracter may also display behaviors of complaining, whining and sarcasm to distract.

Leveler – the leveler has an emotional balance and can relate to all of the other categories. They are assertive and have a goal of solving a problem. The leveler is the congruent part within this system.

When we see these behaviors being displayed, it sparks a desire to ask a question to find out if these parts represent an incongruence. If they do, we can help ourselves or others to move toward congruence. Of course, the Satir Categories do not need to be displayed; they are simply examples and clues for some incongruent parts.

Now, we are going to look at three NLP processes using parts: Parts Integration, Six Step Reframe and Communicating with Symptoms. As with all NLP techniques, learning from a book can be challenging as you are learning at a level of being consciously unskilled. We have mentioned this before and will again now, the best way to actually learn and develop competence of these skills is to attend a live NLP training where you can see a teaching demonstration and get supervised practice at learning these skills. When the steps of these techniques are followed, you will have a better understanding of your parts and hopefully you will be able to negotiate integration or behavior changes as appropriate.

Parts Integration

Based on the work of Fritz Perls (Gestalt Therapy) and Virginia Satir, Parts Integration is an NLP technique that elicits and sorts the polarities of incongruence in order to integrate two conflicting parts, thus creating wholeness within a person. That being said, the purpose of Parts Integration is to do just that, integrate the parts.

When working with parts integration, it is useful to keep some of the **NLP Presuppositions** in mind:
- People are not their behaviors.
- Every behavior has a positive intention.
- Every emotion is useful in some context.
- The most important information about a person is that person's behavior.

This process also presupposes the following aspects about incongruent parts:
- These parts were once part of a congruent wholeness.
- These parts were born from significant emotional events.
- Both parts have the same highest intention.
- The parts usually have their own behaviors, beliefs and values system.
- Reintegration (congruence) of these parts is possible.

When we look at examples of issues suitable for Parts Integration, you will see that the two parts are opposite to each other and the behaviors of each are also opposite to each other. Examples of incongruent parts include:

	A part of me wants a relationship,	But another part of me doesn't want to lose my independence.
Behaviors	• Goes on dates. • Seeks a relationship. • Talks to friends about wanting to be in a relationship.	• Sabotages relationships. • Makes excuses to not go out. • Avoids commitment. • Screens phone calls and messages.

A part of me wants to be good with money and create financial security,	But another part just wants to spend the money I have and not be limited.
Behaviors	• Creates a savings plan. • Makes financial investments. • Has future financial goals.	• Sabotages savings by spending. • Goes into debt by using credit cards or loans. • Feels pressured by "having" to save money and not spend.

I want to get out of my current relationship,	But a part of me doesn't want to be alone.
Behaviors	• Sarcasm. • Finding fault in partner and the relationship. • Unhappy in the relationship. • Tells friends that she wants to leave the relationship.	• Makes excuses for the relationship not being right. • "Puts up with" a bad relationship. • Tells friends that it will get better with time.

Eliciting and Integrating Parts Process

Before starting this process, identify the desired outcome and ensure the desired outcome is ecological for yourself and anyone it may affect.

1. **Identify the conflicting and incongruent parts.**

2. **Spatially anchor each part.**
   Imagine that you can imagine what each part looks, feels and sounds like as a symbol or shape. Place each part in space, in your hands or on a surface in front of you. This personifies each part and creates it into "something" the conscious mind can identify. We are not making

any meaning of the symbol, just creating something to communicate with.

3. **Identify the highest intention of each part.**
   Ask each part in turn questions to *chunk it up* to its highest intention. Questions include:
   - What is the intention of this part?
   - When you have x what does that do for you?
   - When you have x what does that allow you?

   When eliciting answers for these questions, listen for intentions versus behaviors. Chunk the first part to its highest abstract intention and chunk up to that same intention for the second part. Because these parts are in direct conflict with the opposite of itself the intentions will be the same.

4. **Notice that both parts were once a part of the same congruent part.**

5. **Identify the advantages and resources of each part.**
   Ask each part in turn what the attributes, advantages, skills, and behaviors each has that are useful and resourceful for themselves, each other, and you.

6. **Transform and integrate the parts.**
   Imagine the symbols that represent these parts can come together to create a new symbol that represents a congruent, whole part that has the same highest intention, advantages, and resources of each part – and can work together as one whole system for your highest benefit. Then, bring that new combined part inside.

7. **Test and Future Pace.**
   Imagine a time in the future where this conflict may have arisen in the past and notice what happens instead.

Six-Step Reframe

The Six-Step Reframe is a process developed by John Grinder and Judith DeLozier. Similar to the Parts Integration process, this NLP process separates behavior from intention, but this time we are not intending to integrate the parts. Instead, we are reframing the intention of parts in order to negotiate a path of working together. After all, *when we know better we can do better.* By separating behavior and intention, this can lead a person to more choices, better understanding and a way of enlisting the internal parts to cooperate with each other, thus being able to work together.

This process is useful for working with individuals as well as groups and teams of people. In contrast to Parts Integration, this process does not presuppose that the parts we are working with used to be a part of the greater whole, nor does it presuppose we can integrate these parts. In fact, we are working this time with parts that do not belong together, but their incongruence works against each other to create incongruence. You will see from these examples that the two parts do not necessarily relate to each other and they are not opposite to each other, just in conflict to each other. Most of the time, but not always, parts used with the Six-Step Reframe are external conflicts instead of internal conflicts like we see mainly in Parts Integration. Examples of parts to use for Six-Step Reframe include:

I would like a new job,	But it's too hard to find one in this economy.

I'd like to complete a degree or course,	But I don't have the time to study.

I want to start a business and work for myself,	But I want the security of having a job.

I'd like to learn more about NLP,	But I don't have the money.

We can also use Six-Step Reframe for a group, family, couple, or team of people. We simply use two opposing points of view.

Six-Step Reframe Process
1. **Identify the conflicting parts.**

2. **Separate behavior from intention.**
    Identify the behavior of each part and chunk up to its highest intention. It is not necessary for the parts to reach the same highest intention, because we are not integrating these parts but rather negotiating with them. There is a good chance that these parts may not have been a part of the same system.

    Ask each part in turn questions to *chunk it up* to its highest intention. Questions include:
    *   What is the intention of this part?
    *   When you have x what does that do for you?
    *   When you have x what does that allow you?
    When eliciting answers for these questions, listen for intentions versus behaviors.

3. **Use a conditional close.**
    In order to work together, the parts need to agree that they can and will. This pre-permission frame is necessary so you can work with any potential objections. Until this point, each part has been working independently and often in opposition to the other. Now that they know each has a positive intention, they can also begin to work together.

> a   Reiterate the positive intention of each part and validate that each intention is a good intention for you.
>
> b   If the intention is the same for both parts, ask "if both parts got X, would they agree to that?"
>
> c   If the intention is different for both parts, ask "if part A got Y and Part B got Z, would they agree to that?"
>
> d   If there is disagreement, continue to reframe the positive intent of both, identify positive resources or advantages of both and then use the conditional close again until you get agreement.

4. **Create alternate behaviors to satisfy the intention.**
   Identify 2-3 alternative behaviors that can be used to reach the positive intention of each part that does not alienate or discount the other part. If needed, enlist the assistance of a "creative part."

5. **Give permission to the parts.**
   Ask if each part gives permission to itself and to the other part to work toward its positive intention for the goodness of both and self.

6. **Ecology Check**
   Ensure that the new behaviors and intentions are in alignment with you and ecological to you and anyone it may effect.

7. **Test and Future Pace**

Communicating with Symptoms

People often experience pain when they are incongruent. A headache, backache, stomachache; even the pain of depression, anxiety, fear, stress, and the behavior of smoking or drinking can exemplify incongruence. This process was originally developed by Suzi Smith and Tim Hallbom based on the work of Robert

Dilts. Ultimately, we are working with just one part in this process as opposed to two as in the Parts Integration and Six-Step Reframe.

Because *the mind and body are connected, they affect each other*. Often the pain we notice in our life is a symptom of something else happening in our lives, and it is our body's way of getting our attention. Frequently, the part manifests itself into a physical sensation or behavior to get our intention to pay attention to what it wants and needs.

Once we become aware of a symptom, we can treat it like a part and find out what its intention is and what it wants and what it is trying to communicate to us. By knowing this, we can do something about it. For example, a headache for someone might be the body's way of telling them to slow down and take a break. Knowing this information allows the person with a headache to have a choice. Knowing this may not remove the headache, but getting its intention met will (i.e., the headache might not go away until this person slows down and takes a break).

Examples of symptoms suitable to use with the Communicating with Symptoms process:
- Any physical pain or ache including headache, stomachache, backache, neck ache, nausea, leg cramps, carpal tunnel, etc.
- Chronic fatigue, auto immune deficiency, food intolerance, etc.
- Weight gain or loss, binge eating, water retention, etc.
- Physical illness including cold, flu, cancer, constipation, etc.
- Addictions such as: smoking, alcohol, drugs, gambling, sex, etc.
- Emotional distress including fears, phobias, anxiety, depression, stress, anger, sadness, guilt, etc.

Communicating with Symptoms Process

1. **Identify the symptom, behavior, or problem that is causing a conflict.**

2. **Separate the behavior from the person.**
    Imagine an image that represents this part to appear outside of you, as if it is floating in front of you. What does it look like, tactilely feel like and sound like?

3. **Identify the positive intention of the part.**
    Ask each part in turn questions to *chunk it up* to its highest intention. Questions include:
    *   What is the intention of this part?
    *   When you have x what does that do for you?
    *   When you have x what does that allow you?

    When eliciting answers for these questions, listen for intentions versus behaviors.

4. **Contextualize the intention of the part.**
    Allow the conscious and unconscious mind to realize that this part has good intentions and it has been working as a separate system. Ask questions such as:
    *   Do you like the intention of this part?
    *   Does this part know that it's hurting you or holding you back instead of helping you?
    *   Does this part mean to be keeping you from its positive intention by using its old behaviors and methods?
    *   Does this part know that it's draining you instead of empowering you?

5. **Identify positive resources the part has.**
    Elicit and access positive attributes, advantages, skills, and behaviors that this part has which are useful and resourceful to you.

6. **Create alternative behaviors to satisfy the intention.**
   Identify 2-3 alternative behaviors that can be used to reach the positive intention.

7. **Ecology check.**
   Ensure that the new behaviors and intentions are in alignment with you and ecological to you and anyone it may affect.

8. **Test and future pace.**

Day 24 –
Beliefs

Janice was twenty-four and she had recently moved in with her boyfriend. Together they were hosting a house warming party for themselves and decided that cooking a roast would be most appropriate for their main meal. Scott, her partner, was preparing the roast in the kitchen when Janice walked in. He had it seasoned and ready to put in the oven. Janice saw the roast and told him that he was doing it wrong; in order to make the roast as juicy as possible he had to cut it in half. Scott had never heard of this technique and told her that he had made a roast before and he would be doing it his way. With a big sigh, Janice exclaimed, "Fine, do it your way, you always do!"

The aftermath of this one remark created a catastrophe of derogatory remarks, raised voices, condemnation of ever moving in together and the house warming party cancelled. With frustration and remorse, Janice called her mother to vent and talk about the situation.

"Why did you tell him to cut the roast in half?" Janice's mother asked.

With a long pause, Janice responded sheepishly, "Isn't that how you cook a roast?"

"Well, you can cut in half, but the best way is to keep it whole."

Now with more vigor and frustration in her voice Janice declared, "I learned how to cook a roast from you! I watched you for years, and you always cut the roast in half before you cooked it!"

Contemplating this news, Janice's mother replied, "Oh, you must be thinking about when you were little! The house we had back then just had a small oven, so to fit the roast in I had to cut it in half!"

According to sociologist Morris Massey, the majority of the beliefs that we have in life were created during the Imprint Period of our lives, the ages of 0-7 (see day 7 for more information). Until the age of 7 we are just little sponges soaking up information. This information becomes our truths of life, our beliefs.

We have a belief about nearly everything, and our beliefs motivate us to do what we do. Recall from Neurological Levels, beliefs are about why we do something. When a person asks the question, "Why do I do this?", the answer is most likely "Because you have a belief that supports it." That works for just about everything:

- Why do I binge eat?
  - I believe controlling how I eat means I'm in control of my life.
- Why am I bad at relationships?
  - I believe that relationships are too hard.
- Why can't I hold a job?
  - I believe I'm not working in the career I'm meant to.
- Why am I a good friend?
  - I believe friendships are important.
- Why do I get promotions at work?
  - I believe I'm a good and conscientious worker.

We have both resourceful and unresourceful beliefs. Resourceful beliefs are those that help to move us toward a desired state and strengthen the foundation of who we are and are based on a foundation of beneficial behaviors and capabilities. Whereas unresourceful beliefs are those that hold us back, interfere in our progress and sometimes make us doubt ourselves and our identity. Unresourceful beliefs are often based on a shaky foundation of incongruent behaviors and a lack of capabilities.

The easiest way to ascertain a person's beliefs is to listen to their language and watch their behavior. Language tells us a lot about the person we are. What you focus on is what you attract. Therefore, if you are thinking about what you can't do, or that you are not good enough – that will come your way. However, if your language is telling you and you are believing "I can do that, let me give it a go," then you can do that as well.

When watching behavior, if you notice a behavior that is not aligned with a person's intention, there is often an unresourceful belief behind it. For example, if a person says they would like to get a new job yet their behavior is one that is procrastinating applying for jobs, it would be worthwhile to look at any unresourceful beliefs the person may have about getting a new job. This person may have beliefs like "I'm not qualified enough for a new job," "No other job will pay me what I'm getting here," "It's too much effort to get a new job," or even "I don't like stepping out of my comfort zone." Any of these beliefs create an interference of getting a new job.

Often people have conflicting beliefs like "I've outgrown my current job and I'm ready for a promotion, but I'm not qualified enough to get a new job." This conflicting belief is known as a double bind. The way out of a double bind is to change one of the beliefs. This doesn't necessarily mean change the belief of "I'm not qualified enough," because that might be very true. It might be to change the overall belief to something like "I've outgrown my current job and I now want to get qualified enough to move to the next level." This statement (belief) provides a person with the opportunity to move forward, where the first just stops a person in their tracks.

Where Do Beliefs Come From?

Ultimately, beliefs are derived from the world around us, and they make up a big part of an individuals model of the world. While the majority of our beliefs are created by the age of seven, we are continually updating, learning and altering the truths in our life. We are trying out new things, observing other people and making new findings everyday. I (Heidi) recently worked with a client who was miserable at his job. While I was talking to him I found out that he had an office job and he enjoyed working outdoors and using his hands to create things. Specifically, he loved nature and landscaping. But he had a belief that he would never ever do manual work for a job. His father had been a laborer and always struggled to put food on the table and keep a steady job. To my client, a manual job meant instability, and an office job, like his current one, meant stability. We were able to rearrange his beliefs to support his love of the outdoors, which helped to reframe what doing a labor type job means. For the past few years, he has been working with the Parks and Recreation team on landscapes. He has never been happier and more fulfilled in his job in his life. And he gets paid well and has a very stable career.

Our beliefs can change. Sometimes it takes a while to change a belief and sometimes it can happen instantaneously. I have a friend who used to be a very fast driver. She customarily drove over the speed limit. She got pulled over frequently and was told often to slow it down. Nothing could change her belief that speeding was OK for her. Until a close friend of hers was killed in a car accident by a speeding driver. It took only one event to change her beliefs and her driving behavior forever.

With the use of NLP, we don't have to experience tragedies to change a belief, and it doesn't have to take a long time. In fact, NLP can help change a belief in a very short amount of time, as long as there is an intention and a desired state. Over the next few days we'll be looking at some ways to change beliefs. First, let's look into your world.

What do you believe to be true? As we have mentioned, your beliefs make a big impact on who you are. If you had different beliefs, you would be a different person. On day 9 we looked at values. Remember, a value is what is important to you. Each of our values is supported by beliefs. Some of those beliefs will be resourceful and some will be unresourceful. If they are unresourceful, there is a good chance that there will be incongruence or the values for that area will not be met.

Let's revisit the example in day 9. Diane wanted to change jobs because there was something "not right" in her current job, but she was unable to put her finger on the problem. When we elicited her values, this is what we found:

Value	Is this value being met?
Use/Learn Skills	Yes
Respect	*No*
Independence	Yes
Work/Life Balance	*No*
Good Money	Yes

We could go one step further with Diane and elicit the beliefs she has about her values. We could do this about each one as an exercise for her to understand more about herself and why these values are important, or we can elicit the beliefs only about the values that are not being met. In this case, we elicited only the beliefs about respect and having work/life balance. Here is what we found:

Values of Career	Beliefs and Patterns
Respect	- I know I've done a good job when people comment on my work.
	- If I don't have respect, I'm not motivated to do well.
	- Other people's opinions of me and my work matter to me.
Work/Life Balance	- There is never enough time to spend with my family and friends.
	- It's good to live a balanced life.
	- If you work too hard, life will be boring.

If any of the beliefs are unaligned with the value, we can change or alter the belief by reframing the belief or using specific NLP techniques for changing beliefs and patterns. In Diane's case, she had a few beliefs that were incongruent with her values, namely:

- Other people's opinions of me and my work matter to me.
- There is never enough time to spend with my family and friends.

The first of those two beliefs is incongruent simply because this value within her career is not being met. If it was being met, that would presuppose that she is getting the feedback and respect she wants and desires. However, her need for other people's opinion may hold her back from doing her best and consequently receiving the respect she wants.

The second belief is a double bind, "I want to balance my work and life, but there isn't enough time." As long as this belief exists in its present form Diane's value of having work/life balance will not be met.

Some NLP techniques identify the source of origin, and it's interesting to know where our beliefs come from; however, this is not really important information. So many people come into our office, tell us their problem and then ask us, "Why do I do this? When I know why I do this, then I can stop doing it." We have found that that isn't really true. Our general answer for the "Why?" question is "because."

After all, if a person needs help with anger management and we identify the source of origin of her anger problems being when she was three years old her toy was unjustly taken from her, does that mean she is no longer angry? No, now she knows why she is angry. Sure, it might help to make sense of her world, but for most people it will simply give them justification for their current behaviors.

Just as we discussed in the Meta Model day, NLP rarely uses the question "Why" as it mainly produces reasons and justification. Instead, even when we look for the source of origin of a belief, we are doing so with the intention of finding resources or *learnings* which may not be apparent. This can give us more empowerment and choice for the future.

Here is an example of how a belief gets set while simply being in the wrong place at the wrong time (if such a thing exists). One man we worked with was having trouble with relationships. He was successful at business, but not in relationships. We used an NLP technique using his timeline and unconscious mind. We went back to a memory of when he was 18-20 months old; sitting in a high chair eating. He recalled a conversation between his uncle and his father. His uncle had said something along the lines of "you can't run a successful business and be in a good relationship at the same time." At this simple age, his unconscious mind stored a limiting belief that a person can't be successful at relationships and business at the same time.

Was this beneficial for him as an adult? Absolutely not. And was his uncle speaking in his own truth or in jest? We have no way of knowing that. He was just speaking. For his uncle, it was probably true within his model of the world at that time. We don't know what happened a week from then, a year from then, or 10 years from then. But it may have been true for his uncle then. And, in the unconscious mind of this little boy, he picked this statement up and stored it as a truth. This truth or belief created interference from having both a successful business and a relationship.

A tool that we would like to introduce to you today is one we go into extensively in our Level 2 training, NLP Master Practitioner Certification. It is based on the work of Connirae Andreas on language patterns; more information can be found on the audio program by Connirae called Advanced Language Patterns. This tool is about finding **full belief statements**.

On day 7 we looked at language and talked specifically about linguistic presuppositions. We discussed that we communicate mainly at the surface level which excludes about 90% of what we mean. Let's look at the same example again that we saw on day 7. Someone says to you:

> **I should exercise more.**
>> What might you presuppose here? Maybe that I don't exercise at all. Perhaps you could presuppose that I have a desire to exercise. Or, maybe that I don't like to exercise. It could be presupposed that I know how to exercise, have a place to exercise, find importance or value in exercise. Maybe a thought could come to mind that I already do exercise, but not enough. And so many other presuppositions based on this one statement.

We can ask two simple questions to elicit a full belief statement and therefore gain even more understanding about a person's model of the world. When we can find a person's full belief statement we are uncovering the cause and effect statement or the complex equivalent (see day 10 for more definitions). This helps us to pinpoint where the belief comes from and possibly the actual issue behind it, therefore even giving more insight into the person's own model of the world. The two questions we ask, in order, are:

1. How do you know that? (effect statement)
2. What causes that? (cause statement)

Once we have the answers to these questions we string the answers together in a certain order to create a full belief statement. Let's put this into action:

Amanda:	I should exercise more.
Laureli:	How do you know that?
Amanda:	My jeans are fitting too tight.
Laureli:	What causes that?
Amanda:	I eat too much junk food.
Laureli:	You eat too much junk food and your jeans are fitting too tight, therefore you should exercise more?

When a person hears their full belief statement said back to them, this is often a reframe or pattern shift of thinking. In Amanda's case, her issue really isn't about exercising more (while that might not hurt her), it is actually about eating too much junk food.

You string the full belief statement together in this way:

Cause statement **and** _effect statement_ **therefore** _belief_.

It is best to use their words verbatim, not the words that come from your model of the world.

You eat too much junk food **and** _your jeans are fitting too tightly_ **therefore** _you should exercise more._

Let's look at a few more:

Mitchell:	I'll never get paid what I'm worth.
Heidi:	How do you know that?
Mitchell:	I've applied for a lot of jobs and never get them.
Heidi:	What causes that?
Mitchell:	I don't have the right education they are looking for.
Heidi:	You don't have the right education they are looking for and you've applied for a lot of jobs and never get them, therefore you'll never get paid what you're worth?

This example also shifts the focus to the real issue, having the right education. In this case, Mitchell is now more consciously aware of his thoughts and he can have more choice.

Katie:	I'm too busy to do what is really important.
Laureli:	How do you know that?
Katie:	My list of desires is just getting longer.
Laureli:	What causes that?
Katie:	My work is so demanding and it takes up too much of my time.
Laureli:	Your work is so demanding and it takes up too much of your time and your list of desires is just getting longer, therefore you are too busy to do what is really important.

Again, this example offers us another illustration into the power of eliciting full belief statements. Now that Katie is more aware consciously that she can't do what is really important to her because her work is demanding and takes more time, she has some possible options. She could ask for help at work, she could reprioritize work, she could put up some boundaries to ensure she has time for herself. Of course, the options that Katie chooses are hers and based on her model of the world.

Utilizing **Meta Questions** (see chapter 10) is also a great way to gain more understanding about beliefs. By asking a simple question; "What do you believe about that", you can uncover the beliefs that reside around beliefs. Here is an example of this tool in action:

Jennifer:	I get so angry about religion.
Heidi:	What do you believe about religion?
Jennifer:	I believe that it is hypocritical and unfair.
Heidi:	And what do you believe about that?
Jennifer:	I believe that God wouldn't condemn people, and religions do.
Heidi:	And what do you believe about God not Condemning people?
Jennifer:	Well, that my God will love me regardless of my choices.

By asking this simple question, it is possible to understand more about the frames of a belief and what beliefs are behind the beliefs we have. In Jennifers' example, her belief is more about the acceptance of her choice rather than religion in general. Even if it is about religion in general, the beliefs behind this have to do with acceptance of her choices. When we know this information, we can do better at helping and respecting people's model of the world.

Humans are complex. I'm not sure if dogs and cats have beliefs or not, but I'd like to think that if they did, they would be simple like "I believe I'll get fed today" and "I know I'm loved." There is a really good chance that being left alone when the puppy was three months old isn't going to leave them with issues of abandonment in their dog years. Because beliefs are so easily set, it is important to be careful about what we say and who we say it to. Remember from day 3 when we discussed the prime directives of the unconscious mind, the unconscious mind takes everything personally and is a servant to follow orders. Words have power.

Over the next few days we will be delving into some of the NLP techniques dealing with timelines. This will give us an opportunity to see how we can change and make alterations to some deeper beliefs and take more personal power back. In the meantime, start to notice what some of your resourceful beliefs are; they help you to be who you are. And notice some of your unresourceful beliefs; they sometimes stop you from being all you can be.

Day 25 –
Understanding Timeline

In 1492 Columbus set sail for the New World. The Great Wall of China was built in 246BC. The United Nations was formed in 1945. It is believed that the 2017 Rugby League World Cup will be co-hosted by Australia and New Zealand. Star Wars was released in 1977. Sydney hosted the Summer Olympics in 2000, Rio will host them in 2016. Coca Cola was invented in 1892. The internet was created in 1989. By 2014 Virgin Galactic is supposed to fly their first spacecraft with paying passengers. In 2025 Oprah Winfrey will be 71 years young. Roberto Benigni won an Oscar for Life is Beautiful in 1998. By 2020 it is expected that all cars being built will be hybrid. McDonald's started in 1955.

With little to no effort you were able to easily think about each of the above historical and future events. Each one of us easily has the ability to access past information and project future information, just by a thought. We do it every day. It is said that everything happens twice, first in your imagination and then in reality. If you think about what you are doing this upcoming weekend, you imagine it happening before it even happens. If you recall what you did last weekend, you again use your imagination to bring to mind what happened; after all you have to use your imagination, you can't physically do it again.

When people tell us that they have a bad imagination, we know that is an untrue belief. Everyone has a great imagination; the difference between a belief that says that you have a good or bad imagination is simply the process of accepting what first comes into your mind without second guessing, analyzing or needing to understand or make sense of what is coming into your awareness. Einstein is quoted as saying "Imagination is more important than knowledge. For knowledge is limited to all we now know and understand, while imagination embraces the entire world, and all there ever will be to know and understand."

We bring up the topic of imagination simply because once we start talking about Timeline, some people want more detail or information about what their mind is presenting them. We ask you to simply accept what is being presented. After all, it is a present, a gift.

Indira Gandhi was the Prime Minister of the Republic of India for a total of fifteen years. In the early 1970's (before the birth of her granddaughter in 1972), in an interview Indira was asked who she sought for advice. The Prime Minister replied, "When I seek wisdom and guidance I seek counsel from my grandmother and my granddaughter. My grandmother has passed away and my granddaughter is not yet born."

How Your Mind Stores Time

Recall from Day 2 we talked about the three minds; your conscious, unconscious, and higher conscious mind. Your unconscious mind has a way of storing time; and how you store time has some meaning into you and possibly even why you do what you do. When you think about the past, this past memory comes to you from a certain direction. It might be from the left or right, from in front or behind you, from above or below; there isn't a right or wrong answer, there is just a direction. The same thing is true for the future and even the present.

The unconscious mind is symbolic and metaphorical about everything. If a person refers to their past with a hand gesture over their shoulder or say something like "that's behind me," there is a good chance they store their past behind them. If a person uses a hand gesture in front of them to represent something they haven't yet done, their future may be stored in front of them. Often people look to their left or right when referring to their past or future. Again, this could be an indicator of how this person stores time.

In fact, as soon as we are talking about the location of a thought, we are actually accessing the submodalities of time. Someone's past might be behind them (location) and very close to them (distance), and they may have a feeling that the past is pushing them around. Similarly, I (Heidi) worked with a woman who stored her past above her and she said she always felt weighed down by the past. We have found that if a person's future is too far away, some people feel that there is no use in planning because it's just too far (even tomorrow is the future!). Or if their future is too close or too big (size), it is overwhelming and also a trigger for being stuck.

Even submodalities like color versus black and white, bright versus dim, focused versus defocused can make a difference in the timeline. If a person has a hard time accessing or remembering past events, it might be useful to elicit their timeline and understand how they store time, in particular their past. Many people who have a hard time accessing the past have stored their past as a dark place. We can use submodalities to change this and make it brighter or lighter. Some people benefit from using their imagination to do this by imagining a light switch and turning on the light. If, for example, the future looks hazy, cloudy or defocused, it might not be a pleasant thing to think about. Therefore you could help the person to clear it up and bring it into focus.

The concept of timelines and using the submodality of timelines was first officially introduced to NLP by Connirae and Steve Andreas. In 1983, Bandler began to reveal the general structure of submodalities and that created a curiosity in the Andreas' about the submodalities of time. They found that people not only had widely differing timelines, but the shape of a timeline determined aspects of personality. They also found that by changing a person's timeline they could change these personality traits without changing any individual events within the timeline. In a workshop on Advanced Submodalities taught in 1984, Connirae and Steve shared this new information with their students. At the 1985 NLP Conference in Denver, Colorado Steve made a three-hour presentation about timeline entitled Just in Time.

The number of different oriented timelines that we have come across in the many years we've been doing this is amazing. Again, there is no wrong or right. How some people store time, however, doesn't work as well as others. For example, if a person stored both their past and future in front of them, the unconscious mind may get confused about where it is going. If the past and future looked like the below image, the past may get in the way of thinking about the future.

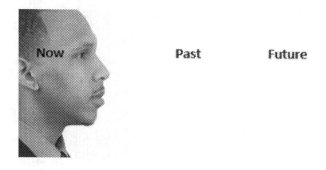

Based on how the timeline is situated, we can presuppose what meaning it might have for someone, and to verify our supposition, we can ask questions to clarify. In the early 2000's, Heidi started to notice many of her clients that came to see her were high achievers, but not actually achieving much. She became very curious about what was happening that might be similar with them all. She looked into various meta programs, beliefs, and values and didn't find many similarities. Then she looked at how each stored their timeline, in particular, how they stored their future. The below illustrates what she found.

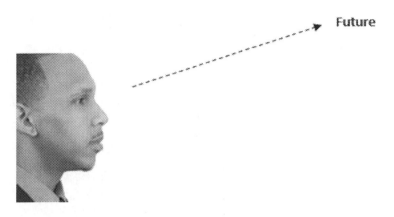

Future

The common denominator behind this over achieving mindset and underachieving behavior was the storage of the future above and in front of them, so they had to virtually look up to see their future. Heidi asked questions such as:

Does it ever feel like you're climbing a hill to get to your future? Does it sometimes feel like you take one step forward and then slip back? Do your goals sometimes feel just out of your grasp? Do your goals ever feel too high to be achieved?

Interestingly, the majority of these questions were answered affirmatively. Heidi then set about to alter or change the timeline to see what difference it made. To change a timeline you simply move the submodalities; we'll look at this in more detail in a moment. In this case, Heidi invited her clients to simply drop their future to be aligned with their eye gaze. The result: things became easier and these high achievers became high producers as well; this time without the lofty goals.

We can make meaning of a timeline, and remember if you do, check your assumptions because they will most likely be coming from your own model of the world. NLP allows us enough flexibility that if our assumption does not fit with the person we are talking with, we can drop our notions and go with theirs.

After all, who is best to tell you about another person's model of their own world?

Eliciting the Timeline

Let's take a quick look at how you store time, without much thinking, just answer the following questions.

1. Remember what you had for dinner last night. Where does this past memory come to you from? Point in that direction.
2. Imagine what you will wear two days from now. Where does this future memory come to you from? Point in that direction.
3. And, as you think about now, right here and right now. Where is your Now? Is it inside or outside of you?

If you could draw your timeline, what would it look like?

As we mentioned before, store time can tell us about the personality of a person. Based on meta-programs introduced in the early 1980's, the categories of **In Time** and **Through Time** were used to understand the time orientation of individuals.

In Time

If your timeline runs inside you, regardless of where your past and future are situated, this timeline is known as In Time. Most likely it is your Now that is inside you. Having your timeline inside you creates many possible personality characteristics including: getting lost in time, associated to now, prone to being late, not aware of 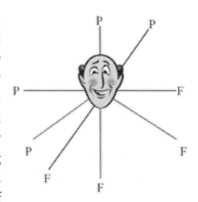 time passing, tend to not plan, and prefers spontaneity to plans.

Through Time

If your timeline is all outside you, regardless of how your past and future are situated, this is known as Through Time. The personality characteristics of having a Through Time timeline includes: takes time personally, dissociated from now, finds it hard to do nothing, aware of time passing and are good with time, natural with time management, tends to plan ahead and is aware of deadlines.

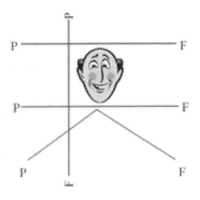

Changing the Timeline

As we have discussed, changing a timeline is as simple as moving around submodalities. Of course, there needs to be an intention to change a timeline, and a need to do it. After all, the way you store time may work perfectly well for you. There are uses, however, in changing a timeline. For example, you may want to consider changing a timeline if:

- The submodalities are incongruent.
    - The past may be in front of the person.
    - The complete timeline is inside of a person.
    - The future is high or behind a person.
    - Part or all of the timeline is dark or hard to see.
    - The past/future is too close or too far away.
- You want change from in time to through time.

To change a timeline, first access the current location and relevant submodalities and propose the person to move or make appropriate changes. When the timeline has been changed, test the change for suitability by asking a question like "What do you notice now about this new location?" You can also suggest the changes stay by locking it into place with their unconscious mind.

We can also use anchors to initiate a timeline change. If, for example, a person was through time and they wished to be more in time at home to play with their children or relax and do nothing, an anchor to move them from through time to in time might be useful. In this case, the anchor could be a word, touch, or movement that unconsciously changes the timeline from being oriented as through time to in time.

Being able to change a timeline and the metaphors of a timeline provides us with even more possibilities to be in charge of our mind and results. We invite you to change the orientation of your timeline for a few hours, just to see what the difference is. What would it be like to be in time if you are normally through time oriented? Or to have your past in front of you and the future behind you? You can always change it back!

Clearing the Now

In 2004, after working with a number of clients that presented with overwhelm, Heidi devised this NLP technique of clearing the now. Remember, your conscious mind can hold 7 +/- 2 chunks of information, more than this and we often feel very overwhelmed, easily confused and at times extremely tired. Often, if a person is holding more than 7-9 chunks, many of those chunks do not belong in their "now" or their present conscious awareness.

What you did yesterday, an hour ago or even 10 minutes ago belongs in the past. What you will do tomorrow, where you're taking your family on the weekend or what you might be learning from this book tomorrow, all belong in the future. What belongs in the now is just this. You, this book, and anything else that might be happening right here and now.

The intention of this process is to clear your now and organize your past and future so your unconscious mind has an easier time accessing and storing information. We have found that many people have a belief of "If I don't hold something in my mind at all times, I'll forget it." Yet, when was the last time you forgot how to breathe or tie your shoes without thinking about it?

The following process has been scripted so you can use this with someone else. After familiarizing yourself with it, simply read what is in bold.

1. **Close your eyes and relax and notice that you can see and feel your now.**

2. **I'd also like you to notice what is in your now… what is in your now?** You may get a list, or a simple explanation – but most often you will find that there is a lot more in their now, than what is happening… now. **Good, and notice too how it is organized. And now, I'd like you to notice that your unconscious mind can organize what is in your now… putting the like with the like – family with family, work with work and so on… that's right… and let me know when it is all organized.** Wait for response.

3. **Good, now I'd like you to allow your unconscious mind to notice what is in your now that isn't really a now thing… for example, that thing that you are going to do later today – it may be better in the future… and that thing that you just did before coming here, it may be better in the past. Notice that your unconscious mind can organize and transport those things in your now that belong in your future and past and put them there – in your future and past… good, and let me know when that is done…** wait for response… keep them cleaning out their now until the only thing left is you and your

client – their now… everything else should be either in the future or past. Once that has been completed:

4. **Good, now I'd like you to go into where you store your future – and notice what is here… allow your unconscious mind to now organize the things here – putting the like with the like, even organizing the near future and the distant future… let me know when this is all organized…** wait for response…

5. **Good, now I'd like you to go into where you store your past – and notice what is here… allow your unconscious mind to now organize the things here – putting the like with the like let me know when this is all organized…** wait for response…

6. **Good, now float back to now and notice the expansiveness of having just this, just here and just now in your awareness. So much more can be possible now, can't it… When you're ready, come back to now and open your eyes.**

Today we've been looking at how you store time, the meanings of your timeline and how you can change it and clear it when appropriate. Tomorrow we will be looking at how you can use aspects of your timeline to make specific changes, alterations, and enhancements to events within your timeline. As you have seen, time is an important quality which can prove to be useful with the skills of NLP.

Day 26 –
Timeline Processes

There are two main ways to use timelines within NLP. The first we looked at yesterday; it deals with changing the structure of the timeline by altering the submodalities. By first understanding in detail how a person's timeline is structured, we can reorient the timeline to support the kind of person they want to be. When the structure of a timeline is changed the person lives with a new relationship to time. The second way to use timelines is what we'll be looking at today: working with the events within the timeline to alter or enhance these memories by adding resources and sometimes using different perceptual position to view events and gain more understanding from a different point of view.

Even without a great conscious memory, it is fairly simple to access past events on the timeline. Doing this does take a fair amount of trust of your unconscious mind. Remember, your unconscious mind stores every memory that you have ever, ever, ever had. Just because you may not consciously remember something doesn't mean you don't remember it. We can also revisit the NLP Presupposition that states: *You have all the resources you need to achieve your desired outcome.* This presupposition is based on the notion that in each event in life, you are automatically storing resources (attitudes, behaviors, skills, learning, etc.) that will help you to be better tomorrow. Therefore, we can access via the timeline resources and events in the past which we don't have conscious access to.

On day 11 we looked at States and State Management. Anytime we are eliciting a state, we are actually accessing our past timeline. Let's look at the words used to elicit a state: Can you recall a time when you were energized? Can you remember a specific time?

Go ahead and go back to that time now, just step into that time when you felt very energized – see what you saw, hear what you heard and really feel what it feels like to be energized.

Accessing Past Resources

We can use the timeline to access resources to be used now and in the future, we can also access resources that would have been beneficial in the past. Let's take a look first at accessing resources for now and the future.

If a person were to give a speech to a large group of people they don't know, what resources might be useful? Perhaps confidence, knowledge of what they are talking about, and energy could be useful. By eliciting past events when a person has had these states we can add them as resources now. This can be done either by creating an anchor of some sort, or by simply inviting their unconscious mind to bring those resources to the now and seeing through their present eyes and body and recognizing how having those states would alter and enhance their ability to give this speech.

By accessing past resources, we are using our history in a positive manner to influence the present. There is no need to recreate the wheel every time. Recently we worked with a young woman who worked in a sales capacity and wanted to have the "knack" that her colleagues seemed to have. She believed that she had to over prepare her sales meetings in order to flow and be comfortable, when her colleagues seemed to just be able to spontaneously flow and be comfortable with little preparation. She identified through second positioning her colleagues that they were comfortable, authentic and natural in their presentation style. We accessed each of these states from her past and brought these states to her present. When we tested what she was experiencing as she thought about her next unknown spontaneous sales meeting she replied, "I have the knack!"

Accessing Future Resources

We can also access resources for the present that we may have in the future. One of the very first NLP processes that Heidi experienced was one lead by Robert McDonald call the Wise Old Sage. This process has to do with seeing and talking to your older self. This is a great exercise to do with yourself. Here is the gist of how it works:

Imagine a person across from you who is kind and loving toward you. As you watch this person, you can recognize that this person is actually you; an older and wiser you. Very old, near the end of your life, but not dying. Feel the love and compassion from this person sitting opposite you, and then move to their space and sit down in this person, seeing the present you through their eyes. Through the eyes of a wiser, more mature and more knowing self.

From here, you can share knowledge, understanding, and gain learning from your older self. Yes, you are using your imagination and the unconscious mind doesn't know the difference between imagination and reality. From your older self you can gain so many resources that you can bring back to your present self and walk into your future with more purpose, personal power, and positive intention.

Additionally, we can access resources from a future event that we have planned which hasn't yet happened. This is useful if you are unsure of what to do or how to do it, and also useful if you are feeling unresourceful feelings such as worry, anxiety, or fear about a future event. This is a simple process known as **Clearing Anxiety and Worry**; let's look at this technique through an example.

Emily was planning a dinner party at her house with some close friends the next weekend. However, she was wracked with fear and worry that everything would go wrong. Her thoughts rolled around in her mind, "What if I burn the food," "What if no one likes what I've cooked," "What if no one shows up," "What if…"

On the verge of canceling a lovely dinner with friends, she made an appointment to see Laureli for some coaching. This type of worrying showed up in many areas of her life and she wanted to stop this pattern. After assessing Emily's present state, Laureli asked her what she wanted. What would the best outcome be? With that in mind, Laureli then invited Emily to use her timeline and float into the future, to after the successful completion of her dinner party. She then enquired, "Where are those old worries?" to which Emily responded, "They are gone." Logically of course, they would be gone because the event completed successfully. Laureli then asked Emily to unconsciously store any learning, resources, and understandings that will help her to create this outcome now. Finally, she had Emily come back to the room and access those resources, learning, and understanding to have them as a way to begin and end the task.

This is a simple process that can be taught to people who are prone to worrying and anxiety. One definition of worrying is a hallucination of what hasn't yet happened. This is a great process that tells the unconscious mind, "I really do have what it takes to do this!" It's a great reminder *that you are in charge of your mind, and therefore your results.*

Gestalt

A big part of the beginning of NLP was within Gestalt Therapy. The word Gestalt is a German word, roughly translated to a grouping or culmination of something; usually in NLP, this *something* is normally emotions and behaviors. Gestalt Therapy is a form of psychotherapy that focuses on personal responsibility and making self-regulating adjustments in a situation. It was developed in the 1940's and 1950's by Fritz Perls, Laura Perls, and Paul Goodman. You may recall that one of the people modeled in the beginning of NLP was Fritz Perls.

Richard Bandler was originally a student at Foothills College in Los Altos, California, before transferring to the University of California, Santa Cruz. While in Santa Cruz, Bandler began studying Gestalt Therapy. It has been shared by one of the other early NLPers, Frank Pucelik, that he and Bandler studied and modeled Fritz Perls doing Gestalt Therapy with clients. Bandler worked for the publishing company *Science and Behavior Books* and had access to tapes and transcripts and began to copy the therapeutic approach of Fritz Perls. After a while, they were doing a "cleaner" version of what Fritz was doing because they were modeling what they observed working, not the theory behind it.

Bandler and Pucelik started a Gestalt practice group and attracted the attention of other students and also an Associate Professor of Linguistics, John Grinder. Shortly thereafter, Bandler and Grinder worked on what we now know as Neuro-Linguistic Programming. Gestalt is a large part of NLP, the Wise Old Sage technique we looked at early comes from a Gestalt technique known as the Empty Chair. Bandler, Grinder, and a team of developers helped to find ways to use aspects of Gestalt and Family Therapy to affect and make direct changes to the gestalts people have in life.

As we mentioned, a gestalt is a grouping or culmination of something, like an emotion. So, we each have gestalts about everything – happiness, anger, love, joy, sadness, etc. The unresourceful gestalts sometimes contain so many repressed memories yet an ammunition of unconscious information that it creates a self-fulfilling prophecy. One of the best ways to describe a gestalt is like a chain of pearls. Let's imagine a gestalt of anger. Each of the pearls on the chain represents an event which contains unresolved anger. Once the strand gets long enough (which doesn't take much), it takes only a look from someone, or the sound of their voice, or something very minute to break the chain, sending all of the pearls scattering everywhere (a burst of anger would be the emotional outcome). The chain then reformats itself, this time with a new pearl, making the chain even stronger.

From our research and understanding after working with people and gestalts for so many years, each of these pearls contains three elements: (1) the memory of the event, (2) the emotions of the event, and (3) the learning from the event. Therefore, when someone is working from a gestalt, at that precise time, they have access to fewer resources yet have the resources they need.

Again, let's use anger as the example. Barry was an executive at a telecommunications company and he had been told over many years that he needed to attend an anger management course. It wasn't until Barry was diagnosed with high blood pressure and told that his anger might actually kill him that he did something about it. In general, Barry wasn't an angry man, but he was a man that you didn't want to be around when he erupted. It seemed to Barry and everyone around him that something else took over when he was angry, and he felt very out of control of his emotions and behaviors. After an episode of anger, he would often get equally as angry at himself in privacy because he knew better. However, a gestalt is an anchor for a response (anger), and when triggered, the gestalt takes over as an automatic response, and it is as if we are out of control.

The origin of this gestalt is most likely sometime during the Imprinting Period between the ages of 0-7. Although we have no scientific proof, we have also found many gestalts that have been passed down genealogically through the genes. I'm sure you've overheard a comment such as, "You have your grandfather's anger," perhaps a genealogical gestalt is the answer to how this could occur. The first event of a gestalt is normally one that is significant in nature; in NLP we call this a **significant emotional event** or SEE. In the event of an SEE, the unconscious mind, which naturally stores a memory and learning of an event while letting go of any unuseful emotions, does not have its same faculties. Instead, it stores everything together: the learning, emotion, and memory. Imagine one solitary pearl. The next time something like this happens, the unconscious mind again stores this information as a second pearl. Then, the unconscious mind starts to look for similar instances and the emotion behind the gestalt becomes a self-fulfilling prophecy. In Barry's case, there was something specific that triggered his anger, yet he was unconsciously unaware of what it was.

We can use the timeline to trace back the source of origin or root cause of a gestalt, and we can then identify consciously and unconsciously what there was to have learned from this event, what emotions were present that can be let go and we can dissociate from the memory and store it with the others.

Although not directly modeled, the therapeutic timeline based work in NLP can be closely related to Boud, Keogh, and Walker's model of learning. Their model consisted of three stages:
1. Returning to and replaying the experience,
2. Attending to the feelings that the experience provoked, and
3. Re-evaluation of the experience.

In recollecting what took place during the experience, they assert that exploring "the feelings evoked during the experience" is of particular importance. More specifically, we need to work through any negative feelings that have arisen and eventually set those aside, while retaining and enhancing positive feelings. If the negative feelings are not addressed, what commonly happens is that learning and transition becomes blocked (trapped in a gestalt). In the re-evaluation stage, our aim is to use this experience as a way of getting ready for new experiences and new learning.

A reasonable definition of learning could be, "Learning is a relatively permanent change in behavior or in behavioral potentiality that results from experience." Or as Maples and Webster state more simply, "Learning can be thought of as a process by which behavior changes as a result of experiences."

Bateson asserts "that lessons too complex to grasp in a single occurrence spiral past again and again, small examples gradually leading to greater and greater implications." In other words, we continually recycle our past experiences, especially those events that were ambiguous, mysterious and incomplete. What was once barely intelligible may be deeply meaningful a second time, and even a third. Bateson went on to observe that one way to acknowledge this spiral is to encounter familiar issues within unfamiliar environments.

The meaning of experience is never permanently fixed; thus, the text of experience is always open to reinterpretation. Usher, Bryant, and Johnston have proposed a "map" of experimental learning. With this model, "learning does not simplistically derive from experience; rather, experience and learning are mutually positioned in an interactive dynamic."

Clearing Patterns

One aspect of NLP is about the patterns and programs we run in life. If we come across a pattern of emotion, behavior, or thought that is not congruent with what we want, there are many ways to change that pattern. Today we will be looking at two change techniques that are intended to change the perception of the past, gain access to more resources and therefore create a new and more beneficial pattern for the future.

Unconscious Pattern Change

This technique, like many others, requires the use of imagination and trust of the unconscious mind. Until this technique is understood at an unconscious level, it is often easier to be lead through it by an NLP Practitioner. Once you are more familiar with the steps and intention of each step, it becomes easier to facilitate yourself through this process. As before, we recommend learning NLP in a supervised environment where you can receive feedback and learn the best ways to lead and be lead.

In this particular technique, we will be working to clear or release a gestalt by using the unconscious mind to find its root cause. There is an extremely good chance that you do not consciously know the root cause. Even if you think you do, we encourage you to stay open to other possibilities. Earlier we talked about Barry. He was quite sure that his anger stemmed from being in the Army, yet when we traveled along his timeline to access the source of origin, the memory that came to mind was of him sitting in a highchair screaming and angry because he wanted to get down yet he was trapped.

It is important to note at this time it is not important whatsoever that you consciously recall the memory. When we use the technique, we will notice emotions, but visual recall is unimportant. Some people access past memories visually, many do not.

1. Think about the emotion, behavior, or thought you want to clear.

2. Access the timeline and trust your unconscious mind to take you to the exact moment in the past where this pattern began. Trust your unconscious mind to take you there, even without needing to know where or when you were.

3. When you get to this time where the pattern began, notice what emotions were present.

4. Trust your unconscious mind to store any learning or resources that were available, yet you didn't know or see them at the time. *The storing of learning is a very unconscious process, you don't have to consciously be aware of what there was to have learned.*

5. When you know the learning has been stored, float out of this event and further into the past, so you are above and before this event happened. Where are the emotions? Have they disappeared?

6. Allow your unconscious mind to look forward to now and trust your unconscious mind to float back to now, but only as quickly as you can store the learning from any other similar events, store the learning and let go of the emotions all the way back to now.

When you test this process, the outcome should be a dissociated memory of the emotions of the gestalt versus the actual emotions.

Visual Kinesthetic Dissociation

The VK Dissociation process, as it is commonly known, is a powerful technique for dealing with painful or traumatic experiences. The intention of this process is to dissociate or separate a visual experience from the feelings it produces. For example, a person may have a visual anchor that creates a strong sense of unwanted feelings, without any actual action taking place. This association of an image and a feeling is known as a synesthesia. The VK Dissociation is one of the techniques that the NLP Research and Recognition team received a grant for to study with war veterans (see www.nlprandr.org for more information).

This is one of the earliest techniques developed in 1976 by Bandler and Grinder. It is a synthesis of techniques used by Dr. Milton Erickson and the spatial sorting process used in Gestalt Therapy. Over the years the process has been updated to include the use of a person's timeline, which makes it easier to follow.

1. Recall for a moment the experience which you are associated with (present state).

2. Remember a time before this event when you were safe, before it had happened. In your mind see this time, being safe, on a movie screen in black and white. As if you are watching an old movie of someone else.

3. Now, recall a time after present state when you were safe and resourceful again. *If there hasn't yet been a time, project*

into the future and imagine a time. Step into this time after the event, when you were safe again. See it through your own eyes as a full color movie, feel the feelings of being safe and being resourceful.

4. In a moment, you are going to rewind this movie very fast all the way back to the black and white image. Ready, rewind. *This should take 2-3 seconds.*

5. Now, seeing the black and white image, fast forward all the way to the color movie.

6. Continue to rewind and fast forward rapidly, shifting the eyes as you move in your mind. Do this 5-6 times before asking, "Now, think of your old present state. What do you notice?" If the strong emotions are still present, continue to fast forward and rewind.

The power of the unconscious mind is amazing. We have assisted thousands of people over the years with these timeline techniques. People who used to cower at the sight or thought of something are now living happy, peaceful lives without their trauma from the VK Dissociation process. Individuals who have had years of unresourceful emotions, behaviors, and thoughts are working with new unconscious patterns. And people who had previously felt as if they didn't have the tools to succeed reached within themselves to access resources and accomplish what they set out to do. These are just a few timeline based techniques, ultimately the possibilities are endless.

If there is a desired state which is more beneficial than what a person has now, there is a way to alter the present experience and make a shift. Using timeline techniques is a powerful and non-evasive way to work with past events and help the unconscious mind to let go of the past and access resources for the present and future. As Dr. Milton Erickson said, "It's never too late to have a happy childhood."

Psychological Comparison

Because the foundations of NLP are within psychotherapy, we find it interesting to compare NLP with some of the other therapeutic modalities, which are somewhat similar.

Model	Focus	Agents of Change	Theorists
I. Social	Interaction of person, behavior and environment	Change in how one interacts and behaves in a social context	Bandura, Rotter
II. Behavioral	Observable behavior	Learning via conditioning and modeling	Guthrie, Hull, Pavlov, Skinner, Thorndike, Tolman, Watson
III. Cognitive	Thoughts and thought processes	Change in how one understands and thinks about the world	Ausubel, Bruner, Gagne, Koffka, Kohler, Lewin, Perls, Piaget
IV. Humanistic	Subjective experience	Support of individual natural motivation to seek full potential.	Maslow, Rogers
V. NLP	How senses are used to create representations of the world	Enrichment and alterations of representations	

Day 27 –
Strategies

Golf. It seems to be one of those games that people either love or hate. There really doesn't seem to be much in between. Those that love it are not necessarily good at the game, but they love it nonetheless.

Have you ever tried to create a bouquet of flowers to look as good as a professional florist? Sure, they've gone to school for this skill, but some people can do it naturally. It's amazing.

Other people find a zone while they are running and they can continue to do this sport for hours at a time. Personally (Heidi), I only want to be running if someone is chasing me! Yet, it would be good to find that kind of zone. Some people find it while meditating, or cooking, or knitting. In fact, we all have the ability to find our zone.

Have you ever wondered how some people can do things so easily? Have you ever wondered how you can be motivated about one thing and not about another? Are you curious why some people do what they do? Something that makes a great NLPer is curiosity. Curiosity about how things work, and this curiosity comes without rules about how things should be done. To be able to have an investigatory mind is a good thing; it allows you to be curious, find the recipe for how something is done and then use that recipe to replicate what you've found. As Bandler said, "NLP is an attitude and a methodology which leaves behind a trail of techniques."

Have you ever baked a pie? I love baking pies. If you've never done it, it might seem a bit daunting. After all, it's a pie. But, once you have made a pie you know that it is one of the easiest deserts to make (even your own crust). All you need is a step-by-step recipe, the ingredients, and some time.

You already do this in life. You have a recipe for everything that you do. Everything. How you get up in the morning, how you fall in love, how you keep a job, how you motivate yourself, how you procrastinate, how you brush your teeth, how you stay healthy (or not), how you laugh, how you tell a joke, how you live. Some of the recipes work extremely well, others need a bit of help, but they all work without you thinking about it.

The recipes that we use in our lives are called **Strategies** in NLP. A Strategy is the internal sequence and the order you do something to get a specific result. Our strategies are very unconscious – in fact, if you asked a florist how she arranges the flowers so beautifully, she may know the external steps of arranging flowers, but there is a great chance that she doesn't know what her internal steps are. The same is true with the golfer and runner. They may know what they do externally to enjoy the game or get into their zone, but the internal strategy is most likely a mystery.

Strategies are a mystery simply because we are unconsciously skilled at so much of what we do in life. You don't have to think about or even know your strategy for waking up, you just do it. You don't have to think about how many times you chew your food before you swallow, you just do it. You don't have to think about getting dressed, breathing, going to the bathroom, smiling, falling asleep, or laughing at a joke; it just happens.

When was the last time that something happened in life and you got angry? Before you got angry, did you stop for a moment and think to yourself, "This would be a good time to use my emotion of anger, I'm going to get angry now"? Or, the last time you heard a good joke, did you pause at the end and contemplate, "That was a good really good joke, I'd like to produce a belly laugh now"? Most likely not. To have or have to have that much conscious input into our responses would make us into robots instead of the humans that we are.

But, when you did get angry (we all get angry, we may just each show it differently), your mind and body did something so quickly without you thinking about it that produced the state of anger. When you see someone that you find attractive, your mind has a recipe that it is following to give you the conscious awareness of being attracted to someone. If you are good at being relaxed in tense situations, this means your mind is able to easily follow its recipe for relaxing without thought. There is a good chance that you won't know specifically how your unconscious mind gets you to a certain state but one this is certain; your unconscious mind follows a specific sequence to get you there.

We have strategies for everything. Here are just a few examples:

Love	Decision	Relaxation	Creativity	Tension
Hate	Motivation	Disgust	Sports	Procrastination
Learning	Happiness	Fun	The Zone	Sex
Boredom	Loneliness	Forgetting	Meditating	Remembering
Parenting	Managing	Buying	Waking Up	Wealth

Using a simple tool you can elicit someone else's strategy and use it with them. For example, if you can identify the motivation strategy of your children, you can use that strategy to get them into a motivated state when necessary. Or, if you are selling something, you can elicit someone's buying strategy and use their specific strategy with them. You could even elicit someone's decision making strategy and use their strategy to help guide them to the direction you want them to make.

One note here before we go on. Often people ask us a question like, "So am I going to be using a person's strategy to manipulate them?" And the short answer is no. With any aspect of NLP, you cannot make someone do something they do not want to do. We make a concerted effort to keep ecology in mind when working with any NLP techniques, Strategies included. If I am trying to sell a $2,000 watch to someone who doesn't need the watch, can't afford the watch and doesn't want the watch, no matter what tools I use I am not going to sell that watch. However, if I'm trying to sell this $2,000 watch to someone who needs a watch, is in the market for a high-end watch and is comparing my watch with my competitor's watch, if I can elicit his buying strategy and use it with him, I will have a much better opportunity of making that sale. Manipulation, no. Influential communication with ecology, yes. By understanding someone's strategy you can simply make it easier to communicate your message in their way to get the outcome you are after.

OK – let's move on. We looked at the tool for eliciting strategies a few days ago. **Eye Accessing Cues.** By watching someone's eye patterns while in a conversation about how they do something, you will be able to elicit a person's strategy. Let me tell you two things up front: (1) eliciting your own strategy is challenging. Short of taking a video of yourself we haven't found a good way to get an accurate understanding – so this is mainly a tool to use with other, and (2) while not impossible, learning how to elicit a strategy from a book is difficult. This is absolutely one of those skills that need hands on, practical guidance and coaching to master. However, once you do master this skill it becomes one that you can use all the time.

As you've noticed by now from watching eye patterns over the past thirteen days, people's eyes move a lot. We know from the chapter on Accessing Cues that where a person's eyes go has meaning. We can ascertain if someone is seeing, hearing, feeling or thinking something just by watching their eyes. An NLP Strategy is elicited in three steps:

1. **Associate someone into a past experience you want to elicit the strategy of.**

2. **Engage them in a conversation about how they did what they are doing.**
3. **Watch for accessing cues based on the how.**

We won't beat around the bush here – there is a lot going on to master this skill and it will take some time. And, that time is worth it. While you are first learning to understand eye patterns, it is sometimes hard to also be involved in a conversation. So, the first step to being good with Strategies is to be good with eye patterns. Then, the next step is to be able to listen, follow and participate in a conversation while identifying eye patterns and at the same time identifying if what someone is telling you is just the story (painting the picture) or if they are telling you about the actual strategy.

One way to differentiate between story and strategy is by listening to what they are telling you. If it is information to help you understand where they are, what they're doing, who they're with, why they are there or anything else that paints the picture, it is just content and part of the story. You are listening specifically for the story to shift to how they did something.

- How they knew they were attracted to someone.
- How they knew they were going to make a specific decision.
- How they knew it was time to exercise.
- How they knew to buy a certain item.
- How they knew the spelling of a specific word.

A few months ago, I was chatting to a friend about being healthy. She told me that her motivation for exercising was very low and she wanted to figure out how to motivate herself. Well, this was a great opportunity to use strategies. In a conversation, I simply found out something else that she is easily motivated by – going to the horse races was her answer. So I asked her to remember when she was going to the last race and invited her to step back into the time just before she went, when she was motivated and excited and ready to go to the races. Then I asked her to tell me how she knew she wanted to go to the races.

My friend is the same as most people – before she actually got to the how, she told me about where it was, when it was, why she went, how she got there, who she went with, what she wore, who she placed bets on, and finally, after me reiterating "how did you know you wanted to go to the races," her story changed into finding out about the race and deciding to go. It was this specific part of her story that I was extremely interested in.

In this part of the conversation, which spanned over about 2 minutes of our 15-minute chat about the races, her eyes made some very distinct and direct movements. Eye movements from a Strategy will normally be quite sharp and quick. And, even more interesting, the person's words may not match their eye movement. For example, a person might say I felt really good to be outside, but their eyes moved to Vr. If this were a part of a strategy, the notation you would make would be Vr, since this is where their eyes went.

For my friend, when she was telling me about finding out about the race and deciding to go, her eyes moved in this order: Vc, Id, K.

From this Strategy I know the following information: when she gets motivated she does so because she: (1) sees a constructed image in her mind, (2) talks to herself, and then (3) gets a feeling.

This was our conversation once I knew her Strategy:

> Heidi: Can you imagine what you would see (Vc) if you were exercising regularly.
>
> Amber: I'd see a more fit and healthy me.

Heidi:	And when you are more fit and healthy, what do you say to yourself (Id) about exercise?
Amber:	Well, that it's easy, it's good for me and I can do it.
Heidi:	Excellent! And when you do it, what do you feel (K)?
Amber:	A sense of excitement, motivation and a desire to do it!
Heidi:	Cool, so do that again. Imagine seeing a fit and healthy you, hear what you tell yourself and then feel that sense of motivation. Do that a few times.

What we just did was we triggered Amber's motivation strategy for exercise by modeling her strategy for doing something else she was motivated to do. The mind just knows the state of motivation, it doesn't really care what the topic is.

Let's look a bit more in depth at what is going on to make a Strategy work. In Amber's situation, she has a three-step motivation strategy: Vc, then Id, then K. In that order and sequence.

Step 1 –	Visually construct an image. For Amber, this could be imagine doing a task, or imagine being done with a task. You will need to calibrate for a best-fit.
Step 2 –	Talk to yourself about the topic. For Amber, this was motivating self-talk. It could have been very logical. Again, you'll need to calibrate.

Step 3 –   Feel a feeling. Amber had a good kinesthetic feeling of excitement and motivation. The emotions, feelings, and states could be different for everyone. For Amber, this could have been feeling the sweat on her skin, feeling her heart beat and even feeling the motion of a treadmill.

The very first accessing cue of a strategy is known as the **Lead Representational System** (LRS). The LRS will be different for every Strategy a person has and is not at all related to a person's Primary Representational System (see Day 6). If the LRS is not activated, the Strategy won't be triggered. And, if the sequence of accessing cues does not happen, the Strategy won't finish. The order of the Strategy is of utmost importance.

In Amber's Strategy, if she doesn't get a constructed image, her Strategy will never start. And, even if she gets a constructed image, if she doesn't then talk to herself, the Strategy will never finish. Finally, after Vc and Id, Amber's Strategy requires a positive K, which is the motivation. If the feeling is negative, the Strategy won't be complete and the motivation will not come. Only when her recipe for motivation is followed exactly will her Strategy become engaged. This explains why in normal situations she wasn't getting motivated for exercise – her motivation Strategy was not being triggered. Instead of employing her motivation strategy, Amber may have been unconsciously using her *I-deserve-a-break-today* strategy.

You can teach a person's strategy to them or simply use their sequence via words for them in the future. For example, next time I wanted to motivate Amber to do something, let's say I wanted to motivate Amber to come to the museum with me, I could say something like:

Can you imagine some of the new displays at the museum? I know there is a new Human Body exhibit – imagine seeing inside of the working body and how interesting that would be (Vc). What do you think about that? The workings of the body. I told myself before that if I can find a way to know more, I should (Id). It's a good feeling to know more – so I wonder, when do you feel like coming with me (K)?

Will this work every time? No. But, knowing her Strategy, I am likely to be more influential when I can communicate at an unconscious level with Amber and appeal to her internal Strategy rather than just my words alone.

If you know your own strategy, you can kick-start it like this too. And you can also feed back a person's strategy to them to engage the Strategy at will, like I did with Amber above. If I want someone to make a decision in my favor, I can elicit their decision making strategy and then use my words in that order to fire the strategy, I could even use my words in an email in the order of their Strategy. If I am using a person's unconscious recipe to entice their Strategy to fire off while communicating with them, I am more likely to get my desired state.

Getting your skills of identifying and making meaning of eye patterns is the first step to building success with this tool, and differentiating content (story) from the strategy is the second most important skill to have. Once you have developed these skills, the world is full of strategies and you can become a master at influencing with ecology, by using a person's strategy.

Strategy Elicitation

When eliciting a Strategy, the person's words are only important to differentiate between words that are telling the story or about the strategy. We are only interested in the words that correlate to the strategy.

1. **Associate to a remembered experience relating to the strategy you wish to elicit.**
   - Buying – can you remember when you bought your necklace? In your mind, can you go back to when you bought it – right back, as if you're there now?
   - Motivation – can you remember a time when you were really motivated? In your mind, take yourself back there now – step into what it is like to be really motivated.
   - Decision – can you recall a time when you made a good decision very easily? Step back to that time now. Feel what you felt and see what you saw when you made that good decision.

2. **Elicit what was happening from a *how* point of view.**
   - Buying – when you bought your necklace, *how* did you know to buy that one? What was going on?
   - Motivation – when you were motivated, *how* did you do this? *How* did you get motivated? What was happening?
   - Decision – when you made this good decision, *how* did you do it? What was going on?

3. **Watch for eye accessing cues based on the *how*.**
   a   The content or the *story* is not important to the strategy.
   b   The strategy will come solely from the eye movements, not words.
   c   Most strategy eye movements will be very sharp and quick versus searching type movements.
   d   Most strategies have 2-5 steps which will begin to loop.

4. **Feed back the strategy sequence and calibrate.**
   Use your words as a story to feed back what you believe the strategy to be and calibrate for correctness.

Day 28 –
Neurological Levels

"You cannot solve a problem at the same level it was created,
you have to go to a higher level." – Albert Einstein

Have you ever felt completely congruent about something? Aligned in your behaviors, beliefs, and identity? This full-level congruence feels great, doesn't it? How about the other way around? Have you ever felt incongruent about something, but in a way that you can't quite pinpoint? Is it sometimes like you are doing all the right things, but you are not moving anywhere? Or maybe you know what to do, but you just can't get yourself to do it. This can be on a personal level or even within a team, group, or company.

When we can identify where we are stuck we have a greater opportunity to work on what isn't working and create more alignment with ourselves, our team mates, our family, or with a project, problem issue, or idea. To identify this, we use the NLP tool of **Neurological Levels** to pinpoint a level of incongruence and then, as Einstein purports, work at the level above it.

Neurological Levels was adapted by Robert Dilts from the work of anthropologist Gregory Bateson. Bateson identified four basic levels of learning and change, each one having a higher degree of abstraction than the one below it.

In the Dilts model of Neurological Levels, there are six hierarchical levels. Each experience we have flows through these levels to help create our model of the world. By listening to someone's language, it is possible to ascertain which Neurological Level they are on – and perhaps stuck on at times, unable to move forward or backward. Neurological Levels are very useful when building a deeper level of rapport, when identifying where someone is stuck, and when doing personal change work using the skills of NLP.

Today we will be looking at each level independently, so you can gain an understanding of how to identify where a person may be trapped and how you can work at the higher level. We will also be looking at an alignment process you can use to realign the levels and create congruence within these levels.

The Neurological Levels

There are six Neurological Levels, and according to Robert Dilts they are in a hierarchy – each one leading and creating a foundation for the next. However, Dr. Michael Hall looks at it differently – he sees Neurological Levels as more of an investigatory tool without sequence or order. In our professional opinion, we lean more toward Dilts' idea of a hierarchy; we will explain our reasoning as we process through the levels. The individual levels, in order from highest to lowest are:

- Greater Whole
- Identity
- Values & Beliefs
- Capabilities
- Behaviors
- Environment

Now, let's take a look at the levels from bottom up. We will use three running examples throughout these levels; we will give you examples of statements you might hear at each level to indicate that a person is stuck at that level. The examples are:

- **Example 1:** a woman who is underperforming in her job
- **Example 2:** a man who has just ended a relationship
- **Example 3:** a teenager who is having a hard time studying for exams

Environment – *where and when*

The level of Environment deals with the **Where and When** something is happening. No matter what is happening in our lives we have an environment, which is why this is the base level of Neurological Levels. A lot of the time, when someone is *stuck* at the level of environment they have a lot of excuses for what is going on.

In order to help someone at the level of environment, we can go to the level above this (behaviors) to create behaviors that will help to combat the environment issues. For example, if someone can't read because the room is too dark (environment), they could employ a behavior of turning on more lights, getting a lamp or moving to a brighter place.

- **Example 1:** It's just too noisy to get anything done. I can't concentrate here. Every time I start something new I get interrupted.
- **Example 2:** This is just the wrong time for me to be in a relationship. I can't find the right woman in this city. She lived too far away for me.
- **Example 3:** My desk is too cramped to study at. I don't have a good place to study. My brother keeps bothering me.

Behaviors – *what*

The level of Behaviors is about **What** a person is doing. While people are not their behaviors, a person's behavior is one of the most important information we can find about a person. If a person's behavior is not aligned with their intentions, there will be incongruence. And, if a person does not see an alternative behavior, they may need some new skills (capabilities) to help them reach new understanding.

In order to assist someone who is stuck at the behavior level, we can go to the level of capabilities. For example, if someone is trying to lose weight yet they keep binge eating (behavior), they may benefit from gaining the capability of using determination, strong will, and having the ability to say no.

- **Example 1:** I can't get myself motivated. I keep doing the easy tasks first. It seems like I have to redo a lot of my work.
- **Example 2:** I put up walls when someone gets too close. I stopped calling her so she would get the hint. I get jealous and clingy with women I date.
- **Example 3:** I try to do too many things at once. I need to allocate specific time to study. I check my emails while I'm studying.

Capabilities – *how*

The level of Capabilities looks at **How** a person does what he does. This is about the skills and strategies a person uses to accomplish (or not accomplish a task). Remember the NLP Presupposition that says *everyone has all of the resources to achieve their desired results*? This Neurological Level is about just that. Sometimes people do have the skills, but they lack the belief. Therefore, to assist someone with a capability deficit, we cannot only *teach* them skills (if applicable), but we can also work with the beliefs a person has.

For example, if someone said, "I'm just awful at keeping my car on the road," I can presuppose that this lack of capabilities is upheld by a belief of "I'm a bad driver," or something of that nature. Until we address the issue at the level above it (beliefs and values), there is a chance that skill boosting alone won't fix it.

- **Example 1:** I don't know how to use our new database. I need someone to show me how to do my job better. I'm really bad at managing my time.
- **Example 2:** I don't know how to love. I wish someone would teach me how to trust people. How do other people make relationships work?
- **Example 3:** I need a good structure for studying. How do some people just remember information so easily? I don't know how to study properly.

Beliefs and Values – *why*

The level of Beliefs and Values is about **Why** a person does what they do. We've already looked at values, which are what is important to a person. In the next few days we'll look at what is true to a person; their beliefs. This is an important level because, in our professional experience, the majority of issues reside at this level. Our beliefs and values are one of the strongest indicators of patterns of emotions, behaviors, and thoughts.

Interestingly, there are many NLP techniques that work at this level, yet they are actually working at the level of Identity. For example, if someone has a belief that they cannot communicate effectively, this belief will impact on who they are and how they present themselves to the world. By changing this belief, their identity will invariably change too.

- **Example 1:** It's not important for me to be the best. I'll never be a great employee. I can't do my job any better.
- **Example 2:** There just aren't any good women for me. It's important for me to find someone who will be a good mother. I can't show my emotions.
- **Example 3:** I'll never remember everything. It takes me a long time to learn something. Some people just have a gift for doing well on tests.

Identity – *who*

The level of Identity is about **who** a person is. Each of us may have a different identity based on all of the previous levels, starting with environment. To illustrate this, think about who you are at home and at work. You may be a different person at each. Imagine you are in very important meeting, there is a good chance that your identity would be different in this meeting versus if you were at a park playing with children. The environment, the behaviors you have, what you are capable of, and the beliefs and values you hold create who you are in a certain context.

We find that people often get *stuck* at the level of identity if they have undergone changes or have somehow let life get in the way of living. To assist someone who is stuck at this level, we work with the unconscious mind at the level of Greater Whole to create a new identity based on the person's desired state.

- **Example 1:** I'm a loser. I'm an underperformer. Lowest on the totem pole; that's me.
- **Example 2:** I'm a loaner. I'm a perpetual bachelor. I'm a heart breaker.
- **Example 3:** I'm dumb. I'm a slow learner. Just call me stupid.

Greater Whole – *what else*

The level of Greater Whole looks at the big question **what else**. This is the most abstract Neurological Level and often the most important. Some words to describe the Greater Whole include spirituality, nothingness, everything, purpose, collective consciousness, or soul space. Ultimately, it is that place which exists everywhere, yet nowhere, and is above and beyond our conscious awareness. Some people who are on a search for meaning or life's purpose may get stuck at this level, yet in our experience this only happens if someone is trying to be too conscious (thinking) about being unconscious.

By listening to the words a person uses, we can often identify what Neurological Level a person is caught in. This can allow us to better respect the person's model of the world, choose the right NLP tool to use and even to help them understand what is going on in their life with more clarity.

Working within the Levels

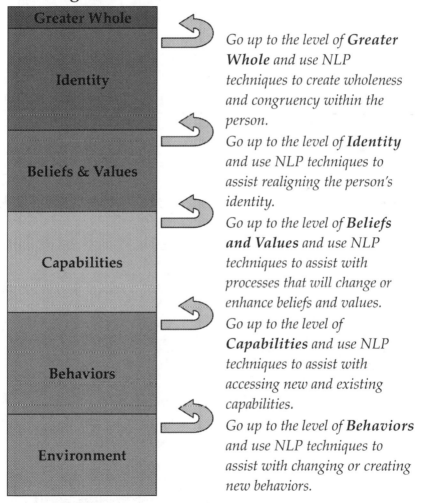

Go up to the level of **Greater Whole** and use NLP techniques to create wholeness and congruency within the person.

Go up to the level of **Identity** and use NLP techniques to assist realigning the person's identity.

Go up to the level of **Beliefs and Values** and use NLP techniques to assist with processes that will change or enhance beliefs and values.

Go up to the level of **Capabilities** and use NLP techniques to assist with accessing new and existing capabilities.

Go up to the level of **Behaviors** and use NLP techniques to assist with changing or creating new behaviors.

A tool that encompasses the Neurological Levels which is often used to create more clarity and understanding is known as **Neurological Levels Alignment**. This is one of the main processes we use when people are fixed at the level of identity.

The Neurological Levels Alignment process is useful to align the levels when there is an issue, problem, or stuckness that you may not be aware of the cause or origin. This is a process that usually produces clarity, understanding, and an internal progress forward, rather than change or clearing as some other processes.

Often we do this process as a standing and moving technique using spatial anchors. That is, you will physically step into each different level and associate with it. This often assists the person's unconscious mind to be more free and associative with these states. It is important to trust your unconscious mind rather than contemplate and think too much.

Neurological Levels Alignment

Meta	Environment	Behavior	Capability	Beliefs & Values	Identity	Greater Whole

1. Stand in **meta position** and think of the issue you would like more clarity about.
2. Step forward into the level of **environment** and notice what you see and hear when you are in the environment where this issue takes place.
3. Step forward into the level of **behavior** and notice the behaviors you have when this issue is happening.
4. Step forward into the level of **capabilities** and notice what you feel, see and hear that you are capable of.
5. Step forward into the level of **beliefs and values** and notice what beliefs you have about this issue and what is important to you about it.

6. Step forward into the level of **identity** and notice who you are when this issue is happening.

7. Step forward into the level of **greater whole** and just let yourself be here for a moment. Letting go of everything and just connecting to that which is above and beyond and greater than you. Let your unconscious mind store any learning or understanding from this level which will assist you going forward.

8. Step back to the level of **identity** and notice what is different. Who are you now? Store any learnings from this level and bring all of those learnings back with you.

9. Step back to the level of **beliefs and values** and notice what you believe to be true now. Again, store any learning or understanding at the unconscious level.

10. Step back to the level of **capabilities** and notice what you are capable of now. Trust your unconscious mind to store any additional learning and bring all of your learning back again.

11. Step back to the level of **behaviors** and notice what new and resourceful behaviors you have now. Store more learning from this level which will continue to help you.

12. Step back to the level of **environment** and notice how even where and when this issue used to happen is different. Again, trust your unconscious mind to store any learning from this level.

13. Step back to **meta position** and once again think about the issue. Notice what has changed, what you now know and what options you now have.

14. Come back to now and open your eyes.

Day 29 –
Outcomes and Goals

What if every person on this planet had within them the latent prospect of greatness and true unlimited abilities? What if just by expanding your awareness and thinking in new ways, you could literally rewire your own brain to have the life you want?

NLP gives us the understanding and methodology to help people think and develop beyond their "now" awareness, by using past experiences to create the present and future that they want.

One of our favorite inspirational quotes that remind us that we are more comes from Marianne Williamson: *"Our deepest fear is not that we are inadequate. Our deepest fear is that we are powerful beyond measure. It is our light, not our darkness that most frightens us. We ask ourselves, who am I to be brilliant, gorgeous, talented, and fabulous? Actually, who are you not to be? You are a child of God. Your playing small does not serve the world. There is nothing enlightened about shrinking so that other people won't feel insecure around you. We are all meant to shine, as children do."*

A very important component of creating anything in your life is to realize that your unconscious mind is constantly eavesdropping on everything you say, do and think and making it real. We are the creator of our reality, good or bad; it's how we manage our thoughts and actions that make the difference.

A study conducted in 1979 on students in the Harvard MBA program is a popular example of setting goals. The students were asked this simple question: Have you set clear, written goals for your future and made plans to accomplish them?

Only three percent of the graduates had written goals and plans; 13 percent had goals, but they were not in writing; and a whopping 84 percent had no specific goals at all.

Ten years later, the members of the class were interviewed again, and the findings, while somewhat predictable, were nonetheless amazing.

The 13 percent of the class who had goals were earning, on average, twice as much as the 84 percent who had no goals at all. The three percent who had clear, written goals were earning, on average, ten times as much as the other 97 percent put together. In spite of such proof, most people don't have clear, measurable goals that they consciously work toward.

We realize that what a person earns is not the only measure of success; however this study really emphasizes the power of the mind and the intention behind the goal. What we want to share is how to set yourself up for however you measure success. Knowing how to set your goals and outcomes is important, how to keep on course is of key importance.

ATTENTION + INTENTION = TARGET
Start by setting a goal and an outcome and know what your intention is for having the goal, so you can pay attention as you keep on target. There is an intention behind everything that you do. You got out of bed today, not because it was your goal, but because there was an intention behind it. Perhaps it was to start the day, or go to work, or school, or attend to something. If for some reason you start to pay attention to other distractions that come along while you are getting out of bed, then they become what you focus on. This can hinder how effectively you get out of bed and perhaps how you experience your day. Being aware of the intention is part of goal setting as it tells you what you need to be paying attention to. We often say, "Energy flows where attention goes." When you focus your attention on your intention, it keeps you on target.

Intentions are what you intend to happen, not a laundry list of what you want. It may be useful to think about intentions in terms of what/how you intend to be versus what you intend to do.

For instance, my intention as I (Laureli) write this chapter is for it to be understandable to everyone who reads it. With this intention in mind, I can pay attention to being comprehensive while still being conversational as I write. In our NLP trainings and with many of our clients, we have a task of writing a daily intention. Having a daily intention can help you to attract to you what you want and set you up for success moment to moment. Some examples of intentions that people use daily include:

- Today I intend to have fun.
- Today I intend to be a good learner.
- Today I intend to listen to others.
- Today I intend to stay on time.
- Today I intend to be healthy.
- Today I intend to stay open to possibilities.
- Today I intend to acknowledge people.

Some other examples are: to connect with others, be caring, attract wealth, be healthy, be in my genius mind, observe, giving, and loving.

We find that when people set an intention every morning it sets their day. It is like writing a diary at the beginning of the day stating how it will be versus at the end of the day how it unfolded without direction. We encourage you begin making an intention each day for the next two weeks, so you can experience how it affects your life. The rewards will be plentiful.

Every thought we think, every word we speak, and every action we take happens because of what we are paying attention to, consciously or unconsciously. Where our attention is focused moves us in the direction of a future experience or outcome.

When a person sets an intention, they are creating a connection with their future by linking knowledge from the past and how they conduct themselves in the present. The words used when setting an intention send a message to the unconscious mind, which is activated whenever you focus attention and action toward it. This is where the magic happens.

We would like to share a quote from the movie *What the Bleep Do We Know* by Dr. Joe Dispenza. He is sharing information about how he creates his day. We find that this quote captures the essence of setting intentions and what can happen.

> *"I wake up in the morning, and I consciously create my day the way I want it to happen. Now, sometimes, because my mind is examining all the things that I need to get done, it takes me a little bit to settle down, and get to the point, of where I'm actually intentionally creating my day. But here's the thing. When I create my day, and out of nowhere, little things happen that are so unexplainable, I know that they are the process or the result of my creation. And the more I do that, the more I build a neural net, in my brain, that I accept that that's possible. It gives me the power and the incentive to do it the next day. I say, I'm taking this time to create my day, and I'm infecting the Quantum Field. I'll use living as a genius, for example. And as I do that, during parts of the day, I'll have thoughts that are so amazing, that cause a chill in my physical body, that have come from nowhere. Then, I remember that thought has an associated energy that has produced an effect in my physical body. Now, that's a subjective experience, but the truth is that I don't think that unless I was creating my day to have unlimited thought, that the thought would come."*

Goals

A goal without an outcome is just a dream.

Goals are lifelines to the future and are an important part of the human experience. We develop and grow and bring about a phenomenal change in our lives as we achieve our goals. When people set a goal it is because it gives them a target or an outcome. In fact, goals and outcomes work together. Having a goal without an outcome is like running a marathon without a finish line. Goals are what you want and outcomes are what you get.

Goals are driven the same way as an intention because both are about what you want. However, the goal is usually the big picture and the intentions of the goal are more specific. Someone may have a goal to lose weight and their intentions may be to look better, fit into their clothes, be healthier and have more energy. If this person is paying attention to what they are being deprived of, or thinking about food, they are probably going to end up fighting with themselves and possibly not achieving their weight loss outcome. The goal may remain the same, but the outcome may not be achieved or it may change. It is much harder to stay on target when you are paying attention to anything else but your intention. The trick is to know when you are off course so you can make corrections; you can only do this if you know where you are heading.

Apollo 8, the first manned mission to orbit the moon, was almost dropped because the engineers could not figure out how to keep the rocket on course. They could only keep it on course 20% of the time, thus being off course 80% was not acceptable. However, they decided to approach the issue in a different way. Instead of focusing on being off course, they developed a superior measurement gauge that allowed them to monitor their course as they made constant small corrections. The result was they maintained their course by monitoring and making adjustments the entire journey. Like our ancestors who navigated the seas, they kept their eye on destination as they made their way through untold obstacles.

> *"The greatest achievement was at first, and for*
> *a time, but a dream." --Napoleon Hill*

The main reasons people do not achieve their goals are:

- They do not take ownership of them, they wait for someone or something to fulfill their goals.
- They don't dedicate time to achieve the goals.
- They focus on what they don't want or other distractions.
- They blame other people for not allowing them.
- They are not motivated enough to complete them.

Creating a Well-Formed Outcome

In NLP, we have a set of six criteria that thoroughly refine the objectives of the goal to create what is referred to as a **well-formed outcome** (WFO). It is more systematic than the well-known process of SMART (specific, measurable, attainable, realistic, and timely) goal, as it has all the criteria already built in. It is more formed that the SAFE (see, accept, feel and express) tool and more encompassing than the 7-habits goal setting formula. In fact, in our opinion, from all of the goal setting tools we have examined, the NLP Well-Formed Outcome is by far more superior to all.

By creating a well-formed outcome, you are directing your mind and your behaviors with steps that can be measured, timed and checked for ecology. Generally, goals and outcomes are in alignment with your conscious and unconscious mind; however, there are some cases when a goal or desire is in conflict. When this happens it causes a clash of wills within the person. This can happen when there is something called a secondary gain or where an unconscious intent takes preference over a conscious goal. For example, one of our clients had just completed her certificate in remedial massage. It was her goal and dream to have her own practice and do the work she loved. As we were formulating her well-formed outcome, she found what we called secondary gain. She realized that if she had a successful practice, then she would have to move from her subsidized government housing which she loved, as she would no longer qualify to live there. By knowing this, we were able to help her with her limiting beliefs in order for her to align her outcome.

Remember, NLP is outcome and solution based, thus a well-formed outcome gives us steps to co-create that makes it achievable, powerful and verifiable. Let us look at the steps to creating a well-formed outcome.

Well-Formed Outcome

Allow yourself at least 20-30 minutes to complete a well-formed outcome. The following example looks at someone who wants to lose weight.

1. **Describe what specifically you want.** State this as a positive versus what you do not want. Many people know what they do not want and sometimes start out listing those first.

   Example: *I want to lose weight. If someone said, "I don't want to be fat," I would ask, "When you are no longer fat what will you be?"*

2. **State what you can do and what is within your control.** Make a list of things that you can specifically do to move in the direction of the outcome?

   Example: *I can exercise three times a week, watch what I eat and cut sugar out of my diet.*

3. **Where, when and how specifically will you get your outcome.** Define and emphasize the specific environment

if appropriate environment, the context or situation required to reach the outcome. State specifics to give the unconscious mind directions.

Example: *instead of "I want to lose weight," state specifically how much weight to lose within a given time such as three pounds over two months.*

4. **Describe in sensory words specifics about your outcome.** What would you see, hear, feel.

   Example: *instead of "I want to be a size 10" say, "I want to see myself fit into my clothes, feel comfortable with what I'm wearing, feel like I have more energy and feel healthier." When stated in visual auditory and kinesthetic language it makes it real and less vague.*

5. **Put the outcome into sizeable steps that are doable.** What steps will you take to create this?

   Example: *instead of "I will lose 20 pounds" state, "I will exercise on Mondays, Wednesday and Fridays, keep to my daily diet, and lose three pounds a month."*

6. **Discover the resources you have and will need to get your outcome.** List the resources you have and the resources you need to reach your outcome.

   Example: *I have a system that I can follow; I have the time to exercise, I have the discipline to follow through. I need motivation or small rewards to keep me vested; I need a personal trainer; I need to be kind to myself and praise myself more.*

7. **Specify the evidence of when you will have your outcome.** How will you know when you have reached your outcome? Make this full of rich imagery so you can picture yourself having these things happen.

Example: *I will fit into a size 10, my scales show that I've lost my desired weight; I wear a bikini to the beach. I would say to myself, well done, I knew you could do this.*

8. **Check the ecology.** Does this outcome fit in your life and have no consequences to yourself or others or is it incongruent? Sometimes we do have outcomes that affect others, this is not a problem. It is important that you look at the big picture to determine if your outcome will give you what you want so you can be you. Sometimes by not changing we enable others to be co-dependent or lazy. When you change, other people can change. It has to start somewhere.

By setting your WFO, you have given your unconscious mind steps and evidence to pull you toward your goals and outcome. Remember to pay attention to your outcomes intention. If you find yourself becoming distracted, we suggest you stop and review your well-formed outcome and make adjustments to keep on course.

Future Goal

Once you have created a well-formed outcome you can use a simple NLP technique known as Future Goal. This technique will help to solidify your outcome and orient your future to welcome it. This is a timeline process where you will drop your outcome into your future. This will allow your unconscious mind to draw you toward it.

1. **What is your outcome?** Using your answers from your WFO, be specific. Remember to state it positively, make it specific, give it a time frame and that it is measurable.

2. **How will you know when you have this? What is your evidence of having achieved this goal or outcome now?** Review # 7 from the well-formed outcome.

3. **Close your eyes and imagine you have this goal now. Notice what it feels like to have accomplished this goal. Notice what you see, hear and feel.** *Get an image or representation of your outcome and let yourself imagine it as vividly as possible.* **Now make this even more compelling by turning up the volume, increase the feelings, making the pictures you have brighter** (fine tune the submodalities), **make it so compelling and when it is as good as it can get, turn it into a photo that you can hold in your hand.** *This will dissociate you from the outcome. This is an important step because if it were to be put in associated, the unconscious mind may think it has already achieved it and not draw you toward it.*

4. **Now imagine you can float above yourself holding that photo and allow your unconscious mind to float out into the future, to an unspecified time in the near future and allow your unconscious mind to take charge now. And watch as you now release that photo and you watch it float down, down into your timeline, and it lands in the exact right place.**

5. **Turn and look toward now, and notice all of the events between then and now are realigning themselves to support you in having achieved this goal now.**

6. **And float back to now and open your eyes.**

Author of Creative Visualizations, Shakti Gawain wrote, *"Every moment of your life is infinitely creative and the universe is endlessly bountiful. Just put forth a clear enough request and everything your heart desires must come to you."*

When we are creating our future, we are directing our mind to think and take action toward our desired outcome and taking charge of our lives. We use well-formed outcomes all the time. Anytime we have a goal that we want to achieve, we spend time creating a well-formed outcome, and then putting that goal into the future. As you are already aware from the past twenty-nine days, the unconscious mind is very powerful. And, while we have tools that will help us to live our lives better, we might as well use them!

Day 30 –
Putting It All Together

This entire topic of NLP is a huge one. In the past thirty days, we have barely scratched the surface of NLP knowledge, skills, and techniques. In a book or in a classroom there is only so much learning that can happen. However, as we've iterated before, the best way to learn NLP is by partaking in a live classroom situation where you can be supervised, stretched, challenged, corrected and developed in your NLP skills.

Recall the New Guinea proverb: *knowledge is only a rumor until it is in your muscle*. Reading this book has given you knowledge. However, without experience it will continue to be just a rumor.

As you have seen, there is so much that NLP can be used for. We can easily categorize the use of NLP into three categories:

- Personal Development – using NLP with yourself

- Business – using the NLP knowledge and techniques in a business setting

- Coaching – using the NLP knowledge and techniques with other (life coaching, parenting, teaching, training, therapy, etc.)

Ultimately, we have found that once a person learns NLP it is virtually impossible to limit its use in one area. Even just knowing and understanding the NLP Presuppositions starts to reframe and alter old ways of thinking and being.

Remember – NLP is an outcome solution based tool. We have to know where we are going before applying NLP; and you can't make someone change if they don't want to. We like to think of NLP as a *do-with* tool versus *do-to* like some other tools which can fit into personal development, business, and coaching tools.

Today we will be looking at how we can bring what we have been talking about for the past month to a close. To begin this task, we'd like to introduce you to the **NLP Formula.**

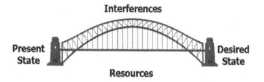

The NLP Formula

No matter how you are using NLP, there is a simple formula to follow. It contains four specific steps:

1. **Present State** – The first thing we want to do before anything else, with ourselves or others is to identify a present state. The present state is where you are at the moment in a given context or in general. To identify a person's Present State we generally use an NLP technique known as Personal History. You can find two versions later in this chapter.

2. **Desired State** – Now that you know where you are, the next step is to identify where you want to be. If there is no desired state other than the present state, then there is really nothing to do. If however the desired state is different, we can start to delve into the specifics of what someone wants. To elicit a person's Desired State we typically use a processed called **Achievable Outcome**. You can find two versions later in this chapter.

3. **Interferences** – Throughout asking various questions to identify a person's present state and desired state, you would have been using a variety of NLP techniques, namely meta model, calibration, sensory acuity, and listening to the language patterns of the person you are working with (or yourself). You are identifying interferences; that is, anything that might block, limit, hinder or get in the way of moving from the present state to the desired state. Interferences might be unresourceful beliefs, unuseful behaviors, habits, thoughts, or emotions, incongruent parts, negative self talk, etc.

4. **Resources** – The final aspect we are interested in for this formula is resources. Resources are anything that can be useful or beneficial for a person including attitudes, attributes, things, skills, etc. Money, time, curiosity, confidence, charisma, and desire are all examples of resources. We are interested in two main aspects about resources: those resources you have which will help to achieve the desired state, and those you need to achieve the desired state.

Once this formula is understood we can then apply various NLP techniques to clear, change and eliminate interferences and build and access resources. Given the number of NLP techniques available, the NLP Formula makes it easier to choose what technique to apply in various situations. No two people, issues, or desired states are the same.

Often our students ask us questions like this one: "I have a friend who is a smoker and wants to stop, what NLP techniques should I use?" No matter what the content of this question contains, our answer is relatively the same each time: "It depends completely upon the person's present state, desired state, interferences, and resources they have and need." That is the long version of "there is no one-size fits all." However, as long as you know the information that makes up the NLP Formula, you can help just about anyone with just about anything.

NLP is not a quick fix, nor is it a one-time-stop to fix something. Some people claim that NLP can cure, fix, alter or change something with just one technique, or just one NLP session. NLP is fast. NLP does work well. And NLP encompasses so much. Yes, some things can change very quickly – however, our goal is always to create long-lasting change, not just a quick change. In order to create a long-lasting change, we want to understand and apply as many NLP techniques as necessary to assist someone. Generally, we are working with an individual for two to ten one-hour NLP sessions. In each session we are using 2-3 different NLP techniques and always coming back to the NLP Formula to see where we are on the journey toward the Desired State. Sometimes the techniques we choose are simply asking questions, using the meta model, sharing a metaphor and reframing. As you have seen, NLP is so much more than closed eyed change processes.

Day-to-Day NLP Skills

If you ask either of us how much NLP are we using in our lives, we'll say quite a bit. After all, it's our job! However, we mean the day-to-day skills of NLP. While we use NLP techniques like Parts Integration, Anchoring, Submodalities, etc., these tools are used much less than the major part of NLP – that is, using the language of the mind to affect patterns we run. Each day, and probably most moments of each day, we are using the skills of NLP that really can make a profound difference in life.

> **NLP Presuppositions** are not just ideas that NLP is based on, they can be a very useful tool to help you navigate life. Recalling, remembering and using them help you to have more flexibility, choice, and wholeness.

Rapport is an imperative skill that can be used multiple times each day. Building an unconscious connection with another person will allow communication to flow easier and it is also easier to respect another person's model of the world when you have rapport.

Primary Representational Systems help you to discover the primary manner in which a person communicates. You can use this information to mirror back to a person in order to communicate at a more unconscious level. This is also a person's learning style and can be used to help facilitate the learning process.

Meta Model allows you to uncover information through asking questions which has been distorted, deleted and generalized. With the Meta Model, not only are you able to better understand someone's model of the world, you also have the opportunity to provide more choice and options from making discoveries.

Sensory Acuity & Calibration is a skill that is very useful for identifying incongruence, unconscious nonverbal communication and helps you to ask better questions to calibrate the meanings of verbal and nonverbal changes.

Meta Programs provide you with an opportunity to understand someone's model of the world and to communicate more effectively with a person. You are able to listen to a person's words and observe behavior to identify various meta programs and use those specific meta programs to mirror back to a person, therefore communicating at a more unconscious level.

Eye Accessing Cues is a fascinating tool that you can use to recognize what modality a person is accessing in their mind. This information is useful to ask better questions, identify possible incongruence and understand a person's model of the world.

Perceptual Positions allows you to see something from a different perspective. By associating into yourself (first position) you have the opportunity to connect with emotions and create a heightened sense of awareness. Second position helps you to understand something from another person's perspective, or to take a dissociated view from yourself. Third position, or meta position, is the magical fly on the wall perspective; this objective position gives you the chance to make even more choices and see alternatives more clearly.

Reframing is a skill which is useful with yourself or someone else to help gain a new perspective about the content or context of a situation. This allows you to shake up a person's model of the world and helps to gain more choice.

State Management can be a moment-to-moment skill. Because you are in charge of your mind you are in charge of your results. By identifying your present state, you have the option to continue, enhance or change the state you are in at any moment in time.

Neurological Levels is an outstanding investigatory tool that can assist you to identify where you or someone is fixed. Remember, most often we need to go to the level above the one which we are stuck at to make a change.

Ericksonian Hypnotic Suggestions are valuable in everyday conversation. This tool provides you the opportunity to be unconsciously influential.

NLP Techniques

If you are a coach, therapist, personal trainer, parent, or other type of "helper," you may have more opportunity to use and practice the skills of using the NLP change and enhancement techniques as compared with others. However, you do have some new tools to use when appropriate. We want to reiterate that the best way to learn the use of these skills is by attending a live training, where you can practice and refine the skills in a learning environment.

Eliciting Values is a great investigation tool which will help you to know why something in life doesn't seem right, it can also be used to build motivation, hire the right employees, maintain a good relationship and maintain congruence by respecting your model of the world, or with a person you are involved with.

Submodalities are a simple, yet effective tool that you can use to understand a person's model of the world and provides you with a skill to enhance and change emotions, thoughts, and behaviors.

Swish Pattern is a technique used to change an unwanted habit or behavior into a more resourceful one.

Compulsion Blowout Technique is a technique used to alter a compulsive emotion, thought, or behavior so it is no longer acting as an interference.

Resource Anchor is a technique used to consciously set a positive anchor for the purpose of using it in a future situation.

Collapse Anchor is a technique used to eliminate a negative anchor while replacing it with an accessed resourceful state.

Circle of Excellence is a useful technique of creating an easily transportable resource anchor.

Parts Integration is a technique that is used to communicate with two internal and incongruent parts. The intention is to identify the positive intention of both parts and integrate them to create congruence and wholeness.

Six Step Reframe is a technique that is useful with groups, families and individuals who have opposing points of view, but those opposing parts never did belong to the same whole part. It is a great tool for negotiating and finding a win-win solution.

Communicating with Symptoms is a technique used to communicate with any kind of symptom (pain, emotion, thought, behavior, etc.) in order to find its positive intention and discover what it is wanting to communicate to you so you have the chance to get its desires met.

Eliciting Strategies give you the chance to find out the recipe someone uses to do or not do something. With this knowledge you are able to better respect a person's model of the world, by using his strategy to unconsciously communicate, motivate and access the strategy.

Neurological Levels Alignment is a technique used to align the six neurological levels. This helps to create congruence and choice for a person.

Eliciting and Changing a Timeline provides you with information regarding a person's personality characteristics and allows you to better understand their model of the world. When you change a person's timeline you are helping them to utilize time in a way that is more efficient and aligned with their desired state.

Unconscious Pattern Change is a technique used with the unconscious mind to find the root cause and change how a person filtered the past to create an unresourceful pattern. It is used to clear unresolved negative emotions, unresourceful beliefs, habits, unwanted patterns of behavior, emotion and thought.

Clearing the Now is a technique used to rearrange information in the conscious mind. By shifting the past and future to their respective places, a person has more opportunity to fully live in the present.

Goal in the Future is a technique used to create a goal with well formed conditions and use the unconscious mind to place it in your timeline in the future.

Clearing Anxiety and Worry is a technique which helps a person to gain more understanding, clarity, and resources from an unresourceful state of anxiety or worry.

In order to gain a better understanding of how to elicit the NLP formula, let's now take a look at the first NLP technique we recommend using with a client/other person – **The Client Summary**. The purpose of the Client Summary is to identify a variety of information about a person's Present State and their Desired State.

We have two versions of this tool – one for a Therapeutic approach and the second for a Coaching perspective.

From the vantage point of using NLP with others we differentiate Coaching and Therapy in the following manner:

- **Coaching** – goal focus with a specific measureable outcome. For example: find a new job, start a business, weight loss, quit smoking, improve communication, create a financial portfolio, write a book, etc.

- **Therapy** – emotional, behavioral and belief based work to assist someone to build resources and release interferences. For example: depression, anxiety, stuckness, fears, develop motivation, increase confidence, health issues, etc.

A great thing about NLP as a tool to use with others – unlike traditional Coaching NLP has tools to help a person to overcome intereferense that may be holding them back from achieving a goal; and unlike traditional counselling or psychotherapy NLP contains tools to help move a person toward their desired state without getting lost in the history and problem.

With both of these tools you are using many of your NLP skills including Meta Model, Eye Accessing Cues, Meta Programs, Listening Skills, Rapport, and more.

Client Summary – Therapy Focus

1. What can I help you with?
2. How does this issue show up in your life?
3. Is there ever a time when you don't have this?
4. What have you done about it?
5. Tell me about any past events that are close or related to this issue.
6. Do any of these past events still influence you present? If so, how?
7. Tell me about your childhood, growing up and family in relation to this issue.
8. What else is important for me to know about you and your life and this issue?
9. Let's get more specific about what you want – explain it to me in more details. (Specific, clean and with VAK modalities).
10. For what purpose do you want this outcome?
11. Have you ever had or done this before?
12. What evidence will you notice in your life when you have this outcome?
13. What resources do you have to get this outcome?
14. What resources do you need to get this outcome?
15. What will you gain or lose by getting this outcome?
16. Is there anything that you are not getting, which if you got would allow you to easily have this outcome?

Cleint Summary – Coaching Focus

1. What can I help you with, what is your goal?
2. For what purpose do you want this?
3. Is there anything that prevents you from having this?
4. So far, what have you done to work toward your goal?
5. Are there any emotions, behaviours or thoughts holding you back from having this?
6. Do you notice any of these (from above) as patterns in your life that would be useful for us to address? (if so, possibly revert to the NLP Therapy Client Summary).
7. Let's get more specific about what you want – tell me more about this goal in more detail. (Specific, clean and with VAK modalities).
8. Where are you now in relation to this goal? What have you done about it?
9. Have you ever had or done this before?
10. What evidence will you notice in your life when you have this outcome?
11. What resources do you have to get this outcome?
12. What resources do you need to get this outcome?
13. What will you gain or lose by getting this outcome?
14. Is there anything that you are not getting, which if you got would allow you to easily have this outcome?
15. How will I be best able to support you in achieving this goal?

Using Your NLP Techniques

Communication Skills

- **Understanding Others**
  - Calibration / Sensory Acuity
  - Eye Accessing Cues
  - Meta Model
  - Meta Programs
  - Chunking Up and Down
  - Submodalities
  - Eliciting Values
  - Elicit Timeline
  - Elicit Strategies
  - Personal History
  - Achievable Outcome
  - Well Formed Outcome

- **Being Understood**
  - Rapport
  - Primary Rep System
  - Eye Accessing Cues
  - Reframing
  - Second Perceptual Position
  - Meta Model
  - Calibration / Sensory Acuity
  - Meta Programs
  - Submodalities

Changing and Clearing Interferences

- Reframing
- Perceptual Positions
- Submodality Changes
- Swish Pattern
- Compulsion Blowout
- Parts Integration
- Six Step Reframe
- Communicate w/ Symptoms
- Collapse Anchor
- Timeline Pattern Change
- Clearing the Now
- Change Time Line
- Clear Anxiety / Worry
- VK Dissociation

Accessing and Building Resources

- Discuss the three minds
- Discuss Prime Directives
- Discuss Presuppositions
- Congruence
- Reframing
- Modal Operators
- Well Formed Outcome
- Elicit States
- State

- Management
- Resource Anchor
- Perceptual Positions
- Integrating Anchors
- Eliciting Values
- Eliciting Strategies
- Communicating w/ Symptoms
- Clearing the Now

Building or Clearing

Which comes first, building or clearing? Again, there is no hard and fast rule. When we are working with clients, when we are deciding what NLP techniques to use, we are either going to be eliciting more information, clearing (interferences) or building (resources). The main question in our minds when deciding what to do first is:

Will a change last without more resources? If yes, then we can clear first. If no, then we will build first. Remember, if you are using NLP to help yourself or someone else through the NLP Formula, you might be working over two to ten one-hour NLP sessions.

Let's look at the following case studies about the same presenting desired state and how we might do things in a different order:

Janet is a thirty-year-old woman who is afraid of public speaking. She passes up work promotions, goes out of her way in meetings to not have to speak up and panics at just the thought of public speaking. She is afraid that she'll embarrass herself by fainting, forgetting what she is supposed to say and ruining her reputation of her good work. She does, however, want to improve her skills and be more confident as a speaker. She says she's never been comfortable speaking to more than two people at a time.

When working with Janet, we want to help her by clearing some of the interferences (fear and self-doubt) and building resources (confidence and self-belief). If we were to clear interferences first, would those resources be able to stay without first building and accessing resources? In Janet's case, we may first want to build resources; by Janet having access to confidence and self-belief, the changes we make to her unconscious patterns of thought, emotion, and behavior are more likely to stay. By building resources first, we are building a strong, stable foundation for change.

Mark is a thirty-two-year old professional man who has a fear of public speaking in front of groups of his peers or people he doesn't know. He has passed up opportunities of high profile projects at work because he would have had to present to groups of people. In his personal life, if Mark is presenting to his friends or family members, he is fine. His desired state is to be more confident and to enjoy public speaking with everyone.

In Mark's case, notice the words *more confidence*. This presupposes that Mark already has the resource of confidence and our job is to help him to access even more of it. Again, we're asking the question: If we were to clear interferences first, would those resources be able to stay without first building and accessing resources? With Mark, we would most likely start with clearing interferences and then building and accessing resources.

Again, there is no right or wrong. As long as you are using and following the NLP Formula, clearing interferences and accessing/building resources that will help a person move from their Present State to Desired State, that is perfect. You can, however, benefit from our years of experience to help you choose where to start. There is no race to the finish; most people have lived with a Present State for quite a long time and working diligently and thoroughly will ensure a successful Desired State.

The Art of NLP

We hope through the past thirty days you have come to appreciate your own model of the world and the skills that NLP can help you with to appreciate others. As you can see, NLP isn't about change, it's about understanding and enhancement. We are proud advocates of using NLP with integrity and ecology. We also believe in applying NLP to yourself first, and then others. Unfortunately, there are many in the NLP world who tend to wear their underwear on the outside of their pants (like Superman) and assert magical qualities of NLP. NLP is good, we know that and we're passionate about that. And we know it is just a tool. NLP is only as good as a person's desired state.

Knowing and practicing NLP does not make one superhuman, it makes us human with some extra tools to understand ourselves and others and enhance or change what is happening based on what we desire.

With these tools you can communicate more effectively, build better rapport, be more flexible in your thinking, elevate your motivation to a new level, make changes to the past, anchor resourceful states to certain situations, be better understood, communicate more directly with the unconscious mind, find your passion, live with more authenticity and simply be a better you.

Here is one thing we know for certain: *NLP works when you work it.*

Laureli has been involved in NLP since 1983 and Heidi since 1997. Our decades of experience have shown us through our clients and lives, and more importantly, our own, that if you want something, you can achieve it. NLP helps to make it easier, yet there is still some work to be done. After all, a goal without action is just a dream.

We hope you take the information you have learned so far and put it to great use. If you have not already completed a live NLP training, we invite you to do so. If you have, you will undoubtedly find this book as a continued resource as you carry on learning, refining and developing your skills. There are so many NLP skills that can be used each and every day, we hope this book has inspired you to do just that.

It has been our pleasure to share our world of NLP with yours.

Where to From Here

As we have just said, it has been our pleasure to share our world of NLP with you, and we look forward to sharing even more with you soon. You may be reading this book as a part of your pre-course learning for our NLP Practitioner Certification training, or perhaps you are just curious about NLP or maybe you are in search of your NLP trainers.

Wherever this book finds you, we are glad that it has and we would like to take this opportunity to share a little more about how you can continue to learn with us.

Learning NLP

Through our NLP Training Company **The Worldwide Institutes of NLP** we provide public NLP certification courses – anyone can learn NLP with us. The only pre-requisite is an interest in learning more about NLP and yourself. During the hands on training with us you will learn and get hands on experience with all of the concepts we have shared with you in the past 30 days plus so much more.

There are three official levels of NLP training:
- **Level 1:** NLP Practitioner Certification
- **Level 2:** NLP Master Practitioner Certification
- **Level 3:** NLP Trainer Certification

Additionally, we provide specific training for anyone who is interested in using NLP as a Coach, Therapist or Consultant.

You can find more information about the programs available at **www.nlpworldwide.com**

We also have developed any online NLP training program at **anywhereNLP.com** – developed and trained by Dr. Heidi, you will be able to access a multi-media classroom where you will be able to continue to learn with video demonstrations, group coaching calls and interactive online forums. The content of the Anywhere NLP program is based on the NLP Practitioner Certification course, however, because this training is not conducted in a live setting with feedback, supervision and guided practice it is not a Certification training – but upon successful completion of the course and assessments you will receive a Certificate of Completion.

Now you have the opportunity to learn with us from **Anywhere** you are. You can find more information about the online NLP training at **www.anywherenlp.com**

See us in Action

Now that you have a better understanding of what NLP is, we would love to introduce a few more concepts with you through an online introduction to NLP. Our **7 Day NLP** program provides you with a short video emailed to you every day for a week. In each video you will see Laureli or Heidi sharing about a different aspect – some of the content from this book will be repeated, but in a different format.

Register for this free online introduction at **www.7daynlp.com**

NLP Success Coaching

If you would like an opportunity to investigate NLP more to see if this modality is something that you would like to learn formally – through our Certification Training or online program, we have a great opportunity for you.

Our **Success Coaching** program provides you with an interactive workbook that you will complete to assess yourself and how you would best benefit from NLP, this workbook is followed by a complimentary 1-hour Coaching session with one of our Associate Coaches.

Not only will you be able to learn more about NLP and how you can use NLP in your life, you will also experience an NLP Coaching Session and learn more about the process of using NLP with others.

To learn more and get started visit: **www.nlpworldwide.com/ nlpsuccessmap**

NLP Coaching or Therapy with Laureli or Heidi
Both Laureli and Heidi still work with clients in a Coaching and Therapy manner. Technology allows us to work with individuals, teams, couples and groups from all over the world. You can learn more about book a full appointment or initial consultation via Skype, phone or in-person in our Sydney office at either of their website:
- www.laureliblyth.com
- www.heidiheron.com

Ask Us a Question
Of course, we are always happy to answer your questions, chat about NLP and find other opportunities to assist you. Simply email, call or find an online avenue to contact us. We can even set up a time to chat in person or online to have a more in-depth conversation. We are always only just a click away!
- Phone: +61 2 9264 4357
- Reach Laureli via email: laureli@nlpworldwide.com
- Reach Heidi via email: heidi@nlpworldwide.com
- Send a general enquiry: info@nlpworldwide.com
- Find us on Facebook: www.facebook.com/nlpworldwide/

References

Andreas, C. & Andreas, S. (1987). *Change your mind and Keep the Change.* Real People Press.

Andreas, S. (2002). *Transforming yourself: becoming who you want to be.* Real People Press.

Battino, R., & South, T. (1999). *Ericksonian Approaches.* Crown House Publishing

Bandler, R. & Grinder, J. (1975). *Patterns of Hypnotic Techniques of Milton H. Erickson, Volume I.* Grinder & Associates

Bodenhammer, B., & Hall, L.M. (2003). *Figuring out people: reading people using Meta Programs.* Crown House Publishing Ltd.

Boud, D., Keogh, R. & Walker, D. (1985). *Reflection: turning experience into learning.* RoutledgeFalmer.

DeLozier, J., & Dilts, R. (2000). *Encyclopedia of systemic Neuro-Linguistic Programming and NLP new coding.* NLP University Press.

Hall, L.M. (2005). *Coaching conversations for transformational change.*

Sperry, R. (1969). *M.S. Handbook of Clinical Neurology.* North-Holland Publishing Company.

Yapko, M. (2003). *Trancework.* Brunner-Routledge